A. B. Paterson

B·R·U·M·BY'S · R·U·N
A N D · O T H E R · V E R S E S

A. B. Paterson

B·R·U·M·B·Y'S · R·U·N

A N D · O T H E R · V E R S E S

ANGUS
& ROBERTSON
PUBLISHERS

ANGUS & ROBERTSON PUBLISHERS

Unit 4, Eden Park, 31 Waterloo Road,
North Ryde, NSW, Australia 2113, and
16 Golden Square, London W1R 4BN,
United Kingdom

First published in Australia
by Angus & Robertson Publishers in 1921
as The Collected Verse of A. B. Paterson
Edited and expanded by A. B. Paterson's
g rand - daughters in 1986
This edition 1988

Copyright © Retusa Pty Ltd 1986

National Library of Australia
Cataloguing-in-publication data.

Paterson, A. B. (Andrew Barton), 1864-1941.
  Brumby's run and other verses.

  ISBN 0 207 15905 X.

  I. Title. II. Title: Collected verse of A. B.
  Paterson.

A821'.2

Printed in Australia by Griffin Press

Introduction

ANDREW BARTON PATERSON, eldest of a family of two sons and five daughters, was born on 17th February 1864 at Narambla, near Orange, New South Wales. His father, Andrew Bogle Paterson, came of an old Scotch family, and his mother was Rose, daughter of Robert Johnstone Barton, of Boree Station. Their home was Illalong, a station in the Yass district. Andrew Bogle Paterson had lost heavily in two previous grazing ventures in north-west New South Wales and Queensland, and now, a few years after the birth of his son, Illalong passed into the hands of a mortgagee, but he remained as manager.

There Andrew Barton Paterson lived until he was about ten years of age. Then, after some preparatory education, he attended Sydney Grammar School. He spent his vacations at the station, a good rider, enjoying the activities and associations which later provided material for his writings. Indoors, though without means to be lavish, there was comfort and also books and the cultivated interests that go with them. Literary inclinations in the family are indicated by the fact that Paterson's father preceded him as a contributor of verse to the *Bulletin*, and afterwards a sister, Jessie, also had verses published in its columns. During schooldays in Sydney Paterson lived congenially at Gladesville with his grandmother, Mrs Robert Barton. She, too, wrote verse, and circulated it privately among her friends, some of whom were prominent in Sydney cultural life of the time. At the age of sixteen he matriculated, and was articled to a firm of solicitors. After being himself enrolled as a solicitor, he became managing clerk for another law firm, and later practised in a partnership with the name of Street and Paterson.

When "Clancy of the Overflow", by "The Banjo", appeared in the 1889 Christmas number of the *Bulletin*, Rolf Boldrewood hailed it as "the best bush ballad since Gordon". Further verses with the same pen-name aroused considerable interest, as well as curiosity concerning the identity of the author, which was not revealed until the publication in 1895 of *The Man from Snowy River and Other Verses*. The success of this book was described in the London *Literary Yearbook* as "without parallel in colonial literary annals" and as giving its author a public wider than that of any other living writer in the language except Kipling. The first edition sold out in a fortnight, the tenth thousand was reached within a year, and altogether sales exceeded 100,000. At the beginning of 1895, while visiting Dagworth, a Queensland sheep station, he wrote the now famous "Waltzing Matilda" verses to a tune which, though an inherent part of a band march published in 1893, seems to be that of an old marching song of Marlborough's soldiers. Back again in Sydney, he fraternized with authors and artists of the time, wrote for the press, then, for the purpose of some descriptive articles for a tourist publication, took ship to Darwin, experiencing the life of that region ashore and afloat.

Towards the end of 1899, having returned to Sydney, he gave up legal practice, and sailed for South Africa as war correspondent for the *Sydney Morning Herald* in the Boer War. Returning to Australia in the latter part of 1900, he almost immediately departed, by way of the Philippines, to China, expecting an opportunity as a war correspondent again; but the fighting connected with the Boxer Rebellion had ended in the meantime, so he went on to London. In 1902, in Sydney once more, he delivered a series of lectures on the Boer War, and repeated them in country towns as well as in Tasmania and New Zealand. In 1903 he married Alice Walker, of Tenterfield, whom he had met during his lecture tour. From 1904 to 1906 he was editor of the *Sydney Evening News*, and in 1907 and 1908 edited the *Town and Country Journal*. In the latter year he acquired an interest in a station, Coodra Vale, on the Upper Murrumbidgee, in country he knew and loved, and made his home there with his wife and their son and daughter. Soon after the 1914-18 war broke out, he sold this property and went to London, hoping for an appointment as a war correspondent. He was disappointed in this, but anxious for war service, though he was now fifty years of age, he became an ambulance driver in France for the Australian hospital at Wimereux. In 1916 he was appointed Remount Officer to the A.I.F. in Egypt, with the rank of Major. There his wife joined him and worked for the British Red Cross. They returned to Australia in 1919 and settled with their two children in Sydney, and he continued to work as a freelance writer. In the New Year honours of 1939 he was made C.B.E. He died at Sydney on 5th February, 1941.

The success of his first book of poems, *The Man from Snowy River and Other Verses* (1895) has already been mentioned. *Rio Grande's Last Race and Other Verses* (1902) was reprinted several times. It contained at the end a number of poems of the Boer War, inevitably suggestive of Kipling, whose influence is rather too plain in a few poems in the other two books. *Saltbush Bill, J.P., and Other Verses* (1917) included some of Paterson's earliest work. The three volumes were in 1921 combined in one as *The Collected Verse of A. B. Paterson*, which has been reprinted many times. He was the author of three books of fiction, namely, a novel, *An Outback Marriage* (1906), *Three Elephant Power and Other Stories* (1917), and another novel, *The Shearer's Colt* (1936). His *Happy Dispatches* (1934) records impressions of notabilities he met while abroad. *The Animals Noah Forgot* (1933) is a collection of verses mostly descriptive of Australian fauna, for juvenile reading. Paterson also compiled a book of *Old Bush Songs, Composed and Sung in the Bush-ranging, Digging and Overlanding Days* (1905). His earliest publication was *Australia for the Australians* (1888), suggesting land reforms as a remedy for the prevalent unemployment and the drift to the cities.

Paterson's poetry has a special connexion with the time when it was written. The Sydney *Bulletin* had been founded in 1880, and, by encouraging Australians to write about life outback, it set bushmen rhyming. This was not entirely new. There were already some bush songs, sung around camp-fires, in huts and shearing-sheds, and on the track. The tunes were mainly those of oversea songs. The words, of unknown authorship, were often similarly imitative, but with more originality because of the Australian themes. It was a local folklore so far as this was possible in a land with so short a history as that of the white man in Australia. The verse of the *Bulletin* bards had a similar but wider significance in a multitude of rhymes of droving and boundary riding and shearing and other station activities, of bushrangers, life on farms and in remote townships, with horse racing and other diversions, often alcoholic. Of the many who wrote them, a score are represented by collections in book form, but the two outstanding names are Paterson and Henry Lawson.

They had different points of view which they aired in the *Bulletin* in a kind of verse debate. A poem like Paterson's "Clancy of the Overflow" was to Lawson a false idealization of bush life, which he accordingly attacked in "Up the Country"; Paterson's reply, "In Defence of the Bush", was just as forceful; Lawson then satirized Paterson as "The City Bushman" in a poem with that title; and Paterson dealt with Lawson and other detractors of the bush in "An Answer to Various Bards". The question of their respective merits as poets does not arise here, and Lawson certainly wrote some excellent bush ballads; but his unfortunate personal experience led him to stress unduly the harsh aspects of the outback, and a corollary of this was the recurring note of social protest in his verse. Neither of these traits, though both had foundation enough, was typical of bush life, with its acceptance of the bad with the good, often sardonic, but not much concerned with any social problems involved. Thus Paterson's simple approach is truer, and his range makes him, as compared with the others besides Lawson, pre-eminent among the balladists.

Allowing for the difference of time, his verses are like the ballads which chronicled common life and doughty deeds in medieval times, and which are now enhanced by the romantic atmosphere of a distant past and its archaic manner. Oral transmission through generations obscured their origin and, in the best of them, distilled the diction finely. More generally, faults are not hard to find, but are accepted as having the common tang of the time. It is somewhat the same with the verbal defects in Paterson's verse. His work has enough quality and resource to show that he could have overcome them, but they are often so much the natural expression of the life he writes about that they help to reveal it, almost as if he were its passive instrument. The gleams of authentic poetry — say, for instance, the opening of "The Travelling Post Office" or passages in "The Man from Snowy River" — occur as casually as the lapses. The worst of these consist of sentimentality in a few detached instances like "Only a Jockey" and "A Bunch of Roses", or when though rarely, as in "Lost", a bush poem emphasizes a sentiment disproportionately. The comic element, on the other hand, is wholesome, and Paterson revels in it. Sometimes it helps to typify a place, as with the two "Dandaloo" poems and "Hay and Hell and Booligal"; or it gives colour to a character such as "Saltbush Bill" or "The Man from Ironbark"; or it may divert incredibility, as in "Father Riley's Horse" and "The City of Dreadful Thirst", with their approach to the supernatural or eerie — for this is perhaps the only phase of balladry that Paterson fails to make convincing, even when he is wholly serious about it in "Rio Grande's Last Race". His comic ballads are outright fun, but they nevertheless vitalize the circumstances and people portrayed.

His verse belongs to the true ballad tradition of tales musically told and heightened with simple glamour. This may consist of some special prowess, as of "The Man from Snowy River"; or heroism like that of the bushranger giving his life to save a comrade in "How Gilbert Died"; or even the exploit of a less romanticized outlaw as in "Conroy's Gap"; or the outcome of a horse race in more than a dozen of Paterson's poems; or it may be concerned with bush life apart from any special event, as in "Clancy of the Overflow" and "A Bushman's Song"; but always there is the tone of period and place and the manner of the people in the telling. He writes as bush folk themselves would if they were able, and it is this that has made his poetry popular with them and with city people to whom it is on that account just as interesting. It is not likely to be less so. Time, with the changes of a mechanical age, has already given a legendary attraction to some of the old bush ways. When the future looks back to the past as we look back to the middle ages, Paterson's poetry will probably have the aura of old minstrelsy. He best of all has sung the action of bush life in that natural music of rhythm and rhyme which has a perpetual general appeal.

FREDERICK T. MACARTNEY

CONTENTS

I

THE MAN FROM SNOWY RIVER
AND OTHER VERSES

PRELUDE

I have gathered these stories afar,
   In the wind and the rain,
In the land where the cattle camps are,
   On the edge of the plain.
On the overland routes of the West,
   When the watches were long,
I have fashioned in earnest and jest
   These fragments of song.

They are just the rude stories one hears
   In sadness and mirth,
The records of wandering years,
   And scant is their worth.
Though their merits indeed are but slight,
   I shall not repine,
If they give you one moment's delight,
   Old comrades of mine.

THE MAN FROM SNOWY RIVER

There was movement at the station, for the word had passed
     around
That the colt from old Regret had got away,
And had joined the wild bush horses — he was worth a thousand
     pound,
So all the cracks had gathered to the fray.
All the tried and noted riders from the stations near and far
Had mustered at the homestead overnight,
For the bushmen love hard riding where the wild bush horses are,
And the stockhorse snuffs the battle with delight.

There was Harrison, who made his pile when Pardon won the cup,
The old man with his hair as white as snow;
But few could ride beside him when his blood was fairly up —
He would go wherever horse and man could go.
And Clancy of the Overflow came down to lend a hand,
No better horseman ever held the reins;
For never horse could throw him while the saddle girths would
     stand,
He learnt to ride while droving on the plains.

And one was there, a stripling on a small and weedy beast,
He was something like a racehorse undersized,
With a touch of Timor pony — three parts thoroughbred at least —
And such as are by mountain horsemen prized.
He was hard and tough and wiry — just the sort that won't say
     die —
There was courage in his quick impatient tread;
And he bore the badge of gameness in his bright and fiery eye,
And the proud and lofty carriage of his head.

But still so slight and weedy, one would doubt his power to stay,
And the old man said, "That horse will never do
For a long and tiring gallop — lad, you'd better stop away,
Those hills are far too rough for such as you."
So he waited sad and wistful — only Clancy stood his friend —
"I think we ought to let him come," he said;
"I warrant he'll be with us when he's wanted at the end,
For both his horse and he are mountain bred.

"He hails from Snowy River, up by Kosciusko's side,
Where the hills are twice as steep and twice as rough,
Where a horse's hoofs strike firelight from the flint stones every
     stride,
The man that holds his own is good enough.

And the Snowy River riders on the mountains make their home,
Where the river runs those giant hills between;
I have seen full many horsemen since I first commenced to roam,
But nowhere yet such horsemen have I seen."

So he went — they found the horses by the big mimosa clump —
They raced away towards the mountain's brow,
And the old man gave his orders, "Boys, go at them from the
    jump,
No use to try for fancy riding now.
And, Clancy, you must wheel them, try and wheel them to the
    right.
Ride boldly, lad, and never fear the spills,
For never yet was rider that could keep the mob in sight,
If once they gain the shelter of those hills."

So Clancy rode to wheel them — he was racing on the wing
Where the best and boldest riders take their place,
And he raced his stockhorse past them, and he made the ranges
    ring
With the stockwhip, as he met them face to face.
Then they halted for a moment, while he swung the dreaded lash,
But they saw their well-loved mountain full in view,
And they charged beneath the stockwhip with a sharp and sudden
    dash,
And off into the mountain scrub they flew.

Then fast the horsemen followed, where the gorges deep and black
Resounded to the thunder of their tread,
And the stockwhips woke the echoes, and they fiercely answered
    back
From cliffs and crags that beetled overhead.
And upward, ever upward, the wild horses held their way,
Where mountain ash and kurrajong grew wide;
And the old man muttered fiercely, "We may bid the mob good
    day,
No man can hold them down the other side."

When they reached the mountain's summit, even Clancy took a
    pull,
It well might make the boldest hold their breath,
The wild hop scrub grew thickly, and the hidden ground was full
Of wombat holes, and any slip was death.
But the man from Snowy River let the pony have his head,
And he swung his stockwhip round and gave a cheer,
And he raced him down the mountain like a torrent down its bed,
While the others stood and watched in very fear.

He sent the flint stones flying, but the pony kept his feet,
He cleared the fallen timber in his stride,
And the man from Snowy River never shifted in his seat —
It was grand to see that mountain horseman ride.
Through the stringybarks and saplings, on the rough and broken
ground,
Down the hillside at a racing pace he went;
And he never drew the bridle till he landed safe and sound,
At the bottom of that terrible descent.

He was right among the horses as they climbed the further hill,
And the watchers on the mountain standing mute,
Saw him ply the stockwhip fiercely, he was right among them still,
As he raced across the clearing in pursuit.
Then they lost him for a moment, where two mountain gullies met
In the ranges, but a final glimpse reveals
On a dim and distant hillside the wild horses racing yet,
With the man from Snowy River at their heels.

And he ran them single-handed till their sides were white with
foam.
He followed like a bloodhound on their track,
Till they halted cowed and beaten, then he turned their heads for
home,
And alone and unassisted brought them back.
But his hardy mountain pony he could scarcely raise a trot,
He was blood from hip to shoulder from the spur;
But his pluck was still undaunted, and his courage fiery hot,
For never yet was mountain horse a cur.

And down by Kosciusko, where the pine-clad ridges raise
Their torn and rugged battlements on high,
Where the air is clear as crystal, and the white stars fairly blaze
At midnight in the cold and frosty sky,
And where around The Overflow the reed beds sweep and sway
To the breezes, and the rolling plains are wide,
The man from Snowy River is a household word today,
And the stockmen tell the story of his ride.

Old Pardon,
the Son of Reprieve

You never heard tell of the story?
  Well, now, I can hardly believe!
Never heard of the honour and glory
  Of Pardon, the son of Reprieve?
But maybe you're only a Johnnie
  And don't know a horse from a hoe?
Well, well, don't get angry, my sonny,
  But, really, a young 'un should know.

They bred him out back on the "Never",
  His mother was Mameluke breed.
To the front — and then stay there — was ever
  The root of the Mameluke creed.
He seemed to inherit their wiry
  Strong frames — and their pluck to receive —
As hard as a flint and as fiery
  Was Pardon, the son of Reprieve.

We ran him at many a meeting
  At crossing and gully and town,
And nothing could give him a beating —
  At least when our money was down.
For weight wouldn't stop him, nor distance,
  Nor odds, though the others were fast,
He'd race with a dogged persistence,
  And wear them all down at the last.

At the Turon the Yattendon filly
  Led by lengths at the mile and a half,
And we all began to look silly,
  While *her* crowd were starting to laugh;
But the old horse came faster and faster,
  His pluck told its tale, and his strength,
He gained on her, caught her, and passed her,
  And won it, hands down, by a length.

And then we swooped down on Menindie
  To run for the President's Cup —
Oh! that's a sweet township — a shindy
  To them is board, lodging, and sup.
Eye-openers they are, and their system
  Is never to suffer defeat;
It's "win, tie, or wrangle" — to best 'em
  You must lose 'em, or else it's "dead heat".

We strolled down the township and found 'em
   At drinking and gaming and play;
If sorrows they had, why they drowned 'em,
   And betting was soon under way.
Their horses were good 'uns and fit 'uns,
   There was plenty of cash in the town;
They backed their own horses like Britons,
   And Lord! how *we* rattled it down!

With gladness we thought of the morrow,
   We counted our wagers with glee,
A simile homely to borrow —
   "There was plenty of milk in our tea".
You see we were green; and we never
   Had even a thought of foul play,
Though we well might have known that the clever
   Division would "put us away".

Experience "*docet*", they tell us,
   At least so I've frequently heard,
But, "dosing" or "stuffing", those fellows
   Were up to each move on the board;
They got to his stall — it is sinful
   To think what such villains would do —
And they gave him a regular skinful
   Of barley — green barley — to chew.

He munched it all night, and we found him
   Next morning as full as a hog —
The girths wouldn't nearly meet round him;
   He looked like an overfed frog.
We saw we were done like a dinner —
   The odds were a thousand to one
Against Pardon turning up winner,
   'Twas cruel to ask him to run.

We got to the course with our troubles,
   A crestfallen couple were we;
And we heard the "books" calling the doubles —
   A roar like the surf of the sea;
And over the tumult and louder
   Rang, "Any price Pardon, I lay!"
Says Jimmy, "The children of Judah
   Are out on the warpath to-day."

Three miles in three heats: Ah, my sonny
   The horses in those days were stout,
They had to run well to win money;
   I don't see such horses about.

Your six-furlong vermin that scamper
  Half a mile with their featherweight up;
They wouldn't earn much of their damper
  In a race like the President's Cup.

The first heat was soon set a-going;
  The Dancer went off to the front;
The Don on his quarters was showing,
  With Pardon right out of the hunt.
He rolled and he weltered and wallowed —
  You'd kick your hat faster, I'll bet;
They finished all bunched, and he followed
  All lathered and dripping with sweat.

But troubles came thicker upon us,
  For while we were rubbing him dry
The stewards came over to warn us:
  "We hear you are running a bye!
If Pardon don't spiel like tarnation
  And win the next heat — if he can —
He'll earn a disqualification;
  Just think over *that*, now, my man!"

Our money all gone and our credit,
  Our horse couldn't gallop a yard;
And then people thought that *we* did it!
  It really was terribly hard.
We were objects of mirth and derision
  To folk in the lawn and the stand,
And the yells of the clever division
  Of "Any price, Pardon!" were grand.

We still had a chance for the money,
  Two heats still remained to be run;
If both fell to us — why, my sonny,
  The clever division were done.
And Pardon was better, we reckoned,
  His sickness was passing away,
So he went to the post for the second
  And principal heat of the day.

They're off and away with a rattle,
  Like dogs from the leashes let slip,
And right at the back of the battle
  He followed them under the whip.
They gained ten good lengths on him quickly,
  He dropped right away from the pack;
I tell you it made me feel sickly
  To see the blue jacket fall back.

Our very last hope had departed —
  We thought the old fellow was done,
When all of a sudden he started
  To go like a shot from a gun.
His chances seemed slight to embolden
  Our hearts; but, with teeth firmly set,
We thought, "Now or never! The old 'un
  May reckon with some of 'em yet."

Then loud rose the warcry for Pardon;
  He swept like the wind down the dip,
And over the rise by the garden,
  The jockey was done with the whip;
The field were at sixes and sevens —
  The pace at the first had been fast —
And hope seemed to drop from the heavens,
  For Pardon was coming at last.

And how he did come! It was splendid;
  He gained on them yards every bound,
Stretching out like a greyhound extended,
  His girth laid right down on the ground.
A shimmer of silk in the cedars
  As into the running they wheeled,
And out flashed the whips on the leaders,
  For Pardon had collared the field.

Then right through the ruck he came sailing —
  I knew that the battle was won —
The son of Haphazard was failing,
  The Yattendon filly was done;
He cut down the Don and the Dancer,
  He raced clean away from the mare —
He's in front! Catch him now if you can, sir!
  And up went my hat in the air!

Then loud from the lawn and the garden
  Rose offers of "Ten to one *on*!"
"Who'll bet on the field? I back Pardon!"
  No use; all the money was gone.
He came for the third heat light-hearted,
  A-jumping and dancing about;
The others were done ere they started
  Crestfallen, and tired, and worn out.

He won it, and ran it much faster
  Than even the first, I believe;
Oh, he was the daddy, the master,
  Was Pardon, the son of Reprieve.

He showed 'em the method to travel —
    The boy sat as still as a stone —
They never could see him for gravel;
    He came in hard-held, and alone.

* * * *

But he's old — and his eyes are grown hollow;
    Like me, with my thatch of the snow;
When he dies, then I hope I may follow,
    And go where the racehorses go,
I don't want no harping nor singing —
    Such things with my style don't agree;
Where the hoofs of the horses are ringing
    There's music sufficient for me.

And surely the thoroughbred horses
    Will rise up again and begin
Fresh races on faraway courses
    And p'raps they might let me slip in.
It would look rather well the race card on
    'Mongst cherubs and seraphs and things,
"Angel Harrison's black gelding Pardon,
    Blue halo, white body and wings".

And if they have racing hereafter,
    (And who is to say they will not?)
When the cheers and the shouting and laughter
    Proclaim that the battle grows hot;
As they come down the racecourse a-steering,
    He'll rush to the front, I believe;
And you'll hear the great multitude cheering
    For Pardon, the son of Reprieve.

Clancy of The Overflow

I had written him a letter which I had, for want of better
   Knowledge, sent to where I met him down the Lachlan, years
     ago;
He was shearing when I knew him, so I sent the letter to him,
   Just "on spec", addressed as follows: "Clancy, of The Overflow".

And an answer came directed in a writing unexpected,
   (And I think the same was written with a thumbnail dipped in
     tar);
'Twas his shearing mate who wrote it, and *verbatim* I will quote it:
   "Clancy's gone to Queensland droving, and we don't know where
     he are."

            * * * *

In my wild erratic fancy visions come to me of Clancy
   Gone a-droving "down the Cooper" where the Western drovers
     go;
As the stock are slowly stringing, Clancy rides behind them singing,
   For the drover's life has pleasures that the townsfolk never know.

And the bush hath friends to meet him, and their kindly voices
     greet him
   In the murmur of the breezes and the river on its bars,
And he sees the vision splendid of the sunlit plains extended,
   And at night the wondrous glory of the everlasting stars.

            * * * *

I am sitting in my dingy little office, where a stingy
   Ray of sunlight struggles feebly down between the houses tall,
And the foetid air and gritty of the dusty, dirty city
   Through the open window floating, spreads its foulness over all.

And in place of lowing cattle, I can hear the fiendish rattle
   Of the tramways and the buses making hurry down the street,
And the language uninviting of the gutter children fighting,
   Comes fitfully and faintly through the ceaseless tramp of feet.

And the hurrying people daunt me, and their pallid faces haunt me
   As they shoulder one another in their rush and nervous haste,
With their eager eyes and greedy, and their stunted forms and
     weedy,
   For townsfolk have no time to grow, they have no time to waste.

And I somehow rather fancy that I'd like to change with Clancy,
   Like to take a turn at droving where the seasons come and go,

While he faced the round eternal of the cashbook and the
    journal —
But I doubt he'd suit the office, Clancy, of "The Overflow".

Conroy's Gap

This was the way of it, don't you know —
  Ryan was "wanted" for stealing sheep,
And never a trooper, high or low,
  Could find him — catch a weasel asleep!
Till Trooper Scott, from the Stockman's Ford —
  A bushman, too, as I've heard them tell —
Chanced to find him drunk as a lord
  Round at the Shadow of Death Hotel.

D' you know the place? It's a wayside inn,
  A low grog-shanty — a bushman trap,
Hiding away in its shame and sin
  Under the shelter of Conroy's Gap —
Under the shade of that frowning range,
  The roughest crowd that ever drew breath —
Thieves and rowdies, uncouth and strange,
  Were mustered round at the Shadow of Death.

The trooper knew that his man would slide
  Like a dingo pup, if he saw the chance;
And with half a start on the mountain side
  Ryan would lead him a merry dance.
Drunk as he was when the trooper came,
  To him that did not matter a rap —
Drunk or sober, he was the same,
  The boldest rider in Conroy's Gap.

"I want you, Ryan," the trooper said,
  "And listen to me, if you dare resist,
So help me heaven, I'll shoot you dead!"
  He snapped the steel on his prisoner's wrist,
And Ryan, hearing the handcuffs click,
  Recovered his wits as they turned to go,
For fright will sober a man as quick
  As all the drugs that the doctors know.

There was a girl in that rough bar
  Went by the name of Kate Carew,
Quiet and shy as the bush girls are,
  But ready-witted and plucky, too.
She loved this Ryan, or so they say,
  And passing by, while her eyes were dim
With tears, she said in a careless way,
  "The Swagman's round in the stable, Jim."

Spoken too low for the trooper's ear,
  Why should she care if he heard or not?
Plenty of swagmen far and near,
  And yet to Ryan it meant a lot.
That was the name of the grandest horse
  In all the district from east to west;
In every show ring, on every course
  They always counted the Swagman best.

He was a wonder, a raking bay —
  One of the grand old Snowdon strain —
One of the sort that could race and stay
  With his mighty limbs and his length of rein.
Born and bred on the mountain side,
  He could race through scrub like a kangaroo,
The girl herself on his back might ride,
  And the Swagman would carry her safely through.

He would travel gaily from daylight's flush
  Till after the stars hung out their lamps,
There was never his like in the open bush,
  And never his match on the cattle camps.
For faster horses might well be found
  On racing tracks, or a plain's extent,
But few, if any, on broken ground
  Could see the way that the Swagman went.

When this girl's father, old Jim Carew,
  Was droving out on the Castlereagh
With Conroy's cattle, a wire came through
  To say that his wife couldn't live the day.
And he was a hundred miles from home,
  As flies the crow, with never a track,
Through plains as pathless as ocean's foam,
  He mounted straight on the Swagman's back.

He left the camp by the sundown light,
  And the settlers out on the Marthaguy
Awoke and heard, in the dead of night,
  A single horseman hurrying by.
He crossed the Bogan at Dandaloo,
  And many a mile of the silent plain
That lonely rider behind him threw
  Before they settled to sleep again.

He rode all night and he steered his course
  By the shining stars with a bushman's skill,
And every time that he pressed his horse
  The Swagman answered him gamely still.

He neared his home as the east was bright,
  The doctor met him outside the town:
"Carew! How far did you come last night?"
  "A hundred miles since the sun went down."

And his wife got round, and an oath he passed,
  So long as he or one of his breed
Could raise a coin, though it took their last
  The Swagman never should want a feed.
And Kate Carew, when her father died,
  She kept the horse and she kept him well:
The pride of the district far and wide,
  He lived in style at the bush hotel.

Such was the Swagman; and Ryan knew
  Nothing about could pace the crack;
Little he'd care for the man in blue
  If once he got on the Swagman's back.
But how to do it? A word let fall
  Gave him the hint as the girl passed by;
Nothing but "Swagman — stable-wall;
  Go to the stable and mind your eye."

He caught her meaning, and quickly turned
  To the trooper: "Reckon you'll gain a stripe
By arresting me, and it's easily earned;
  Let's go to the stable and get my pipe,
The Swagman has it." So off they went,
  And soon as ever they turned their backs
The girl slipped down, on some errand bent
  Behind the stable, and seized an axe.

The trooper stood at the stable door
  While Ryan went in quite cool and slow,
And then (the trick had been played before)
  The girl outside gave the wall a blow.
Three slabs fell out of the stable wall —
  'Twas done 'fore ever the trooper knew —
And Ryan, as soon as he saw them fall,
  Mounted the Swagman and rushed him through.

The trooper heard the hoofbeats ring
  In the stable yard, and he slammed the gate,
But the Swagman rose with a mighty spring
  At the fence, and the trooper fired too late,
As they raced away and his shots flew wide
  And Ryan no longer need care a rap,
For never a horse that was lapped in hide
  Could catch the Swagman in Conroy's Gap.

And that's the story. You want to know
  If Ryan came back to his Kate Carew;
Of course he should have, as stories go,
  But the worst of it is, this story's true:
And in real life it's a certain rule,
  Whatever poets and authors say
Of high-toned robbers and all their school,
  These horse thief fellows aren't built that way.

Come back! Don't hope it — the slinking hound,
  He sloped across to the Queensland side,
And sold the Swagman for fifty pound,
  And stole the money, and more beside.
And took to drink, and by some good chance
  Was killed — thrown out of a stolen trap.
And that was the end of this small romance,
  The end of the story of Conroy's Gap.

OUR NEW HORSE

The boys had come back from the races
  All silent and down on their luck;
They'd backed 'em, straight out and for places,
  But never a winner they struck.
They lost their good money on Slogan,
  And fell most uncommonly flat,
When Partner, the pride of the Bogan,
  Was beaten by Aristocrat.

And one said, "I move that instanter
  We sell out our horses and quit,
The brutes ought to win in a canter,
  Such trials they do when they're fit.
The last one they ran was a snorter —
  A gallop to gladden one's heart —
Two-twelve for a mile and a quarter,
  And finished as straight as a dart.

"And then when I think that they're ready
  To win me a nice little swag,
They are licked like the veriest neddy —
  They're licked from the fall of the flag.
The mare held her own to the stable,
  She died out to nothing at that,
And Partner he never seemed able
  To pace it with Aristocrat.

"And times have been bad, and the seasons
  Don't promise to be of the best;
In short, boys, there's plenty of reasons
  For giving the racing a rest.
The mare can be kept on the station —
  Her breeding is good as can be —
But Partner, his next destination
  Is rather a trouble to me.

"We can't sell him here, for they know him
  As well as the clerk of the course;
He's raced and won races till, blow him,
  He's done as a handicap horse.
A jady, uncertain performer,
  They weight him right out of the hunt,
And clap it on warmer and warmer
  Whenever he gets near the front.

"It's no use to paint him or dot him
  Or put any 'fake' on his brand,
For bushmen are smart, and they'd spot him
  In any saleyard in the land.
The folk about here could all tell him,
  Could swear to each separate hair;
Let us send him to Sydney and sell him,
  There's plenty of Jugginses there.

"We'll call him a maiden, and treat 'em
  To trials will open their eyes,
We'll run their best horses and beat 'em,
  And then won't they think him a prize.
I pity the fellow that buys him,
  He'll find in a very short space,
No matter how highly he tries him,
  The beggar won't *race* in a race."

* * * *

Next week, under "Seller and Buyer",
  Appeared in the *Daily Gazette*:
"A racehorse for sale, and a flyer;
  Has never been started as yet;
A trial will show what his pace is;
  The buyer can get him in light,
And win all the handicap races.
  Apply here before Wednesday night."

He sold for a hundred and thirty,
  Because of a gallop he had
One morning with Bluefish and Bertie,
  And donkey-licked both of 'em bad.
And when the old horse had departed,
  The life on the station grew tame;
The racetrack was dull and deserted,
  The boys had gone back on the game.

* * * *

The winter rolled by, and the station
  Was green with the garland of spring,
A spirit of glad exultation
  Awoke in each animate thing.
And all the old love, the old longing,
  Broke out in the breasts of the boys,
The visions of racing came thronging
  With all its delirious joys.

The rushing of floods in their courses,
   The rattle of rain on the roofs
Recalled the fierce rush of the horses,
   The thunder of galloping hoofs.
And soon one broke out: "I can suffer
   No longer the life of a slug,
The man that don't race is a duffer,
   Let's have one more run for the mug.

"Why, *everything* races, no matter
   Whatever its method may be:
The waterfowl hold a regatta;
   The possums run heats up a tree;
The emus are constantly sprinting
   A handicap out on the plain;
It seems like all nature was hinting,
   'Tis time to be at it again.

"The cockatoo parrots are talking
   Of races to faraway lands;
The native companions are walking
   A go-as-you-please on the sands;
The little foals gallop for pastime;
   The wallabies race down the gap;
Let's try it once more for the last time,
   Bring out the old jacket and cap.

"And now for a horse; we might try one
   Of those that are bred on the place,
But I think it better to buy one,
   A horse that has proved he can race.
Let us send down to Sydney to Skinner,
   A thorough good judge who can ride,
And ask him to buy us a spinner
   To clean out the whole countryside."

They wrote him a letter as follows:
   "We want you to buy us a horse;
He must have the speed to catch swallows,
   And stamina with it of course.
The price ain't a thing that'll grieve us,
   It's getting a bad 'un annoys
The undersigned blokes, and believe us,
   We're yours to a cinder, 'The boys'."

He answered: "I've bought you a hummer,
   A horse that has never been raced;
I saw him run over the Drummer,
   He held him outclassed and outpaced.

His breeding's not known, but they state he
  Is born of a thoroughbred strain,
I paid them a hundred and eighty,
  And started the horse in the train."

They met him — alas, that these verses
  Aren't up to the subject's demands —
Can't set forth their eloquent curses,
  For Partner was back on their hands.
They went in to meet him in gladness,
  They opened his box with delight —
A silent procession of sadness
  They crept to the station at night.

And life has grown dull on the station,
  The boys are all silent and slow;
Their work is a daily vexation,
  And sport is unknown to them now.
Whenever they think how they stranded,
  They squeal just like guinea-pigs squeal;
They bit their own hook, and were landed
  With fifty pounds' loss on the deal.

AN IDYLL
OF DANDALOO

On Western plains, where shade is not,
  'Neath summer skies of cloudless blue,
Where all is dry and all is hot,
  There stands the town of Dandaloo —
A township where life's total sum
Is sleep, diversified with rum.

Its grass-grown streets with dust are deep,
  'Twere vain endeavour to express
The dreamless silence of its sleep,
  Its wide, expansive drunkenness.
The yearly races mostly drew
A lively crowd to Dandaloo.

There came a sportsman from the East,
  The eastern land where sportsmen blow,
And brought with him a speedy beast —
  A speedy beast as horses go.
He came afar in hope to "do"
The little town of Dandaloo.

Now this was weak of him, I wot —
  Exceeding weak, it seemed to me —
For we in Dandaloo were not
  The Jugginses we seemed to be;
In fact, we rather thought we knew
Our book by heart in Dandaloo.

We held a meeting at the bar,
  And met the question fair and square —
"We've stumped the country near and far
  To raise the cash for races here;
We've got a hundred pounds or two —
Not half so bad for Dandaloo.

"And now, it seems, we have to be
  Cleaned out by this here Sydney bloke,
With his imported horse; and he
  Will scoop the pool and leave us broke.
Shall we sit still, and make no fuss
While this chap climbs all over us?"

* * * *

The races came to Dandaloo,
    And all the cornstalks from the West,
On ev'ry kind of moke and screw,
    Came forth in all their glory drest.
The stranger's horse, as hard as nails,
Look'd fit to run for New South Wales.

He won the race by half a length —
    Quite half a length, it seemed to me —
But Dandaloo, with all its strength,
    Roared out, "Dead heat!" most fervently;
And, after hesitation meet,
The judge's verdict was "Dead heat!"

And many men there were could tell
    What gave the verdict extra force:
The stewards, and the judge as well —
    They all had backed the second horse.
For things like this they sometimes do
In larger towns than Dandaloo.

They ran it off; the stranger won,
    Hands down, by near a hundred yards.
He smiled to think his troubles done;
    But Dandaloo held all the cards.
They went to scale and — cruel fate! —
His jockey turned out underweight.

Perhaps they'd tampered with the scale!
    I cannot tell. I only know
It weighed him *out* all right. I fail
    To paint that Sydney sportsman's woe.
He said the stewards were a crew
Of low-lived thieves in Dandaloo.

He lifted up his voice, irate,
    And swore till all the air was blue;
So then we rose to vindicate
    The dignity of Dandaloo.
"Look here," said we, "you must not poke
Such oaths at us poor country folk."

We rode him softly on a rail,
    We shied at him, in careless glee,
Some large tomatoes, rank and stale,
    And eggs of great antiquity —
Their wild, unholy fragrance flew
About the town of Dandaloo.

He left the town at break of day,
　He led his racehorse through the streets,
And now he tells the tale, they say,
　To every racing man he meets.
And Sydney sportsmen all eschew
The atmosphere of Dandaloo.

THE GEEBUNG POLO CLUB

It was somewhere up the country, in a land of rock and scrub,
That they formed an institution called the Geebung Polo Club.
They were long and wiry natives from the rugged mountainside,
And the horse was never saddled that the Geebungs couldn't ride;
But their style of playing polo was irregular and rash —
They had mighty little science, but a mighty lot of dash:
And they played on mountain ponies that were muscular and
    strong,
Though their coats were quite unpolished, and their manes and
    tails were long.
And they used to train those ponies wheeling cattle in the scrub:
They were demons, were the members of the Geebung Polo Club.

It was somewhere down the country, in a city's smoke and steam,
That a polo club existed, called the Cuff and Collar Team.
As a social institution 'twas a marvellous success,
For the members were distinguished by exclusiveness and dress.
They had natty little ponies that were nice, and smooth, and sleek,
For their cultivated owners only rode 'em once a week.
So they started up the country in pursuit of sport and fame,
For they meant to show the Geebungs how they ought to play the
    game;
And they took their valets with them — just to give their boots a
    rub
Ere they started operations on the Geebung Polo Club.

Now my readers can imagine how the contest ebbed and flowed,
When the Geebung boys got going it was time to clear the road;
And the game was so terrific that ere half the time was gone
A spectator's leg was broken — just from merely looking on.
For they waddied one another till the plain was strewn with dead,
While the score was kept so even that they neither got ahead.
And the Cuff and Collar captain, when he tumbled off to die,
Was the last surviving player — so the game was called a tie.

Then the captain of the Geebungs raised him slowly from the
    ground,
Though his wounds were mostly mortal, yet he fiercely gazed
    around;
There was no one to oppose him — all the rest were in a trance,
So he scrambled on his pony for his last expiring chance,
For he meant to make an effort to get victory to his side;
So he struck at goal — and missed it — then he tumbled off and
    died.

* * * *

By the old Campaspe River, where the breezes shake the grass,
There's a row of little gravestones that the stockmen never pass,
For they bear a crude inscription saying, "Stranger, drop a tear,
For the Cuff and Collar players and the Geebung boys lie here."
And on misty moonlit evenings, while the dingoes howl around,
You can see their shadows flitting down that phantom polo
    ground;
You can hear the loud collisions as the flying players meet,
And the rattle of the mallets, and the rush of ponies' feet,
Till the terrified spectator rides like blazes to the pub —
He's been haunted by the spectres of the Geebung Polo Club.

THE TRAVELLING POST OFFICE

The roving breezes come and go, the reed beds sweep and sway,
The sleepy river murmurs low, and loiters on its way,
It is the land of lots o' time along the Castlereagh.

* * * *

The old man's son had left the farm, he found it dull and slow,
He drifted to the great North-west where all the rovers go.
"He's gone so long," the old man said, "he's dropped right out of
    mind,
But if you'd write a line to him I'd take it very kind;
He's shearing here and fencing there, a kind of waif and stray,
He's droving now with Conroy's sheep along the Castlereagh.
The sheep are travelling for the grass, and travelling very slow;
They may be at Mundooran now, or past the Overflow,
Or tramping down the black soil flats across by Waddiwong,
But all those little country towns would send the letter wrong,
The mailman, if he's extra tired, would pass them in his sleep,
It's safest to address the note to 'Care of Conroy's sheep',
For five and twenty thousand head can scarcely go astray,
You write to 'Care of Conroy's sheep along the Castlereagh'."

* * * *

By rock and ridge and riverside the western mail has gone,
Across the great Blue Mountain Range to take that letter on.
A moment on the topmost grade while open fire doors glare,
She pauses like a living thing to breathe the mountain air,
Then launches down the other side across the plains away
To bear that note to "Conroy's sheep along the Castlereagh".

And now by coach and mailman's bag it goes from town to town,
And Conroy's Gap and Conroy's Creek have marked it "further
    down".
Beneath a sky of deepest blue where never cloud abides,
A speck upon the waste of plain the lonely mailman rides.
Where fierce hot winds have set the pine and myall boughs asweep
He hails the shearers passing by for news of Conroy's sheep.
By big lagoons where wildfowl play and crested pigeons flock,
By campfires where the drovers ride around their restless stock,
And past the teamster toiling down to fetch the wool away
My letter chases Conroy's sheep along the Castlereagh.

SALTBUSH BILL

Now this is the law of the Overland that all in the West obey,
A man must cover with travelling sheep a six-mile stage a day;
But this is the law which the drovers make, right easily understood,
They travel their stage where the grass is bad, but they camp where
the grass is good;
They camp, and they ravage the squatter's grass till never a blade
remains,
Then they drift away as the white clouds drift on the edge of the
saltbush plains,
From camp to camp and from run to run they battle it hand to
hand,
For a blade of grass and the right to pass on the track of the
Overland.

For this is the law of the Great Stock Routes, 'tis written in white
and black —
The man that goes with a travelling mob must keep to a half-mile
track;
And the drovers keep to a half-mile track on the runs where the
grass is dead,
But they spread their sheep on a well-grassed run till they go with a
two-mile spread.
So the squatters hurry the drovers on from dawn till the fall of
night,
And the squatters' dogs and the drovers' dogs get mixed in a deadly
fight;
Yet the squatters' men, though they hunt the mob, are willing the
peace to keep,
For the drovers learn how to use their hands when they go with
the travelling sheep;
But this is the tale of a Jackaroo that came from a foreign strand,
And the fight that he fought with Saltbush Bill, the King of the
Overland.

Now Saltbush Bill was a drover tough, as ever the country knew,
He had fought his way on the Great Stock Routes from the sea to
the Big Barcoo;
He could tell when he came to a friendly run that gave him a
chance to spread,
And he knew where the hungry owners were that hurried his sheep
ahead;
He was drifting down in the Eighty drought with a mob that could
scarcely creep,
(When the kangaroos by the thousands starve, it is rough on the
travelling sheep.)

And he camped one night at the crossing place on the edge of the
    Wilga run,
"We must manage a feed for them here," he said, "or the half of
    the mob are done!"
So he spread them out when they left the camp wherever they liked
    to go,
Till he grew aware of a Jackaroo with a station hand in tow,
And they set to work on the straggling sheep, and with many a
    stockwhip crack
They forced them in where the grass was dead in the space of the
    half-mile track;
So William prayed that the hand of fate might suddenly strike him
    blue
But he'd get some grass for his starving sheep in the teeth of that
    Jackaroo.
So he turned and he cursed the Jackaroo, he cursed him alive or
    dead,
From the soles of his great unwieldy feet to the crown of his ugly
    head,
With an extra curse on the moke he rode and the cur at his heels
    that ran,
Till the Jackaroo from his horse got down and he went for the
    drover man;
With the station hand for his picker-up, though the sheep ran loose
    the while,
They battled it out on the saltbush plain in the regular prize ring
    style.

Now, the new chum fought for his honour's sake and the pride of
    the English race,
But the drover fought for his daily bread with a smile on his
    bearded face;
So he shifted ground and he sparred for wind and he made it a
    lengthy mill,
And from time to time as his scouts came in they whispered to
    Saltbush Bill —
"We have spread the sheep with a two-mile spread, and the grass it
    is something grand,
You must stick to him, Bill, for another round for the pride of the
    Overland."

The new chum made it a rushing fight, though never a blow got
    home,
Till the sun rode high in the cloudless sky and glared on the brick-
    red loam,
Till the sheep drew in to the shelter trees and settled them down to
    rest,

Then the drover said he would fight no more and he gave his
    opponent best.
So the new chum rode to the homestead straight and he told them
    a story grand
Of the desperate fight that he fought that day with the King of the
    Overland.
And the tale went home to the public schools of the pluck of the
    English swell,
How the drover fought for his very life, but blood in the end must
    tell.
But the travelling sheep and the Wilga sheep were boxed on the
    Old Man Plain.
'Twas a full week's work ere they drafted out and hunted them off
    again,
With a week's good grass in their wretched hides, with a curse and
    a stockwhip crack,
They hunted them off on the road once more to starve on the half-
    mile track.
And Saltbush Bill, on the Overland, will many a time recite
How the best day's work that ever he did was the day that he lost
    the fight.

A Mountain Station

I bought a run a while ago,
  On country rough and ridgy,
Where wallaroos and wombats grow —
  The Upper Murrumbidgee.
The grass is rather scant, it's true,
  But this a fair exchange is,
The sheep can see a lovely view
  By climbing up the ranges.

And "She-oak Flat" 's the station's name,
  I'm not surprised at that, sirs:
The oaks were there before I came,
  And I supplied the flat, sirs.
A man would wonder how it's done,
  The stock so soon decreases —
They sometimes tumble off the run
  And break themselves to pieces.

I've tried to make expenses meet,
  But wasted all my labours,
The sheep the dingoes didn't eat
  Were stolen by the neighbours.
They stole my pears — my native pears —
  Those thrice-convicted felons,
And ravished from me unawares
  My crop of paddymelons.

And sometimes under sunny skies,
  Without an explanation,
The Murrumbidgee used to rise
  And overflow the station.
But this was caused (as now I know)
  When summer sunshine glowing
Had melted all Kiandra's snow
  And set the river going.

And in the news, perhaps you read:
  "Stock passings. Puckawidgee,
Fat cattle: Seven hundred head
  Swept down the Murrumbidgee;
Their destination's quite obscure,
  But, somehow, there's a notion,
Unless the river falls, they're sure
  To reach the Southern Ocean."

So after that I'll give it best;
  No more with Fate I'll battle.
I'll let the river take the rest,
  For those were all my cattle.
And with one comprehensive curse
  I close my brief narration,
And advertise it in my verse —
  "For Sale! A Mountain Station".

Been There Before

There came a stranger to Walgett town,
  To Walgett town when the sun was low,
And he carried a thirst that was worth a crown,
  Yet how to quench it he did not know;
But he thought he might take those yokels down,
The guileless yokels of Walgett town.

They made him a bet in a private bar,
  In a private bar when the talk was high,
And they bet him some pounds no matter how far
  He could pelt a stone, yet he could not shy
A stone right over the river so brown,
The Darling River at Walgett town.

He knew that the river from bank to bank
  Was fifty yards, and he smiled a smile
As he trundled down, but his hopes they sank
  For there wasn't a stone within fifty mile;
For the saltbush plain and the open down
Produce no quarries in Walgett town.

The yokels laughed at his hopes o'erthrown,
  And he stood awhile like a man in a dream;
Then out of his pocket he fetched a stone,
  And pelted it over the silent stream —
He had been there before: he had wandered down
On a previous visit to Walgett town.

The Man Who Was Away

The widow sought the lawyer's room with children three in tow,
She told the lawyer man her tale in tones of deepest woe.
Said she, "My husband took to drink for pains in his inside,
And never drew a sober breath from then until he died.

"He never drew a sober breath, he died without a will,
And I must sell the bit of land the childer's mouths to fill.
There's some is grown and gone away, but some is childer yet,
And times is very bad indeed — a livin's hard to get.

"There's Min and Sis and little Chris, they stops at home with me,
And Sal has married Greenhide Bill that breaks for Bingeree.
And Fred is drovin' Conroy's sheep along the Castlereagh,
And Charley's shearin' down the Bland, and Peter is away."

The lawyer wrote the details down in ink of legal blue —
"There's Minnie, Susan, Christopher, they stop at home with you;
There's Sarah, Frederick and Charles, I'll write to them to-day,
But what about the other one — the one who is away?

"You'll have to furnish his consent to sell the bit of land."
The widow shuffled in her seat, "Oh, don't you understand?
I thought a lawyer ought to know — I don't know what to say —
You'll have to do without him, boss, for Peter is away."

But here the little boy spoke up — said he, "We thought you knew;
He's done six months in Goulburn gaol — he's got six more to
    do."
Thus in one comprehensive flash he made it clear as day,
The mystery of Peter's life — the man who was away.

THE MAN FROM IRONBARK

It was the man from Ironbark who struck the Sydney town,
He wandered over street and park, he wandered up and down.
He loitered here, he loitered there, till he was like to drop,
Until at last in sheer despair he sought a barber's shop.
"'Ere! shave my beard and whiskers off, I'll be a man of mark,
I'll go and do the Sydney toff up home in Ironbark."

The barber man was small and flash, as barbers mostly are,
He wore a strike-your-fancy sash, he smoked a huge cigar;
He was a humorist of note and keen at repartee,
He laid the odds and kept a "tote", whatever that may be,
And when he saw our friend arrive, he whispered, "Here's a lark!
Just watch me catch him all alive, this man from Ironbark."

There were some gilded youths that sat along the barber's wall.
Their eyes were dull, their heads were flat, they had no brains at
    all;
To them the barber passed the wink, his dexter eyelid shut,
"I'll make this bloomin' yokel think his bloomin' throat is cut."
And as he soaped and rubbed it in he made a rude remark:
"I s'pose the flats is pretty green up there in Ironbark."

A grunt was all reply he got; he shaved the bushman's chin,
Then made the water boiling hot and dipped the razor in.
He raised his hand, his brow grew black, he paused awhile to gloat,
Then slashed the red-hot razor-back across his victim's throat;
Upon the newly-shaven skin it made a livid mark —
No doubt it fairly took him in — the man from Ironbark.

He fetched a wild up-country yell might wake the dead to hear,
And though his throat, he knew full well, was cut from ear to ear,
He struggled gamely to his feet, and faced the murd'rous foe:
"You've done for me! you dog, I'm beat! one hit before I go!
I only wish I had a knife, you blessed murdering shark!
But you'll remember all your life the man from Ironbark."

He lifted up his hairy paw, with one tremendous clout
He landed on the barber's jaw, and knocked the barber out.
He set to work with nail and tooth, he made the place a wreck;
He grabbed the nearest gilded youth, and tried to break his neck.
And all the while his throat he held to save his vital spark,
And "Murder! Bloody murder!" yelled the man from Ironbark.

A peeler man who heard the din came in to see the show;
He tried to run the bushman in, but he refused to go.
And when at last the barber spoke, and said "'Twas all in fun —
'Twas just a little harmless joke, a trifle overdone."

"A joke!" he cried, "By George, that's fine; a lively sort of lark;
I'd like to catch that murdering swine some night in Ironbark."

And now while round the shearing floor the list'ning shearers gape,
He tells the story o'er and o'er, and brags of his escape.
"Them barber chaps what keeps a tote, By George, I've had
    enough,
One tried to cut my bloomin' throat, but thank the Lord it's
    tough."
And whether he's believed or no, there's one thing to remark,
That flowing beards are all the go way up in Ironbark.

THE OPEN STEEPLECHASE

I had ridden over hurdles up the country once or twice,
By the side of Snowy River with a horse they called "The Ace".
And we brought him down to Sydney, and our rider, Jimmy Rice,
Got a fall and broke his shoulder, so they nabbed me in a trice —
Me, that never wore the colours, for the Open Steeplechase.

"Make the running," said the trainer, "it's your only chance
    whatever,
Make it hot from start to finish, for the old black horse can stay,
And just think of how they'll take it, when they hear on Snowy
    River
That the country boy was plucky, and the country horse was
    clever.
You must ride for old Monaro and the mountain boys today."

"Are you ready?" said the starter, as we held the horses back,
All ablazing with impatience, with excitement all aglow;
Before us like a ribbon stretched the steeplechasing track,
And the sunrays glistened brightly on the chestnut and the black
As the starter's words came slowly, "Are — you — ready? Go!"

Well, I scarcely knew we'd started, I was stupid-like with wonder
Till the field closed up beside me and a jump appeared ahead.
And we flew it like a hurdle, not a baulk and not a blunder,
As we charged it all together, and it fairly whistled under,
And then some were pulled behind me and a few shot out and led.

So we ran for half the distance, and I'm making no pretences
When I tell you I was feeling very nervous-like and queer,
For those jockeys rode like demons; you would think they'd lost
    their senses
If you saw them rush their horses at those rasping five foot
    fences —
And in place of making running I was falling to the rear.

Till a chap came racing past me on a horse they called "The
    Quiver",
And said he, "My country joker, are you going to give it best?
Are you frightened of the fences? Does their stoutness make you
    shiver?
Have they come to breeding cowards by the side of Snowy River?
Are there riders on Monaro? —" but I never heard the rest.

For I drove The Ace and sent him just as fast as he could pace it,
At the big black line of timber stretching fair across the track,
And he shot beside The Quiver. "Now," said I, "my boy, we'll race
    it.

You can come with Snowy River if you're only game to face it;
Let us mend the pace a little and we'll see who cries a crack."

So we raced away together, and we left the others standing,
And the people cheered and shouted as we settled down to ride,
And we clung beside The Quiver. At his taking off and landing
I could see his scarlet nostril and his mighty ribs expanding,
And The Ace stretched out in earnest and we held him stride for
    stride.

But the pace was so terrific that they soon ran out their tether —
They were rolling in their gallop, they were fairly blown and
    beat —
But they both were game as pebbles — neither one would show the
    feather.
And we rushed them at the fences, and they cleared them both
    together,
Nearly every time they clouted but they somehow kept their feet.

Then the last jump rose before us, and they faced it game as ever —
We were both at spur and whipcord, fetching blood at every
    bound —
And above the people's cheering and the cries of "Ace" and
    "Quiver",
I could hear the trainer shouting, "One more run for Snowy
    River".
Then we struck the jump together and came smashing to the
    ground.

Well, The Quiver ran to blazes, but The Ace stood still and waited,
Stood and waited like a statue while I scrambled on his back.
There was no one next or near me for the field was fairly slated,
So I cantered home a winner with my shoulder dislocated,
While the man that rode The Quiver followed limping down the
    track.

And he shook my hand and told me that in all his days he never
Met a man who rode more gamely, and our last set to was prime,
And we wired them on Monaro how we chanced to beat The
    Quiver.
And they sent us back an answer, "Good old sort from Snowy
    River;
Send us word each race you start in and we'll back you every
    time."

The Amateur Rider

Him going to ride for us! *Him* — with the pants and the eyeglass
    and all.
Amateur! don't he just look it — it's twenty to one on a fall.
Boss must be gone off his head to be sending our steeplechase crack
Out over fences like these with an object like that on his back.

Ride! Don't tell *me* he can ride. With his pants just as loose as
    balloons,
How can he sit on his horse? And his spurs like a pair of harpoons;
Ought to be under the Dog Act, he ought, and be kept off the
    course.
Fall! why, he'd fall off a cart, let alone off a steeplechase horse.

* * * *

Yessir! the 'orse is all ready — I wish you'd have rode him before;
Nothing like knowing your 'orse, sir, and this chap's a terror to
    bore;
Battleaxe always could pull, and he rushes his fences like fun —
Stands off his jump twenty feet, and then springs like a shot from a
    gun.

Oh, he can jump 'em all right, sir, you make no mistake, 'e's a toff;
Clouts 'em in earnest, too, sometimes, you mind that he don't clout
    you off —
Don't seem to mind how he hits 'em, his shins is as hard as a nail,
Sometimes you'll see the fence shake and the splinters fly up from
    the rail.

All you can do is to hold him and just let him jump as he likes,
Give him his head at the fences, and hang on like death if he
    strikes;
Don't let him run himself out — you can lie third or fourth in the
    race —
Until you clear the stone wall, and from that you can put on the
    pace.

Fell at that wall once, he did, and it gave him a regular spread,
Ever since that time he flies it — he'll stop if you pull at his head,
Just let him race — you can trust him — he'll take first-class care he
    don't fall,
And I think that's the lot — but remember, *he must have his head at
the wall*.

* * * *

Well, he's down safe as far as the start, and he seems to sit on
    pretty neat,

Only his baggified breeches would ruinate anyone's seat —
They're away — here they come — the first fence, and he's head
over heels for a crown!
Good for the new chum, he's over, and two of the others are
down!

Now for the treble, my hearty — By Jove, he can ride, after all;
Whoop, that's your sort — let him fly them! He hasn't much fear of
a fall.
Who in the world would have thought it? And aren't they just
going a pace?
Little Recruit in the lead there will make it a stoutly run race.

Lord! But they're racing in earnest — and down goes Recruit on his
head,
Rolling clean over his boy — it's a miracle if he ain't dead.
Battleaxe, Battleaxe yet! By the Lord, he's got most of 'em beat —
Ho! did you see how he struck, and the swell never moved in his
seat?

Second time round, and, by Jingo! he's holding his lead of 'em well;
Hark to him clouting the timber! It don't seem to trouble the swell.
Now for the wall — let him rush it. A thirty-foot leap, I declare —
Never a shift in his seat, and he's racing for home like a hare.

What's that that's chasing him — Rataplan — regular demon to
stay!
Sit down and ride for your life now! Oh, good, that's the style —
come away!
Rataplan's certain to beat you, unless you can give him the slip;
Sit down and rub in the whalebone now — give him the spurs and
the whip!

Battleaxe, Battleaxe, yet — and it's Battleaxe wins for a crown;
Look at him rushing the fences, he wants to bring t'other chap
down.
Rataplan never will catch him if only he keeps on his pins;
Now! the last fence! and he's over it! Battleaxe, Battleaxe wins!

* * * *

Well, sir, you rode him just perfect — I knew from the first you
could ride.
Some of the chaps said you couldn't, an' I says just like this a' one
side:
Mark me, I says, that's a tradesman — the saddle is where he was
bred.
Weight! you're all right, sir, and thank you; and them was the
words that I said.

ON KILEY'S RUN

The roving breezes come and go
  On Kiley's Run,
The sleepy river murmurs low,
And far away one dimly sees
Beyond the stretch of forest trees —
Beyond the foothills dusk and dun —
The ranges sleeping in the sun
  On Kiley's Run.

'Tis many years since first I came
  To Kiley's Run,
More years than I would care to name
Since I, a stripling, used to ride
For miles and miles at Kiley's side,
The while in stirring tones he told
The stories of the days of old
  On Kiley's Run.

I see the old bush homestead now
  On Kiley's Run,
Just nestled down beneath the brow
Of one small ridge above the sweep
Of river flat, where willows weep
And jasmine flowers and roses bloom,
The air was laden with perfume
  On Kiley's Run.

We lived the good old station life
  On Kiley's Run,
With little thought of care or strife.
Old Kiley seldom used to roam,
He liked to make the Run his home,
The swagman never turned away
With empty hand at close of day
  From Kiley's Run.

We kept a racehorse now and then
  On Kiley's Run,
And neighb'ring stations brought their men
To meetings where the sport was free,
And dainty ladies came to see
Their champions ride; with laugh and song
The old house rang the whole night long
  On Kiley's Run.

The station hands were friends I wot
    On Kiley's Run,
A reckless, merry-hearted lot —
All splendid riders, and they knew
The "boss" was kindness through and through.
Old Kiley always stood their friend,
And so they served him to the end
    On Kiley's Run.

But droughts and losses came apace
    To Kiley's Run,
Till ruin stared him in the face;
He toiled and toiled while lived the light,
He dreamed of overdrafts at night:
At length, because he could not pay,
His bankers took the stock away
    From Kiley's Run.

Old Kiley stood and saw them go
    From Kiley's Run.
The well-bred cattle marching slow;
His stockmen, mates for many a day,
They wrung his hand and went away.
Too old to make another start,
Old Kiley died — of broken heart,
    On Kiley's Run.

The owner lives in England now
    Of Kiley's Run.
He knows a racehorse from a cow;
But that is all he knows of stock:
His chiefest care is how to dock
Expenses, and he sends from town
To cut the shearers' wages down
    On Kiley's Run.

There are no neighbours anywhere
    Near Kiley's Run.
The hospitable homes are bare,
The gardens gone; for no pretence
Must hinder cutting down expense:
The homestead that we held so dear
Contains a half-paid overseer
    On Kiley's Run.

All life and sport and hope have died
    On Kiley's Run.

No longer there the stockmen ride;
For sour-faced boundary riders creep
On mongrel horses after sheep,
Through ranges where, at racing speed,
Old Kiley used to "wheel the lead"
  On Kiley's Run.

There runs a lane for thirty miles
  Through Kiley's Run.
On either side the herbage smiles,
But wretched trav'lling sheep must pass
Without a drink or blade of grass
Thro' that long lane of death and shame:
The weary drovers curse the name
  Of Kiley's Run.

The name itself is changed of late
  Of Kiley's Run.
They call it "Chandos Park Estate".
The lonely swagman through the dark
Must hump his swag past Chandos Park.
The name is English, don't you see,
The old name sweeter sounds to me
  Of "Kiley's Run".

I cannot guess what fate will bring
  To Kiley's Run —
For chances come and changes ring —
I scarcely think 'twill always be
Locked up to suit an absentee;
And if he lets it out in farms
His tenants soon will carry arms
  On Kiley's Run.

FRYING PAN'S THEOLOGY

SCENE: On Monaro.
  Dramatis Personae:
Shock-headed blackfellow,
  Boy (on a pony).
Snowflakes are falling
  So gentle and slow,
Youngster says, "Frying Pan,
  What makes it snow?"
Frying Pan confident
  Makes the reply —
"Shake 'em big flour bag
  Up in the sky!"
"What! when there's miles of it!
  Surely that's brag.
Who is there strong enough
  Shake such a bag?"
"What parson tellin' you,
  Ole Mister Dodd,
Tell you in Sunday-school?
  Big feller God!
He drive His bullock dray,
  Then thunder go,
He shake His flour bag —
  Tumble down snow!"

THE TWO DEVINES

It was shearing time at the Myall Lake,
  And there rose the sound thro' the livelong day
Of the constant clash that the shear blades make
  When the fastest shearers are making play,
But there wasn't a man in the shearers' lines
That could shear a sheep with the two Devines.

They had rung the sheds of the east and west,
  Had beaten the cracks of the Walgett side,
And the Cooma shearers had giv'n them best —
  When they saw them shear, they were satisfied.
From the southern slopes to the western pines
They were noted men, were the two Devines.

'Twas a wether flock that had come to hand,
  Great struggling brutes, that the shearers shirk,
For the fleece was filled with the grass and sand,
  And seventy sheep was a big day's work.
"At a pound a hundred it's dashed hard lines
To shear such sheep," said the two Devines.

But the shearers knew that they'd make a cheque
  When they came to deal with the station ewes;
They were bare of belly and bare of neck
  With a fleece as light as a kangaroo's.
"We will show the boss how a shear blade shines
When we reach those ewes," said the two Devines.

But it chanced next day when the stunted pines
  Were swayed and stirred with the dawn wind's breath,
That a message came for the two Devines
  That their father lay at the point of death.
So away at speed through the whispering pines
Down the bridle track rode the two Devines.

It was fifty miles to their father's hut,
  And the dawn was bright when they rode away;
At the fall of night when the shed was shut
  And the men had rest from the toilsome day,
To the shed once more through the dark'ning pines
On their weary steeds came the two Devines.

"Well, you're back right sudden," the super. said;
  "Is the old man dead and the funeral done?"
"Well, no, sir, he ain't not exactly dead,
  But as good as dead," said the eldest son —

"And we couldn't bear such a chance to lose,
So we came straight back to tackle the ewes."

They are shearing ewes at the Myall Lake,
  And the shed is merry the livelong day
With the clashing sound that the shear blades make
  When the fastest shearers are making play,
And a couple of "hundred and ninety-nines"
Are the tallies made by the two Devines.

In the
Droving Days

"Only a pound," said the auctioneer,
"Only a pound; and I'm standing here
Selling this animal, gain or loss.
Only a pound for the drover's horse;
One of the sort that was ne'er afraid,
One of the boys of the Old Brigade;
Thoroughly honest and game, I'll swear,
Only a little the worse for wear;
Plenty as bad to be seen in town,
Give me a bid and I'll knock him down;
Sold as he stands, and without recourse,
Give me a bid for the drover's horse."

Loitering there in an aimless way
Somehow I noticed the poor old grey,
Weary and battered and screwed, of course,
Yet when I noticed the old grey horse,
The rough bush saddle, and single rein
Of the bridle laid on his tangled mane,
Straightway the crowd and the auctioneer
Seemed on a sudden to disappear,
Melted away in a kind of haze,
For my heart went back to the droving days.

Back to the road, and I crossed again
Over the miles of the saltbush plain —
The shining plain that is said to be
The dried-up bed of an inland sea,
Where the air so dry and so clear and bright
Refracts the sun with a wondrous light,
And out in the dim horizon makes
The deep blue gleam of the phantom lakes.

At dawn of day we would feel the breeze
That stirred the boughs of the sleeping trees,
And brought a breath of the fragrance rare
That comes and goes in that scented air;
For the trees and grass and the shrubs contain
A dry sweet scent on the saltbush plain.
For those that love it and understand,
The saltbush plain is a wonderland.
A wondrous country, where nature's ways
Were revealed to me in the droving days.

We saw the fleet wild horses pass,
And the kangaroos through the Mitchell grass,
The emu ran with her frightened brood
All unmolested and unpursued.
But there rose a shout and a wild hubbub
When the dingo raced for his native scrub,
And he paid right dear for his stolen meals
With the drovers' dogs at his wretched heels.
For we ran him down at a rattling pace,
While the pack horse joined in the stirring chase.
And a wild halloo at the kill we'd raise —
We were light of heart in the droving days.

'Twas a drover's horse, and my hand again
Made a move to close on a fancied rein.
For I felt the swing and the easy stride
Of the grand old horse that I used to ride
In drought or plenty, in good or ill,
That same old steed was my comrade still;
The old grey horse with his honest ways
Was a mate to me in the droving days.

When we kept our watch in the cold and damp,
If the cattle broke from the sleeping camp,
Over the flats and across the plain,
With my head bent down on his waving mane,
Through the boughs above and the stumps below
On the darkest night I would let him go
At a racing speed; he would choose his course,
And my life was safe with the old grey horse.
But man and horse had a favourite job,
When an outlaw broke from a station mob,
With a right good will was the stockwhip plied,
As the old horse raced at the straggler's side,
And the greenhide whip such a weal would raise,
We could use the whip in the droving days.

* * * *

"Only a pound!" and was this the end —
Only a pound for the drover's friend.
The drover's friend that had seen his day,
And now was worthless, and cast away
With a broken knee and a broken heart
To be flogged and starved in a hawker's cart.
Well, I made a bid for a sense of shame
And the memories dear of the good old game.

"Thank you? Guinea! and cheap at that!
Against you there in the curly hat!
Only a guinea, and one more chance,
Down he goes if there's no advance,
Third, and the last time, one! two! three!"
And the old grey horse was knocked down to me.
And now he's wandering, fat and sleek,
On the lucerne flats by the Homestead Creek;
I dare not ride him for fear he'd fall,
But he does a journey to beat them all,
For though he scarcely a trot can raise,
He can take me back to the droving days.

LOST

"He ought to be home," said the old man, "without there's
    something amiss.
He only went to the Two-mile — he ought to be back by this.
He *would* ride the Reckless filly, he *would* have his wilful way;
And, here, he's not back at sundown — and what will his mother
    say?

"He was always his mother's idol, since ever his father died;
And there isn't a horse on the station that he isn't game to ride.
But that Reckless mare is vicious, and if once she gets away
He hasn't got strength to hold her — and what will his mother
    say?"

The old man walked to the sliprail, and peered up the dark'ning
    track,
And looked and longed for the rider that would never more come
    back;
And the mother came and clutched him, with sudden, spasmodic
    fright:
"What has become of my Willie? Why isn't he home tonight?"

Away in the gloomy ranges, at the foot of an ironbark,
The bonnie, winsome laddie was lying stiff and stark;
For the Reckless mare had smashed him against a leaning limb,
And his comely face was battered, and his merry eyes were dim.

And the thoroughbred chestnut filly, the saddle beneath her flanks,
Was away like fire through the ranges to join the wild mob's ranks;
And a broken-hearted woman and an old man worn and grey
Were searching all night in the ranges till the sunrise brought the
    day.

And the mother kept feebly calling, with a hope that would not
    die,
"Willie! where are you, Willie?" But how can the dead reply;
And hope died out with the daylight, and the darkness brought
    despair,
God pity the stricken mother, and answer the widow's prayer!

Though far and wide they sought him, they found not where he
    fell;
For the ranges held him precious, and guarded their treasure well.
The wattle blooms above him, and the bluebells blow close by,
And the brown bees buzz the secret, and the wild birds sing reply.

But the mother pined and faded, and cried, and took no rest,
And rode each day to the ranges on her hopeless, weary quest.

Seeking her loved one ever, she faded and pined away,
But with strength of her great affection she still sought every day.

"I know that sooner or later I shall find my boy," she said.
But she came not home one evening, and they found her lying
  dead,
And stamped on the poor pale features, as the spirit homeward
  pass'd,
Was an angel smile of gladness — she had found the boy at last.

Over the Range

Little bush maiden, wondering-eyed,
  Playing alone in the creek bed dry,
In the small green flat on every side
  Walled in by the Moonbi Ranges high;
Tell us the tale of your lonely life,
  'Mid the great grey forests that know no change.
"I never have left my home," she said,
  "I have never been over the Moonbi Range.

"Father and mother are both long dead,
  And I live with granny in yon wee place."
"Where are your father and mother?" we said.
  She puzzled awhile with thoughtful face,
Then a light came into the shy brown eye,
  And she smiled, for she thought the question strange
On a thing so certain — "When people die
  They go to the country over the range."

"And what is this country like, my lass?"
  "There are blossoming trees and pretty flowers,
And shining creeks where the golden grass
  Is fresh and sweet from the summer showers.
They never need work, nor want, nor weep;
  No troubles can come their hearts to estrange.
Some summer night I shall fall asleep,
  And wake in the country over the range."

Child, you are wise in your simple trust,
  For the wisest man knows no more than you.
Ashes to ashes, and dust to dust:
  Our views by a range are bounded too;
But we know that God hath this gift in store,
  That when we come to the final change,
We shall meet with our loved ones gone before
  To the beautiful country over the range.

Only a Jockey

*"Richard Bennison, a jockey, aged 14, while riding William Tell
in his training, was thrown and killed.
The horse is luckily uninjured." Melbourne wire*

Out in the grey cheerless chill of the morning light,
   Out on the track where the night shades still lurk;
Ere the first gleam of the sun god's returning light,
   Round come the racehorses early at work.

Reefing and pulling and racing so readily,
   Close sit the jockey boys holding them hard,
"Steady the stallion there — canter him steadily,
   Don't let him gallop so much as a yard."

Fiercely he fights while the others run wide of him,
   Reefs at the bit that would hold him in thrall,
Plunges and bucks till the boy that's astride of him
   Goes to the ground with a terrible fall.

"Stop him there! Block him there! Drive him in carefully,
   Lead him about till he's quiet and cool.
Sound as a bell! though he's blown himself fearfully,
   Now let us pick up this poor little fool.

"Stunned? Oh, by Jove, I'm afraid it's a case with him;
   Ride for the doctor! keep bathing his head!
Send for a cart to go down to our place with him" —
   No use! One long sigh and the little chap's dead.

Only a jockey boy! foul-mouthed and bad you see,
   Ignorant, heathenish, gone to his rest.
Parson or Presbyter, Pharisee, Sadducee,
   What did you do for him? — bad was the best.

Negroes and foreigners, all have a claim on you;
   Yearly you send your well-advertised hoard,
But the poor jockey boy — shame on you, shame on you,
   "Feed ye my little ones" — What said the Lord?

Him ye held less than the outer barbarian,
   Left him to die in his ignorant sin;
Have you no principles, humanitarian?
   Have you no precept — "Go gather them in"?

* * * *

Knew he God's name? In his brutal profanity,
   That name was an oath — out of many but one —

What did he get from our famed Christianity?
  Where has his soul — if he had any — gone?

Fourteen years old, and what was he taught of it?
  What did he know of God's infinite grace?
Draw the dark curtain of shame o'er the thought of it,
  Draw the shroud over the jockey boy's face.

How M'Ginnis Went Missing

Let us cease our idle chatter,
  Let the tears bedew our cheek,
For a man from Tallangatta
  Has been missing for a week.

Where the roaring, flooded Murray
  Covered all the lower land,
There he started in a hurry,
  With a bottle in his hand.

And his fate is hid for ever,
  But the public seem to think
That he slumbered by the river,
  'Neath the influence of drink.

And they scarcely seem to wonder
  That the river, wide and deep,
Never woke him with its thunder,
  Never stirred him in his sleep.

As the crashing logs came sweeping,
  And their tumult filled the air,
Then M'Ginnis murmured, sleeping,
  "'Tis a wake in ould Kildare."

So the river rose and found him
  Sleeping softly by the stream,
And the cruel waters drowned him
  Ere he wakened from his dream.

And the blossom-tufted wattle,
  Blooming brightly on the lea
Saw M'Ginnis and the bottle
  Going drifting out to sea.

A Voice from the Town

A sequel to "A Voice from the Bush"

I thought, in the days of the droving,
  Of steps I might hope to retrace,
To be done with the bush and the roving
  And settle once more in my place.
With a heart that was well nigh to breaking,
  In the long, lonely rides on the plain,
I thought of the pleasure of taking
  The hand of a lady again.

I am back into civilisation,
  Once more in the stir and the strife,
But the old joys have lost their sensation —
  The light has gone out of my life;
The men of my time they have married,
  Made fortunes or gone to the wall;
Too long from the scene I have tarried,
  And, somehow, I'm out of it all.

For I go to the balls and the races
  A lonely companionless elf,
And the ladies bestow all their graces
  On others less grey than myself;
While the talk goes around I'm a dumb one
  'Midst youngsters that chatter and prate,
And they call me "the Man who was Someone
  Way back in the year Sixty-eight".

And I look, sour and old, at the dancers
  That swing to the strains of the band,
And the ladies all give me the Lancers,
  No waltzes — I quite understand.
For matrons intent upon matching
  Their daughters with infinite push,
Would scarce think him worthy the catching,
  The broken-down man from the bush.

New partners have come and new faces,
  And I, of the bygone brigade,
Sharply feel that oblivion my place is —
  I must lie with the rest in the shade.

And the youngsters, fresh-featured and pleasant,
  They live as we lived — fairly fast;

But I doubt if the men of the present
  Are as good as the men of the past.

Of excitement and praise they are chary,
  There is nothing much good upon earth;
Their watchword is *nil admirari*,
  They are bored from the days of their birth.
Where the life that we led was a revel
  They "wince and relent and refrain" —
I could show them the road — to the devil,
  Were I only a youngster again.

I could show them the road where the stumps are
  The pleasures that end in remorse,
And the game where the Devil's three trumps are,
  The woman, the card, and the horse.
Shall the blind lead the blind — shall the sower
  Of wind reap the storm as of yore?
Though they get to their goal somewhat slower,
  They march where we hurried before.

For the world never learns — just as we did,
  They gallantly go to their fate,
Unheeded all warnings, unheeded
  The maxims of elders sedate.
As the husbandman, patiently toiling,
  Draws a harvest each year from the soil,
So the fools grow afresh for the spoiling,
  And a new crop of thieves for the spoil.

But a truce to this dull moralising,
  Let them drink while the drops are of gold,
I have tasted the dregs — 'twere surprising
  Were the new wine to me like the old;
And I weary for lack of employment
  In idleness day after day,
For the key to the door of enjoyment
  Is Youth — and I've thrown it away.

A Bunch of Roses

Roses ruddy and roses white,
  What are the joys that my heart discloses?
Sitting alone in the fading light
Memories come to me here to-night
  With the wonderful scent of the big red roses.

Memories come as the daylight fades
  Down on the hearth where the firelight dozes;
Flicker and flutter the lights and shades,
And I see the face of a queen of maids
  Whose memory comes with the scent of roses.

Visions arise of a scene of mirth,
  And a ballroom belle that superbly poses —
A queenly woman of queenly worth,
And I am the happiest man on earth
  With a single flower from a bunch of roses.

Only her memory lives tonight —
  God in His wisdom her young life closes;
Over her grave may the turf be light,
Cover her coffin with roses white —
  She was always fond of the big white roses.

Such are the visions that fade away —
  Man proposes and God disposes;
Look in the glass and I see to-day
Only an old man, worn and grey,
  Bending his head to a bunch of roses.

BLACK SWANS

As I lie at rest on a patch of clover
In the Western Park when the day is done,
I watch as the wild black swans fly over
With their phalanx turned to the sinking sun;
And I hear the clang of their leader crying
To a lagging mate in the rearward flying,
And they fade away in the darkness dying,
Where the stars are mustering one by one.

Oh! ye wild black swans, 'twere a world of wonder
For a while to join in your westward flight,
With the stars above and the dim earth under,
Through the cooling air of the glorious night.
As we swept along on our pinions winging,
We should catch the chime of a church-bell ringing,
Or the distant note of a torrent singing,
Or the far-off flash of a station light.

From the northern lakes with the reeds and rushes,
Where the hills are clothed with a purple haze,
Where the bellbirds chime and the songs of thrushes
Make music sweet in the jungle maze,
They will hold their course to the westward ever,
Till they reach the banks of the old grey river,
Where the waters wash, and the reed beds quiver
In the burning heat of the summer days.

Oh! ye strange wild birds, will ye bear a greeting
To the folk that live in that western land?
Then for every sweep of your pinions beating,
Ye shall bear a wish to the sunburnt band,
To the stalwart men who are stoutly fighting
With the heat and drought and dust storm smiting,
Yet whose life somehow has a strange inviting,
When once to the work they have put their hand.

Facing it yet! Oh, my friend stout-hearted,
What does it matter for rain or shine,
For the hopes deferred and the gain departed?
Nothing could conquer that heart of thine.
And thy health and strength are beyond confessing
As the only joys that are worth possessing.
May the days to come be as rich in blessing
As the days we spent in the auld lang syne.

I would fain go back to the old grey river,
To the old bush days when our hearts were light,
But, alas! those days they have fled for ever,
They are like the swans that have swept from sight.
And I know full well that the strangers' faces
Would meet us now in our dearest places;
For our day is dead and has left no traces
But the thoughts that live in my mind tonight.

There are folk long dead, and our hearts would sicken —
We would grieve for them with a bitter pain,
If the past could live and the dead could quicken,
We then might turn to that life again.
But on lonely nights we would hear them calling,
We should hear their steps on the pathways falling,
We should loathe the life with a hate appalling
In our lonely rides by the ridge and plain.

* * * *

In the silent park is a scent of clover,
And the distant roar of the town is dead,
And I hear once more as the swans fly over
Their far-off clamour from overhead.
They are flying west by their instinct guided,
And for man likewise is his fate decided,
And griefs apportioned and joys divided
By a mighty power with a purpose dread.

THE ALL RIGHT 'UN

He came from "further out",
That land of heat and drought
And dust and gravel.
He got a touch of sun,
And rested at the run
Until his cure was done,
And he could travel.

When spring had decked the plain,
He flitted off again
As flit the swallows.
And from that western land,
When many months were spanned,
A letter came to hand,
Which read as follows:

"Dear Sir, I take my pen
In hopes that all your men
And you are hearty.
You think that I've forgot
Your kindness, Mr Scott,
Oh, no, dear sir, I'm not
That sort of party.

"You sometimes bet, I know,
Well, now you'll have a show
The 'books' to frighten.
Up here at Wingadee
Young Billy Fife and me
We're training Strife, and he
Is a all right 'un.

"Just now we're running byes,
But, sir, first time he tries
I'll send you word of.
And running 'on the crook'
Their measures we have took,
It is the deadest hook
You ever heard of.

"So when we lets him go,
Why, then, I'll let you know,
And you can have a show
To put a mite on.

Now, sir, my leave I'll take,
Yours truly, William Blake.
P.S. Make no mistake,
He's a all right 'un."

* * * *

By next week's *Riverine*
I saw my friend had been
A bit too cunning.
I read: "The racehorse Strife
And jockey William Fife
Disqualified for life —
Suspicious running."

But though they spoilt his game,
I reckon all the same
I fairly ought to claim
My friend a white 'un.
For though he wasn't straight,
His deeds would indicate
His heart at any rate
Was "a all right 'un".

THE BOSS
OF THE ADMIRAL LYNCH

Did you ever hear tell of Chile? I was readin' the other day
Of President Balmaceda and of how he was sent away.
It seems that he didn't suit 'em — they thought that they'd like a
change,
So they started an insurrection and chased him across the range.
They seem to be restless people — and, judging by what you hear,
They raise up these revolutions 'bout two or three times a year;
And the man that goes out of office, he goes for the boundary
quick,
For there isn't no vote by ballot — it's bullets that does the trick.
And it ain't like a real battle, where the prisoners' lives are spared,
And they fight till there's one side beaten and then there's a truce
declared,
And the man that has got the licking goes down like a blooming
lord
To hand in his resignation and give up his blooming sword,
And the other man bows and takes it, and everything's all polite —
This wasn't that kind of a picnic, this wasn't that sort of a fight.
For the pris'ners they took — they shot 'em; no odds were they
small or great,
If they'd collared old Balmaceda, they reckoned to shoot him
straight.
A lot of bloodthirsty devils they were — but there ain't a doubt
They must have been real plucked 'uns — the way that they fought
it out,
And the king of 'em all, I reckon, the man that could stand a
pinch,
Was the boss of a one-horse gunboat. They called her the *Admiral
Lynch*.
Well, he was for Balmaceda, and after the war was done,
And Balmaceda was beaten and his troops had been forced to run,
The other man fetched his army and proceeded to do things
brown,
He marched 'em into the fortress and took command of the town.
Cannon and guns and horses troopin' along the road,
Rumblin' over the bridges, and never a foeman showed
Till they came in sight of the harbour, and the very first thing they
see
Was this mite of a one-horse gunboat a-lying against the quay,
And there as they watched they noticed a flutter of crimson rag,
And under their eyes he hoisted old Balmaceda's flag.

Well, I tell you it fairly knocked 'em — it just took away their
    breath,
For he must ha' known if they caught him, 'twas nothin' but
    sudden death.
An' he'd got no fire in his furnace, no chance to put out to sea,
So he stood by his gun and waited with his vessel against the quay.
Well, they sent him a civil message to say that the war was done,
And most of his side were corpses, and all that were left had run;
And blood had been spilt sufficient, so they gave him a chance to
    decide
If he'd haul down his bit of bunting and come on the winning side.
He listened and heard their message, and answered them all polite,
That he was a Spanish hidalgo, and the men of his race *must* fight!
A gunboat against an army, and with never a chance to run,
And them with their hundred cannon and him with a single gun:
The odds were a trifle heavy — but he wasn't the sort to flinch,
So he opened fire on the army, did the boss of the *Admiral Lynch*.
They pounded his boat to pieces, they silenced his single gun,
And captured the whole consignment, for none of 'em cared to
    run;
And it don't say whether they shot him — it don't even give his
    name —
But whatever they did I'll wager that he went to his graveyard
    game.
I tell you those old hidalgos so stately and so polite,
They turn out the real Maginnis when it comes to an uphill fight.
There was General Alcantara, who died in the heaviest brunt,
And General Alzéreca was killed in the battle's front;
But the king of 'em all, I reckon — the man that could stand a
    pinch —
Was the man who attacked the army with the gunboat *Admiral
    Lynch*.

A BUSHMAN'S SONG

I'm travellin' down the Castlereagh, and I'm a station hand,
I'm handy with the ropin' pole, I'm handy with the brand,
And I can ride a rowdy colt, or swing the axe all day,
But there's no demand for a station hand along the Castlereagh.

So it's shift, boys, shift, for there isn't the slightest doubt
That we've got to make a shift to the stations further out
With the packhorse runnin' after, for he follows like a dog,
We must strike across the country at the old jig-jog.

This old black horse I'm riding — if you'll notice what's his brand,
He wears the crooked R, you see — none better in the land.
He takes a lot of beatin', and the other day we tried,
For a bit of a joke, with a racing bloke, for twenty pounds aside.

It was shift, boys, shift, for there wasn't the slightest doubt,
That I had to make him shift, for the money was nearly out;
But he cantered home a winner, with the other one at the flog —
He's a red-hot sort to pick up with his old jig-jog.

I asked a cove for shearin' once along the Marthaguy:
"We shear non-union, here," says he. "I call it scab," says I.
I looked along the shearin' floor before I turned to go —
There were eight or ten dashed Chinamen a-shearin' in a row.

It was shift, boys, shift, for there wasn't the slightest doubt
It was time to make a shift with the leprosy about.
So I saddled up my horses, and I whistled to my dog,
And I left his scabby station at the old jig-jog.

I went to Illawarra where my brother's got a farm,
He has to ask his landlord's leave before he lifts his arm;
The landlord owns the countryside — man, woman, dog, and cat,
They haven't the cheek to dare to speak without they touch their hat.

It was shift, boys, shift, for there wasn't the slightest doubt
Their little landlord god and I would soon have fallen out;
Was I to touch my hat to him? — was I his bloomin' dog?
So I makes for up the country at the old jig-jog.

But it's time that I was movin', I've a mighty way to go
Till I drink artesian water from a thousand feet below;
Till I meet the overlanders with the cattle comin' down,
And I'll work a while till I make a pile, then have a spree in town.

So, it's shift, boys, shift, for there isn't the slightest doubt
We've got to make a shift to the stations further out;
The packhorse runs behind us, for he follows like a dog,
And we cross a lot of country at the old jig-jog.

How Gilbert Died

There's never a stone at the sleeper's head,
  There's never a fence beside,
And the wandering stock on the grave may tread
  Unnoticed and undenied,
But the smallest child on the Watershed
  Can tell you how Gilbert died.

For he rode at dusk, with his comrade Dunn
  To the hut at the Stockman's Ford,
In the waning light of the sinking sun
  They peered with a fierce accord.
They were outlaws both — and on each man's head
  Was a thousand pounds reward.

They had taken toll of the country round,
  And the troopers came behind
With a black that tracked like a human hound
  In the scrub and the ranges blind:
He could run the trail where a white man's eye
  No sign of a track could find.

He had hunted them out of the One Tree Hill
  And over the Old Man Plain,
But they wheeled their tracks with a wild beast's skill,
  And they made for the range again.
Then away to the hut where their grandsire dwelt,
  They rode with a loosened rein.

And their grandsire gave them a greeting bold:
  "Come in and rest in peace,
No safer place does the country hold —
  With the night pursuit must cease,
And we'll drink success to the roving boys,
  And to hell with the black police."

But they went to death when they entered there,
  In the hut at the Stockman's Ford,
For their grandsire's words were as false as fair —
  They were doomed to the hangman's cord.
He had sold them both to the black police
  For the sake of the big reward.

In the depth of night there are forms that glide
  As stealthy as serpents creep,
And around the hut where the outlaws hide
  They plant in the shadows deep,

And they wait till the first faint flush of dawn
  Shall waken their prey from sleep.

But Gilbert wakes while the night is dark —
  A restless sleeper, aye,
He has heard the sound of a sheepdog's bark,
  And his horse's warning neigh,
And he says to his mate, "There are hawks abroad,
  And it's time that we went away."

Their rifles stood at the stretcher head,
  Their bridles lay to hand,
They wakened the old man out of his bed,
  When they heard the sharp command:
"In the name of the Queen lay down your arms,
  Now, Dunn and Gilbert, stand!"

Then Gilbert reached for his rifle true
  That close at his hand he kept,
He pointed it straight at the voice and drew,
  But never a flash outleapt,
For the water ran from the rifle breach —
  It was drenched while the outlaws slept.

Then he dropped the piece with a bitter oath,
  And he turned to his comrade Dunn:
"We are sold," he said, "we are dead men both,
  But there may be a chance for one;
I'll stop and I'll fight with the pistol here,
  You take to your heels and run."

So Dunn crept out on his hands and knees
  In the dim, half-dawning light,
And he made his way to a patch of trees,
  And vanished among the night,
And the trackers hunted his tracks all day,
  But they never could trace his flight.

But Gilbert walked from the open door
  In a confident style and rash;
He heard at his side the rifles roar,
  And he heard the bullets crash.
But he laughed as he lifted his pistol-hand,
  And he fired at the rifle flash.

Then out of the shadows the troopers aimed
  At his voice and the pistol sound,
With the rifle flashes the darkness flamed,
  He staggered and spun around,

And they riddled his body with rifle balls
   As it lay on the blood-soaked ground.

There's never a stone at the sleeper's head
   There's never a fence beside,
And the wandering stock on the grave may tread
   Unnoticed and undenied,
But the smallest child on the Watershed
   Can tell you how Gilbert died.

THE FLYING GANG

A Railroad Song

I served my time, in the days gone by,
In the railway's clash and clang,
And I worked my way to the end, and I
Was the head of the "Flying Gang".
'Twas a chosen band that was kept at hand
In case of an urgent need,
Was it south or north we were started forth
And away at our utmost speed.
  If word reached town that a bridge was down,
  The imperious summons rang —
  "Come out with the pilot engine sharp,
  And away with the flying gang."

Then a piercing scream and a rush of steam
As the engine moved ahead,
With a measured beat by the slum and street
Of the busy town we fled,
By the uplands bright and the homesteads white,
With the rush of the western gale,
And the pilot swayed with the pace we made
As she rocked on the ringing rail.
  And the country children clapped their hands
  As the engine's echoes rang,
  But their elders said, "There is work ahead
  When they send for the flying gang."

Then across the miles of the saltbush plain
That gleamed with the morning dew,
Where the grasses waved like the ripening grain
The pilot engine flew,
A fiery rush in the open bush
Where the grade marks seemed to fly,
And the order sped on the wires ahead,
The pilot *must* go by.
  The Governor's special must stand aside,
  And the fast express go hang,
  Let your orders be that the line is free
  For the boys of the flying gang.

SHEARING AT CASTLEREAGH

The bell is set aringing, and the engine gives a toot,
There's five and thirty shearers here are shearing for the loot,
So stir yourselves, you penners-up and shove the sheep along,
The musterers are fetching them a hundred thousand strong,
And make your collie dogs speak up — what would the buyers say
In London if the wool was late this year from Castlereagh?

The man that "rung" the Tubbo shed is not the ringer here,
That stripling from the Cooma side can teach him how to shear.
They trim away the ragged locks, and rip the cutter goes,
And leaves a track of snowy fleece from brisket to the nose;
It's lovely how they peel it off with never stop nor stay,
They're racing for the ringer's place this year at Castlereagh.

The man that keeps the cutters sharp is growling in his cage,
He's always in a hurry and he's always in a rage —
"You clumsy-fisted muttonheads, you'd turn a fellow sick,
You pass yourselves as shearers? You were born to swing a pick!
Another broken cutter here, that's two you've broke today,
It's awful how such crawlers come to shear at Castlereagh."

The youngsters picking up the fleece enjoy the merry din,
They throw the classer up the fleece, he throws it to the bin;
The pressers standing by the rack are waiting for the wool,
There's room for just a couple more, the press is nearly full;
Now jump upon the lever, lads, and heave and heave away,
Another bale of golden fleece is branded "Castlereagh".

THE WIND'S MESSAGE

There came a whisper down the Bland between the dawn and dark,
Above the tossing of the pines, above the river's flow;
It stirred the boughs of giant gums and stalwart ironbark;
It drifted where the wild ducks played amid the swamps below;
It brought a breath of mountain air from off the hills of pine,
A scent of eucalyptus trees in honey-laden bloom;
And drifting, drifting far away along the southern line
It caught from leaf and grass and fern a subtle strange perfume.

It reached the toiling city folk, but few there were that heard —
The rattle of their busy life had choked the whisper down;
And some but caught a fresh-blown breeze with scent of pine that
    stirred
A thought of blue hills far away beyond the smoky town;
And others heard the whisper pass, but could not understand
The magic of the breeze's breath that set their hearts aglow,
Nor how the roving wind could bring across the Overland
A sound of voices silent now and songs of long ago.

But some that heard the whisper clear were filled with vague unrest;
The breeze had brought its message home, they could not fixed
    abide;
Their fancies wandered all the day towards the blue hills' breast,
Towards the sunny slopes that lie along the riverside,
The mighty rolling western plains are very fair to see,
Where waving to the passing breeze the silver myalls stand,
But fairer are the giant hills, all rugged though they be,
From which the two great rivers rise that run along the Bland.

Oh! rocky range and rugged spur and river running clear,
That swings around the sudden bends with swirl of snow-white
    foam,
Though we, your sons, are far away, we sometimes seem to hear
The message that the breezes bring to call the wanderers home.
The mountain peaks are white with snow that feeds a thousand
    rills,
Along the river banks the maize grows tall on virgin land,
And we shall live to see once more those sunny southern hills,
And strike once more the bridle track that leads along the Bland.

JOHNSON'S ANTIDOTE

Down along the Snakebite River, where the overlanders camp,
Where the serpents are in millions, all of the most deadly stamp;
Where the station cook in terror, nearly every time he bakes,
Mixes up among the doughboys half a dozen poison snakes:
Where the wily free selector walks in armour-plated pants,
And defies the stings of scorpions, and the bites of bulldog ants:
Where the adder and the viper tear each other by the throat,
There it was that William Johnson sought his snakebite antidote.

Johnson was a free selector, and his brain went rather queer,
For the constant sight of serpents filled him with a deadly fear;
So he tramped his free selection, morning, afternoon and night,
Seeking for some great specific that would cure the serpent's bite.
Till King Billy, of the Mooki, chieftain of the flour bag head,
Told him, "Spos'n snake bite pfeller, pfeller mostly drop down
    dead;
Spos'n snake bite old goanna, then you watch a while you see,
Old goanna cure himself with eating little pfeller tree."
"That's the cure," said William Johnson, "point me out this plant
    sublime",
But King Billy, feeling lazy, said he'd go another time.
Thus it came to pass that Johnson, having got the tale by rote,
Followed every stray goanna, seeking for the antidote.

* * * *

Loafing once beside the river, while he thought his heart would
    break,
There he saw a big goanna, fighting with a tiger snake,
In and out they rolled and wriggled, bit each other, heart and soul,
Till the valiant old goanna swallowed his opponent whole.
Breathless, Johnson sat and watched him, saw him struggle up the
    bank,
Saw him nibbling at the branches of some bushes, green and rank;
Saw him, happy and contented, lick his lips, as off he crept,
While the bulging in his stomach showed where his opponent slept.
Then a cheer of exultation burst aloud from Johnson's throat;
"Luck at last," said he, "I've struck it! 'tis the famous antidote.

"Here it is, the Grand Elixir, greatest blessing ever known,
Twenty thousand men in India die each year of snakes alone.
Think of all the foreign nations, negro, chow, and blackamoor,
Saved from sudden expiration, by my wondrous snakebite cure.
It will bring me fame and fortune! In the happy days to be,
Men of every clime and nation will be round to gaze on me —
Scientific men in thousands, men of mark and men of note,

Rushing down the Mooki River, after Johnson's antidote.
It will cure *delirium tremens*, when the patient's eyeballs stare
At imaginary spiders, snakes which really are not there.
When he thinks he sees them wriggle, when he thinks he sees them
    bloat,
It will cure him just to think of Johnson's Snakebite Antidote."

Then he rushed to the museum, found a scientific man —
"Trot me out a deadly serpent, just the deadliest you can;
I intend to let him bite me, all the risk I will endure,
Just to prove the sterling value of my wondrous snakebite cure.
Even though an adder bit me, back to life again I'd float;
Snakes are out of date, I tell you, since I've found the antidote."

Said the scientific person, "If you really want to die,
Go ahead — but, if you're doubtful, let your sheepdog have a try.
Get a pair of dogs and try it, let the snake give both a nip;
Give your dog the snakebite mixture, let the other fellow rip;
If he dies and yours survives him, then it proves the thing is good.
Will you fetch your dog and try it?" Johnson rather thought he
    would.
So he went and fetched his canine, hauled him forward by the
    throat.
"Stump, old man," says he, "we'll show them we've the genwine
    antidote."

Both the dogs were duly loaded with the poison gland's contents;
Johnson gave his dog the mixture, then sat down to wait events.
"Mark," he said, "in twenty minutes Stump'll be a-rushing round,
While the other wretched creature lies a corpse upon the ground."
But, alas for William Johnson! ere they'd watched a half-hour's spell
Stumpy was as dead as mutton, t'other dog was live and well.
And the scientific person hurried off with utmost speed,
Tested Johnson's drug and found it was a deadly poison weed;
Half a tumbler killed an emu, half a spoonful killed a goat,
All the snakes on earth were harmless to that awful antidote.

* * * *

Down along the Mooki River, on the overlanders' camp,
Where the serpents are in millions, all of the most deadly stamp,
Wanders, daily, William Johnson, down among those poisonous
    hordes,
Shooting every stray goanna, calls them "black and yaller frauds".
And King Billy, of the Mooki, cadging for the cast-off coat,
Somehow seems to dodge the subject of the snakebite antidote.

AMBITION AND ART

Ambition
I am the maid of the lustrous eyes
  Of great fruition,
Whom the sons of men that are over-wise
  Have called Ambition.

And the world's success is the only goal
  I have within me;
The meanest man with the smallest soul
  May woo and win me.

For the lust of power and the pride of place
  To all I proffer.
Wilt thou take thy part in the crowded race
  For what I offer?

The choice is thine, and the world is wide —
  Thy path is lonely.
I may not lead and I may not guide —
  I urge thee only.

I am just a whip and a spur that smites
  To fierce endeavour.
In the restless days and the sleepless nights
  I urge thee ever.

Thou shalt wake from sleep with a startled cry,
  In fright upleaping
At a rival's step as it passes by
  Whilst thou art sleeping.

Honour and truth shall be overthrown
  In fierce desire;
Thou shalt use thy friend as a stepping-stone
  To mount thee higher.

When the curtain falls on the sordid strife
  That seemed so splendid,
Thou shalt look with pain on the wasted life
  That thou hast ended.

Thou hast sold thy life for a guerdon small
  In fitful flashes;
There has been reward — but the end of all
  Is dust and ashes.

For the night has come and it brings to naught
  Thy projects cherished,

And thine epitaph shall in brass be wrought —
  "He lived and perished."

Art

I wait for thee at the outer gate,
  My love, mine only;
Wherefore tarriest thou so late
  While I am lonely?

Thou shalt seek my side with a footstep swift,
  In thee implanted
Is the love of Art and the greatest gift
  That God has granted.

And the world's concerns with its rights and wrongs
  Shall seem but small things —
Poet or painter, a singer of songs,
  Thine art is all things.

For the wine of life is a woman's love
  To keep beside thee;
But the love of Art is a thing above —
  A star to guide thee.

As the years go by with thy love of Art
  All undiminished,
Thou shalt end thy days with a quiet heart —
  Thy work is finished.

So the painter fashions a picture strong
  That fadeth never,
And the singer singeth a wondrous song
  That lives for ever.

IN DEFENCE
OF THE BUSH

So you're back from up the country, Mister Lawson, where you
    went,
And you're cursing all the business in a bitter discontent;
Well, we grieve to disappoint you, and it makes us sad to hear
That it wasn't cool and shady — and there wasn't plenty beer,
And the loony bullock snorted when you first came into view;
Well, you know it's not so often that he sees a swell like you;
And the roads were hot and dusty, and the plains were burnt and
    brown,
And no doubt you're better suited drinking lemon squash in town.

Yet, perchance, if you should journey down the very track you
    went
In a month or two at furthest you would wonder what it meant,
Where the sunbaked earth was gasping like a creature in its pain
You would find the grasses waving like a field of summer grain,
And the miles of thirsty gutters blocked with sand and choked with
    mud,
You would find them mighty rivers with a turbid, sweeping flood;
For the rain and drought and sunshine make no changes in the
    street,
In the sullen line of buildings and the ceaseless tramp of feet;
But the bush hath moods and changes, as the seasons rise and fall,
And the men who know the bush land — they are loyal through it
    all.

But you found the bush was dismal and a land of no delight,
Did you chance to hear a chorus in the shearers' huts at night?
Did they "rise up, William Riley" by the camp-fire's cheery blaze?
Did they rise him as we rose him in the good old droving days?
And the women of the homesteads and the men you chanced to
    meet —
Were their faces sour and saddened like the "faces in the street",
And the "shy selector children" — were they better now or worse
Than the little city urchins who would greet you with a curse?
Is not such a life much better than the squalid street and square
Where the fallen women flaunt it in the fierce electric glare,
Where the sempstress plies her sewing till her eyes are sore and red
In a filthy, dirty attic toiling on for daily bread?
Did you hear no sweeter voices in the music of the bush
Than the roar of trams and buses, and the war whoop of "the
    push"?

Did the magpies rouse your slumbers with their carol sweet and
  strange?
Did you hear the silver chiming of the bellbirds on the range?
But, perchance, the wild birds' music by your senses was despised,
For you say you'll stay in townships till the bush is civilised.
Would you make it a tea garden and on Sundays have a band
Where the "blokes" might take their "donahs", with a "public"
  close at hand?
You had better stick to Sydney and make merry with the "push",
For the bush will never suit you, and you'll never suit the bush.

LAST WEEK

Oh, the new chum went to the backblock run,
But he should have gone there last week.
He tramped ten miles with a loaded gun,
But of turkey or duck he saw never a one,
For he should have been there last week,
   They said,
There were flocks of 'em there last week.

He wended his way to a waterfall,
And he should have gone there last week.
He carried a camera, legs and all,
But the day was hot, and the stream was small,
For he should have gone there last week,
   They said,
They drowned a man there last week.

He went for a drive, and he made a start,
Which should have been made last week,
For the old horse died of a broken heart;
So he footed it home and he dragged the cart —
But the horse was all right last week,
   They said,
He trotted a match last week.

So he asked the bushies who came from far
To visit the town last week,
If they'd dine with him, and they said, "Hurrah!"
But there wasn't a drop in the whisky jar —
"You should have been here last week,"
   He said,
"I drank it all up last week!"

THOSE NAMES

The shearers sat in the firelight, hearty and hale and strong,
After the hard day's shearing, passing the joke along:
The "ringer" that shore a hundred, as they never were shorn
    before,
And the novice who, toiling bravely, had tommyhawked half a
    score,
The tar boy, the cook, and the slushy, the sweeper that swept the
    board,
The picker-up, and the penner, with the rest of the shearing horde.
There were men from the inland stations where the skies like a
    furnace glow,
And men from the Snowy River, the land of the frozen snow;
There were swarthy Queensland drovers who reckoned all land by
    miles,
And farmers' sons from the Murray, where many a vineyard smiles.
They started at telling stories when they wearied of cards and
    games,
And to give these stories a flavour they threw in some local names,
And a man from the bleak Monaro, away on the tableland,
He fixed his eyes on the ceiling, and he started to play his hand.

He told them of Adjintoothbong, where the pine-clad mountains
    freeze,
And the weight of the snow in summer breaks branches off the trees,
And, as he warmed to the business, he let them have it strong —
Nimitybelle, Conargo, Wheeo, Bongongolong;
He lingered over them fondly, because they recalled to mind
A thought of the old bush homestead, and the girl that he left
    behind.
Then the shearers all sat silent till a man in the corner rose;
Said he, "I've travelled aplenty but never heard names like those,
Out in the western districts, out on the Castlereagh
Most of the names are easy — short for a man to say.
You've heard of Mungrybambone and the Gundabluey pine,
Quobbotha, Girilambone, and Terramungamine,
Quambone, Eunonyhareenyha, Wee Waa, and Buntijo —"
But the rest of the shearers stopped him, "For the sake of your jaw,
    go slow,
If you reckon those names are short ones out where such names
    prevail,
Just try and remember some long ones before you begin the tale."

And the man from the western district, though never a word he
    said,
Just winked with his dexter eyelid, and then he retired to bed.

A Bush Christening

On the outer Barcoo where the churches are few,
   And men of religion are scanty,
On a road never cross'd 'cept by folk that are lost,
   One Michael Magee had a shanty.

Now this Mike was the dad of a ten-year-old lad,
   Plump, healthy, and stoutly conditioned;
He was strong as the best, but poor Mike had no rest
   For the youngster had never been christened.

And his wife used to cry, "If the darlin' should die
   Saint Peter would not recognise him."
But by luck he survived till a preacher arrived,
   Who agreed straightaway to baptise him.

Now the artful young rogue, while they held their collogue,
   With his ear to the keyhole was listenin',
And he muttered in fright while his features turned white,
   "What the divil and all is this christenin'?"

He was none of your dolts, he had seen them brand colts,
   And it seemed to his small understanding,
If the man in the frock made him one of the flock,
   It must mean something very like branding.

So away with a rush he set off for the bush,
   While the tears in his eyelids they glistened —
"'Tis outrageous," says he, "to brand youngsters like me,
   I'll be dashed if I'll stop to be christened!"

Like a young native dog he ran into a log,
   And his father with language uncivil,
Never heeding the "praste" cried aloud in his haste,
   "Come out and be christened, you divil!"

But he lay there as snug as a bug in a rug,
   And his parents in vain might reprove him,
Till his reverence spoke (he was fond of a joke)
   "I've a notion," says he, "that'll move him.

"Poke a stick up the log, give the spalpeen a prog;
   Poke him aisy — don't hurt him or maim him,
'Tis not long that he'll stand, I've the water at hand,
   As he rushes out this end I'll name him.

"Here he comes, and for shame! ye've forgotten the name —
   Is it Patsy or Michael or Dinnis?"

Here the youngster ran out, and the priest gave a shout —
  "Take your chance, anyhow, wid 'Maginnis'!"

As the howling young cub ran away to the scrub
  Where he knew that pursuit would be risky,
The priest, as he fled, flung a flask at his head
  That was labelled "Maginnis's Whisky!"

And Maginnis Magee has been made a J.P.,
  And the one thing he hates more than sin is
To be asked by the folk who have heard of the joke,
  How he came to be christened "Maginnis"!

How the Favourite Beat Us

"Aye," said the boozer, "I tell you it's true, sir,
  I once was a punter with plenty of pelf,
But gone is my glory, I'll tell you the story
  How I stiffened my horse and got stiffened myself.

"'Twas a mare called the Cracker, I came down to back her,
  But found she was favourite all of a rush,
The folk just did pour on to lay six to four on,
  And several bookies were killed in the crush.

"It seems old Tomato was stiff, though a starter;
  They reckoned him fit for the Caulfield to keep.
The Bloke and the Donah were scratched by their owner,
  He only was offered three-fourths of the sweep.

"We knew Salamander was slow as a gander,
  The mare could have beat him the length of the straight,
And old Manumission was out of condition,
  And most of the others were running off weight.

"No doubt someone 'blew it', for everyone knew it,
  The bets were all gone, and I muttered in spite,
'If I can't get a copper, by Jingo, I'll stop her,
  Let the public fall in, it will serve the brutes right.'

"I said to the jockey, 'Now, listen, my cocky,
  You watch as you're cantering down by the stand,
I'll wait where that toff is and give you the office,
  You're only to win if I lift up my hand.'

"I then tried to back her — 'What price is the Cracker?'
  'Our books are all full, sir,' each bookie did swear;
My mind, then, I made up, my fortune I played up
  I bet every shilling against my own mare.

"I strolled to the gateway, the mare in the straight way
  Was shifting and dancing, and pawing the ground,
The boy saw me enter and wheeled for his canter,
  When a darned great mosquito came buzzing around.

"They breed 'em at Hexham, it's risky to vex 'em,
  They suck a man dry at a sitting, no doubt,
But just as the mare passed, he fluttered my hair past,
  I lifted my hand, and I flattened him out.

"I was stunned when they started, the mare simply darted
  Away to the front when the flag was let fall,

For none there could match her, and none tried to catch her —
    She finished a furlong in front of them all.

"You bet that I went for the boy, whom I sent for
    The moment he weighed and came out of the stand —
'Who paid you to win it? Come, own up this minute.'
    'Lord love yer,' said he, 'why, you lifted your hand.'

"'Twas true, by St Peter, that cursed 'muskeeter'
    Had broke me so broke that I hadn't a brown,
And you'll find the best course is when dealing with horses
    To win when you're able, and *keep your hands down.*"

THE GREAT CALAMITY

MacFierce'un came to Whiskeyhurst
  When summer days were hot,
And bided there wi' Jock McThirst,
  A brawny brother Scot.
Gude Faith! They made the whisky fly,
  Like Highland chieftains true,
And when they'd drunk the beaker dry
  They sang, "We are nae fou!"

"There is nae folk like oor ain folk,
  Sae gallant and sae true."
They sang the only Scottish joke
  Which is, "We are nae fou."

Said bold McThirst, "Let Saxons jaw
  Aboot their great concerns,
But bonny Scotland beats them a',
  The land o' cakes and Burns,
The land o' partridge, deer, and grouse,
  Fill up your glass, I beg,
There's muckle whusky i' the house,
  Forbye what's in the keg."

And here a hearty laugh he laughed,
  "Just come wi' me, I beg."
MacFierce'un saw with pleasure daft
  A fifty-gallon keg.

"Losh, man, that's grand," MacFierce'un cried,
  "Saw ever man the like?
Now, wi' the daylight, I maun ride
  To meet a Southron tyke,
But I'll be back ere summer's gone,
  So bide for me, I beg,
We'll make a grand assault upon
  Yon deevil of a keg."

* * * *

MacFierce'un rode to Whiskeyhurst,
  When summer days were gone,
And there he met with Jock McThirst
  Was greetin' all alone.

"McThirst, what gars ye look sae blank?
  Have all yer wits gane daft?
Has that accursed Southron bank
  Called up your overdraft?

Is all your grass burnt up wi' drouth?
  Is wool and hides gone flat?"
McThirst replied, "Gude friend, in truth,
  'Tis muckle waur than that."

"Has sair misfortune cursed your life
  That you should weep sae free?
Is harm upon your bonny wife,
  The children at your knee?
Is scaith upon your house and hame?"
  McThirst upraised his head:
"My bairns hae done the deed of shame —
  'Twere better they were dead.

"To think my bonny infant son
  Should do the deed o' guilt —
He let the whuskey spigot run,
  And a' the whuskey's spilt!"

                    * * * *

Upon them both these words did bring
  A solemn silence deep,
Gude faith, it is a fearsome thing
  To see two strong men weep.

Come-by-Chance

As I pondered very weary o'er a volume long and dreary —
For the plot was void of interest — 'twas the Postal Guide, in fact,
There I learnt the true location, distance, size, and population
Of each township, town, and village in the radius of the Act.

And I learnt that Puckawidgee stands beside the Murrumbidgee,
And that Booleroi and Bumble get their letters twice a year,
Also that the post inspector, when he visited Collector,
Closed the office up instanter, and re-opened Dungalear.

But my languid mood forsook me, when I found a name that took
        me,
Quite by chance I came across it — "Come-by-Chance" was what I
        read;
No location was assigned it, not a thing to help one find it,
Just an "N" which stood for northward, and the rest was all unsaid.

I shall leave my home, and forthward wander stoutly to the
        northward
Till I come by chance across it, and I'll straightway settle down,
For there can't be any hurry, nor the slightest cause for worry
Where the telegraph don't reach you nor the railways run to town.

And one's letters and exchanges come by chance across the ranges,
Where a wiry young Australian leads a pack horse once a week,
And the good news grows by keeping, and you're spared the pain
        of weeping
Over bad news when the mailman drops the letters in the creek.

But I fear, and more's the pity, that there's really no such city,
For there's not a man can find it of the shrewdest folk I know,
"Come-by-Chance", be sure it never means a land of fierce
        endeavour,
It is just the careless country where the dreamers only go.

* * * *

Though we work and toil and hustle in our life of haste and bustle,
All that makes our life worth living comes unstriven for and free;
Man may weary and importune, but the fickle goddess Fortune
Deals him out his pain or pleasure careless what his worth may be.

All the happy times entrancing, days of sport and nights of
        dancing,
Moonlit rides and stolen kisses, pouting lips and loving glance:
When you think of these be certain you have looked behind the
        curtain,
You have had the luck to linger just a while in "Come-by-Chance".

UNDER THE
SHADOW OF KILEY'S HILL

This is the place where they all were bred;
  Some of the rafters are standing still;
Now they are scattered and lost and dead,
Every one from the old nest fled,
  Out of the shadow of Kiley's Hill.

Better it is that they ne'er came back —
  Changes and chances are quickly rung;
Now the old homestead is gone to rack,
Green is the grass on the well-worn track
  Down by the gate where the roses clung.

Gone is the garden they kept with care;
  Left to decay at its own sweet will,
Fruit trees and flower beds eaten bare,
Cattle and sheep where the roses were,
  Under the shadow of Kiley's Hill.

Where are the children that throve and grew
  In the old homestead in days gone by?
One is away on the far Barcoo
Watching his cattle the long year through,
  Watching them starve in the droughts and die.

One in the town where all cares are rife,
  Weary with troubles that cramp and kill,
Fain would be done with the restless strife,
Fain would go back to the old bush life,
  Back to the shadow of Kiley's Hill.

One is away on the roving quest,
  Seeking his share of the golden spoil,
Out in the wastes of the trackless west,
Wandering ever he gives the best
  Of his years and strength to the hopeless toil.

What of the parents? That unkempt mound
  Shows where they slumber united still;
Rough is their grave, but they sleep as sound
Out on the range as on holy ground,
  Under the shadow of Kiley's Hill.

JIM CAREW

Born of a thoroughbred English race,
  Well-proportioned and closely knit,
Neat of figure and handsome face,
  Always ready and always fit,
Hard and wiry of limb and thew,
That was the ne'er-do-well Jim Carew.

One of the sons of the good old land —
  Many a year since his like was known;
Never a game but he took command,
  Never a sport but he held his own;
Gained at his college a triple blue —
Good as they make them was Jim Carew.

Came to grief — was it card or horse?
  Nobody asked and nobody cared;
Ship him away to the bush of course,
  Ne'er-do-well fellows are easily spared;
Only of women a tolerable few
Sorrowed at parting with Jim Carew.

Gentleman Jim on the cattle camp,
  Sitting his horse with an easy grace;
But the reckless living has left its stamp
  In the deep drawn lines of that handsome face,
And a harder look in those eyes of blue:
Prompt at a quarrel is Jim Carew.

Billy the Lasher was out for gore —
  Twelve-stone navvy with chest of hair,
When he opened out with a hungry roar,
  On a ten-stone man it was hardly fair;
But his wife was wise if his face she knew
By the time you were done with him, Jim Carew.

Gentleman Jim in the stockmen's hut
  Works with them, toils with them, side by side;
As to his past — well, his lips are shut.
  "Gentleman once," say his mates with pride;
And the wildest cornstalk can ne'er outdo
In feats of recklessness, Jim Carew.

What should he live for? A dull despair!
  Drink is his master and drags him down,
Water of Lethe that drowns all care.
  Gentleman Jim has a lot to drown,

And he reigns as king with a drunken crew,
Sinking to misery, Jim Carew.

Such is the end of the ne'er-do-well —
   Jimmy the Boozer, all down at heel;
But he straightens up when he's asked to tell
   His name and race, and a flash of steel
Still lightens up in those eyes of blue —
"I am, or — no, I *was* — Jim Carew."

THE SWAGMAN'S REST

We buried old Bob where the bloodwoods wave
  At the foot of the Eaglehawk;
We fashioned a cross on the old man's grave,
  For fear that his ghost might walk;
We carved his name on a bloodwood tree,
  With the date of his sad decease,
And in place of "Died from effects of spree",
  We wrote, "May he rest in peace".

For Bob was known on the Overland,
  A regular old bush wag,
Tramping along in the dust and sand,
  Humping his well worn swag.
He would camp for days in the river bed,
  And loiter and "fish for whales".
"I'm into the swagman's yard", he said,
  "And I never shall find the rails."

But he found the rails on that summer night
  For a better place — or worse,
As we watched by turns in the flickering light
  With an old black gin for nurse.
The breeze came in with the scent of pine,
  The river sounded clear,
When a change came on, and we saw the sign
  That told us the end was near.

But he spoke in a cultured voice and low —
  "I fancy they've 'sent the route';
I once was an army man, you know,
  Though now I'm a drunken brute;
But bury me out where the bloodwoods wave,
  And if ever you're fairly stuck,
Just take and shovel me out of the grave,
  And, maybe, I'll bring you luck.

"For I've always heard —" here his voice fell weak,
  His strength was well-nigh sped,
He gasped and struggled and tried to speak,
  Then fell in a moment — dead.
Thus ended a wasted life and hard,
  Of energies misapplied —
Old Bob was out of the "swagman's yard"
  And over the Great Divide.

* * * *

The drought came down on the field and flock,
  And never a raindrop fell,
Though the tortured moans of the starving stock
  Might soften a fiend from hell.
And we thought of the hint that the swagman gave
  When he went to the Great Unseen —
We shovelled the skeleton out of the grave
  To see what his hint might mean.

We dug where the cross and the graveposts were,
  We shovelled away the mould,
When sudden a vein of quartz lay bare
  All gleaming with yellow gold.
'Twas a reef with never a fault nor baulk
  That ran from the range's crest,
And the richest mine on the Eaglehawk
  Is known as "The Swagman's Rest".

THE DAYLIGHT IS DYING

The daylight is dying
  Away in the west,
The wild birds are flying
  In silence to rest;
In leafage and frondage
  Where shadows are deep,
They pass to its bondage —
  The kingdom of sleep.
And watched in their sleeping
  By stars in the height,
They rest in your keeping,
  Oh, wonderful night.

When night doth her glories
  Of starshine unfold,
'Tis then that the stories
  Of bushland are told.
Unnumbered I hold them
  In memories bright,
But who could unfold them,
  Or read them aright?
Beyond all denials
  The stars in their glories
The breeze in the myalls
  Are part of these stories.
The waving of grasses,
  The song of the river
That sings as it passes
  For ever and ever,
The hobble chains rattle,
  The calling of birds,
The lowing of cattle
  Must blend with the words.
Without these, indeed, you
  Would find it ere long,
As though I should read you
  The words of a song
That lamely would linger
  When lacking the rune,
The voice of the singer,
  The lilt of the tune.

But, as one half-hearing
  An old-time refrain,
With memory clearing,

Recalls it again,
These tales, roughly wrought of
    The bush and its ways,
May call back a thought of
    The wandering days,
And, blending with each
    In the mem'ries that throng,
There haply shall reach
    You some echo of song.

II

Rio Grande
AND OTHER VERSES

Rio Grande's Last Race

Now this was what Macpherson told
  While waiting in the stand;
A reckless rider, over-bold,
The only man with hands to hold
  The rushing Rio Grande.

He said, "This day I bid goodbye
  To bit and bridle rein,
To ditches deep and fences high,
For I have dreamed a dream, and I
  Shall never ride again.

"I dreamed last night I rode this race
  That I today must ride,
And cant'ring down to take my place
I saw full many an old friend's face
  Come stealing to my side.

"Dead men on horses long since dead,
  They clustered on the track;
The champions of the days long fled,
They moved around with noiseless tread —
  Bay, chestnut, brown, and black.

"And one man on a big grey steed
  Rode up and waved his hand;
Said he, 'We help a friend in need,
And we have come to give a lead
  To you and Rio Grande.

"'For you must give the field the slip,
  So never draw the rein,
But keep him moving with the whip,
And if he falter — set your lip
  And rouse him up again.

"'But when you reach the big stone wall,
  Put down your bridle hand
And let him sail — he cannot fall —
But don't you interfere at all;
  You trust old Rio Grande.'

"We started, and in front we showed,
  The big horse running free:
Right fearlessly and game he strode,
And by my side those dead men rode
  Whom no one else could see.

"As silently as flies a bird,
   They rode on either hand;
At every fence I plainly heard
The phantom leader give the word,
   'Make room for Rio Grande!'

"I spurred him on to get the lead,
   I chanced full many a fall;
But swifter still each phantom steed
Kept with me, and at racing speed
   We reached the big stone wall.

"And there the phantoms on each side
   Drew in and blocked his leap;
'Make room! make room!' I loudly cried,
But right in front they seemed to ride —
   I cursed them in my sleep.

"He never flinched, he faced it game,
   He struck it with his chest,
And every stone burst out in flame,
And Rio Grande and I became
   As phantoms with the rest.

"And then I woke, and for a space
   All nerveless did I seem;
For I have ridden many a race,
But never one at such a pace
   As in that fearful dream.

"And I am sure as man can be
   That out upon the track,
Those phantoms that men cannot see
Are waiting now to ride with me,
   And I shall not come back.

"For I must ride the dead men's race,
   And follow their command;
'Twere worse than death, the foul disgrace
If I should fear to take my place
   Today on Rio Grande."

He mounted, and a jest he threw,
   With never sign of gloom;
But all who heard the story knew
That Jack Macpherson, brave and true,
   Was going to his doom.

They started, and the big black steed
   Came flashing past the stand;

All single-handed in the lead
He strode along at racing speed,
    The mighty Rio Grande.

But on his ribs the whalebone stung,
    A madness it did seem!
And soon it rose on every tongue
That Jack Macpherson rode among
    The creatures of his dream.

He looked to left and looked to right,
    As though men rode beside;
And Rio Grande, with foam-flecks white,
Raced at his jumps in headlong flight
    And cleared them in his stride.

But when they reached the big stone wall,
    Down went the bridle hand,
And loud we heard Macpherson call,
"Make room, or half the field will fall!
    Make room for Rio Grande!"

"He's down! he's down!" And horse and man
    Lay quiet side by side!
No need the pallid face to scan,
We knew with Rio Grande he ran
    The race the dead men ride.

With French to Kimberley

The Boers were down on Kimberley with siege and Maxim gun;
The Boers were down on Kimberley, their numbers ten to one!
Faint were the hopes the British had to make the struggle good,
Defenceless in an open plain the Diamond City stood.
They built them forts from bags of sand, they fought from roof and
    wall,
They flashed a message to the south, "Help! or the town must fall!"
And down our ranks the order ran to march at dawn of day,
For French was off to Kimberley to drive the Boers away.

He made no march along the line; he made no front attack
Upon those Magersfontein heights that drove the Scotchmen back;
But eastward over pathless plains by open veldt and vley,
Across the front of Cronje's force his troopers held their way.
The springbuck, feeding on the flats where Modder River runs,
Were startled by his horses' hoofs, the rumble of his guns.
The Dutchman's spies that watched his march from every rocky
    wall
Rode back in haste: "He marches east! He threatens Jacobsdal!"
Then north he wheeled as wheels the hawk and showed to their
    dismay,
That French was off to Kimberley to drive the Boers away.

His column was five thousand strong — all mounted men — and
    guns:
There met, beneath the world-wide flag, the world-wide Empire's
    sons;
They came to prove to all the earth that kinship conquers space,
And those who fight the British Isles must fight the British race!
From far New Zealand's flax and fern, from cold Canadian snows,
From Queensland plains, where hot as fire the summer sunshine
    glows;
And in the front the Lancers rode that New South Wales had sent:
With easy stride across the plain their long, lean Walers went.
Unknown, untried, those squadrons were, but proudly out they
    drew
Beside the English regiments that fought at Waterloo.
From every coast, from every clime, they met in proud array,
To go with French to Kimberley to drive the Boers away.

He crossed the Reit and fought his way towards the Modder bank.
The foemen closed behind his march, and hung upon the flank.
The long, dry grass was all ablaze, and fierce the veldt fire runs;
He fought them through a wall of flame that blazed around the
    guns!

Then limbered up and drove at speed, though horses fell and died;
We might not halt for man nor beast on that wild, daring ride.
Black with the smoke and parched with thirst, we pressed the
    livelong day
Our headlong march to Kimberley to drive the Boers away.

We reached the drift at fall of night, and camped across the ford.
Next day from all the hills around the Dutchman's cannons roared.
A narrow pass between the hills, with guns on either side;
The boldest man might well turn pale before that pass he tried,
For if the first attack should fail then every hope was gone:
But French looked once, and only once, and then he said, "Push
    on!"
The gunners plied their guns amain; the hail of shrapnel flew;
With rifle fire and lancer charge their squadrons back we threw;
And through the pass between the hills we swept in furious fray,
And French was through to Kimberley to drive the Boers away.

Ay, French was through to Kimberley! And ere the day was done
We saw the Diamond City stand, lit by the evening sun:
Above the town the heliograph hung like an eye of flame:
Around the town the foemen camped — they knew not that we
    came;
But soon they saw us, rank on rank; they heard our squadrons'
    tread;
In panic fear they left their tents, in hopeless rout they fled;
And French rode into Kimberley; the people cheered amain,
The women came with tear-stained eyes to touch his bridle rein,
The starving children lined the streets to raise a feeble cheer,
The bells rang out a joyous peal to say "Relief is here!"
Ay! we that saw that stirring march are proud that we can say
We went with French to Kimberley to drive the Boers away.

BY THE GREY GULF-WATER

Far to the Northward there lies a land,
  A wonderful land that the winds blow over,
And none may fathom nor understand
  The charm it holds for the restless rover;
A great grey chaos — a land half made,
  Where endless space is and no life stirreth;
And the soul of a man will recoil afraid
  From the sphinx-like visage that Nature weareth.
But old Dame Nature, though scornful, craves
  Her dole of death and her share of slaughter;
Many indeed are the nameless graves
  Where her victims sleep by the Grey Gulf-water.

Slowly and slowly those grey streams glide,
  Drifting along with a languid motion,
Lapping the reed beds on either side,
  Wending their way to the Northern Ocean.
Grey are the plains where the emus pass
  Silent and slow, with their staid demeanour;
Over the dead men's graves the grass
  Maybe is waving a trifle greener.
Down in the world where men toil and spin
  Dame Nature smiles as man's hand has taught her;
Only the dead men her smiles can win
  In the great lone land by the Grey Gulf-water.

For the strength of man is an insect's strength,
  In the face of that mighty plain and river,
And the life of a man is a moment's length
  To the life of the stream that will run for ever.
And so it cometh they take no part
  In small-world worries; each hardy rover
Rideth abroad and is light of heart,
  With the plains around and the blue sky over.
And up in the heavens the brown lark sings
  The songs that the strange wild land has taught her;
Full of thanksgiving her sweet song rings —
  And I wish I were back by the Grey Gulf-water.

WITH THE CATTLE

The drought is down on field and flock,
   The river bed is dry;
And we must shift the starving stock
   Before the cattle die.
We muster up with weary hearts
   At breaking of the day,
And turn our heads to foreign parts,
   To take the stock away.
     And it's hunt 'em up and dog 'em,
     And it's get the whip and flog 'em,
For it's weary work is droving when they're dying every day;
     By stock routes bare and eaten,
     On dusty roads and beaten,
With half a chance to save their lives we take the stock away.

We cannot use the whip for shame
   On beasts that crawl along;
We have to drop the weak and lame,
   And try to save the strong;
The wrath of God is on the track,
   The drought fiend holds his sway,
With blows and cries and stockwhip crack
   We take the stock away.
     As they fall we leave them lying,
     With the crows to watch them dying,
Grim sextons of the Overland that fasten on their prey;
     By the fiery dust storm drifting,
     And the mocking mirage shifting,
In heat and drought and hopeless pain we take the stock away.

In dull despair the days go by
   With never hope of change,
But every stage we draw more nigh
   Towards the mountain range;
And some may live to climb the pass,
   And reach the great plateau,
And revel in the mountain grass,
   By streamlets fed with snow.
     As the mountain wind is blowing
     It starts the cattle lowing,
And calling to each other down the dusty long array;
     And there speaks a grizzled drover:
     "Well, thank God, the worst is over,
The creatures smell the mountain grass that's twenty miles away."

They press towards the mountain grass,
   They look with eager eyes
Along the rugged stony pass,
   That slopes towards the skies;
Their feet may bleed from rocks and stones,
   But though the blood-drop starts,
They struggle on with stifled groans,
   For hope is in their hearts.
     And the cattle that are leading,
     Though their feet are worn and bleeding,
Are breaking to a kind of run — pull up, and let them go!
     For the mountain wind is blowing,
     And the mountain grass is growing,
They settle down by running streams ice-cold with melted snow.

The days are done of heat and drought
   Upon the stricken plain;
The wind has shifted right about,
   And brought the welcome rain;
The river runs with sullen roar,
   All flecked with yellow foam,
And we must take the road once more,
   To bring the cattle home.
     And it's "Lads! we'll raise a chorus,
     There's a pleasant trip before us."
And the horses bound beneath us as we start them down the track;
     And the drovers canter, singing,
     Through the sweet green grasses springing,
Towards the far-off mountain land, to bring the cattle back.

Are these the beasts we brought away
   That move so lively now?
They scatter off like flying spray
   Across the mountain's brow;
And dashing down the rugged range
   We hear the stockwhip crack,
Good faith, it is a welcome change
   To bring such cattle back.
     And it's "Steady down the lead there!"
     And it's "Let 'em stop and feed there!"
For they're wild as mountain eagles and their sides are all afoam;
     But they're settling down already,
     And they'll travel nice and steady,
With cheery call and jest and song we fetch the cattle home.

We have to watch them close at night
   For fear they'll make a rush,

And break away in headlong flight
 Across the open bush;
And by the campfire's cheery blaze,
 With mellow voice and strong,
We hear the lonely watchman raise
 The Overlander's song:
  "Oh! it's when we're done with roving,
   With the camping and the droving,
It's homeward down the Bland we'll go, and never more we'll
 roam";
   While the stars shine out above us,
   Like the eyes of those who love us —
The eyes of those who watch and wait to greet the cattle home.

The plains are all awave with grass,
 The skies are deepest blue;
And leisurely the cattle pass
 And feed the long day through;
But when we sight the station gate,
 We make the stockwhips crack,
A welcome sound to those who wait
 To greet the cattle back:
   And through the twilight falling
   We hear their voices calling,
As the cattle splash across the ford and churn it into foam;
   And the children run to meet us,
   And our wives and sweethearts greet us,
Their heroes from the Overland who brought the cattle home.

THE FIRST SURVEYOR

His Widow Speaks

"The opening of the railway line! The Governor and all!
With flags and banners down the street, a banquet and a ball.
Hark to 'em at the station now! They're raising cheer on cheer!
'The man who brought the railway through — our friend the
    engineer!'

"They cheer *his* pluck and enterprise and engineering skill!
'Twas my old husband found the pass behind that big red hill.
Before the engineer was grown we settled with our stock
Behind that great big mountain chain, a line of range and rock —
A line that kept us starving there in weary weeks of drought,
With ne'er a track across the range to let the cattle out.

"'Twas then, with horses starved and weak and scarcely fit to crawl,
My husband went to find a way across that rocky wall.
He vanished in the wilderness, God knows where he was gone,
He hunted till his food gave out, but still he battled on.
His horses strayed — 'twas well they did — they made towards the
    grass,
And down behind that big red hill they found an easy pass.

"He followed up and blazed the trees, to show the safest track,
Then drew his belt another hole and turned and started back.
His horses died — just one pulled through with nothing much to
    spare;
God bless the beast that brought him home, the old white Arab
    mare!
We drove the cattle through the hills, along the new-found way,
And this was our first camping ground — just where I live to-day.

"Then others came across the range and built the township here,
And then there came the railway line and this young engineer.
He drove about with tents and traps, a cook to cook his meals,
A bath to wash himself at night, a chain-man at his heels.
And that was all the pluck and skill for which he's cheered and
    praised,
For after all he took the track, the same my husband blazed!

"My poor old husband, dead and gone with never feast nor cheer;
He's buried by the railway line! — I wonder can he hear
When down the very track he marked, and close to where he's laid,
The cattle trains go roaring down the one-in-thirty grade.
I wonder does he hear them pass and can he see the sight,
When through the dark the fast express goes flaming by at night?

"I think 'twould comfort him to know there's someone left to care,
I'll take some things this very night and hold a banquet there!
The hard old fare we've often shared together, him and me,
Some damper and a bite of beef, a pannikin of tea:
We'll do without the bands and flags, the speeches and the fuss,
We know who *ought* to get the cheers and that's enough for us.

"What's that? They wish that I'd come down — the oldest settler
       here!
Present me to the Governor and that young engineer!
Well, just you tell his Excellence and put the thing polite,
I'm sorry, but I can't come down — I'm dining out tonight!"

MULGA BILL'S BICYCLE

'Twas Mulga Bill, from Eaglehawk, that caught the cycling craze;
He turned away the good old horse that served him many days;
He dressed himself in cycling clothes, resplendent to be seen;
He hurried off to town and bought a shining new machine;
And as he wheeled it through the door, with air of lordly pride,
The grinning shop assistant said, "Excuse me, can you ride?"

"See here, young man," said Mulga Bill, "from Walgett to the sea,
From Conroy's Gap to Castlereagh, there's none can ride like me.
I'm good all round at everything, as everybody knows,
Although I'm not the one to talk — I *hate* a man that blows.
But riding is my special gift, my chiefest, sole delight;
Just ask a wild duck can it swim, a wildcat can it fight.
There's nothing clothed in hair or hide, or built of flesh or steel,
There's nothing walks or jumps, or runs, on axle, hoof, or wheel,
But what I'll sit, while hide will hold and girths and straps are tight:
I'll ride this here two-wheeled concern right straight away at sight."

'Twas Mulga Bill, from Eaglehawk, that sought his own abode,
That perched above the Dead Man's Creek, beside the mountain
    road.
He turned the cycle down the hill and mounted for the fray,
But ere he'd gone a dozen yards it bolted clean away.
It left the track, and through the trees, just like a silver streak,
It whistled down the awful slope towards the Dead Man's Creek.

It shaved a stump by half an inch, it dodged a big white-box:
The very wallaroos in fright went scrambling up the rocks,
The wombats hiding in their caves dug deeper underground,
As Mulga Bill, as white as chalk, sat tight to every bound.
It struck a stone and gave a spring that cleared a fallen tree,
It raced beside a precipice as close as close could be;
And then as Mulga Bill let out one last despairing shriek
It made a leap of twenty feet into the Dead Man's Creek.

'Twas Mulga Bill, from Eaglehawk, that slowly swam ashore:
He said, "I've had some narrer shaves and lively rides before;
I've rode a wild bull round a yard to win a five-pound bet,
But this was the most awful ride that I've encountered yet.
I'll give that two-wheeled outlaw best; it's shaken all my nerve
To feel it whistle through the air and plunge and buck and swerve.
It's safe at rest in Dead Man's Creek, we'll leave it lying still;
A horse's back is good enough henceforth for Mulga Bill."

THE PEARL DIVER

Kanzo Makame, the diver, sturdy and small Japanee,
Seeker of pearls and of pearl shell down in the depths of the sea,
Trudged o'er the bed of the ocean, searching industriously.

Over the pearl grounds, the lugger drifted — a little white speck:
Joe Nagasaki, the "tender", holding the life line on deck,
Talked through the rope to the diver, knew when to drift or to
    check.

Kanzo was king of his lugger, master and diver in one,
Diving wherever it pleased him, taking instructions from none;
Hither and thither he wandered, steering by stars and by sun.

Fearless he was beyond credence, looking at death eye to eye:
This was his formula always, "All man go dead by and by —
S'posing time come no can help it — s'pose time no come, then no
    die."

Dived in the depths of the Darnleys, down twenty fathom and five;
Down where by law and by reason, men are forbidden to dive;
Down in a pressure so awful that only the strongest survive:

Sweated four men at the air pumps, fast as the handles could go,
Forcing the air down that reached him, heated, and tainted, and
    slow —
Kanzo Makame the diver stayed seven minutes below;

Came up on deck like a dead man, paralysed body and brain;
Suffered, while blood was returning, infinite tortures of pain:
Sailed once again to the Darnleys — laughed and descended again!

* * * *

Scarce grew the shell in the shallows, rarely a patch could they
    touch;
Always the take was so little, always the labour so much;
Always they thought of the Islands held by the lumbering Dutch,

Islands where shell was in plenty lying in passage and bay,
Islands where divers could gather hundreds of shell in a day:
But the lumbering Dutch, with their gunboats, hunted the divers
    away.

Joe Nagasaki, the "tender", finding the profits grow small,
Said, "Let us go to the Islands, try for a number one haul!
If we get caught, go to prison — let them take lugger and all!"

Kanzo Makame, the diver — knowing full well what it meant —
Fatalist, gambler, and stoic, smiled a broad smile of content,
Flattened in mainsail and foresail, and off to the Islands they went.

Close to the headlands they drifted, picking up shell by the ton,
Piled up on deck were the oysters, opening wide in the sun,
When, from the lee of the headland, boomed the report of a gun.

Once that the diver was sighted, pearl shell and lugger must go.
Joe Nagasaki decided — quick was the word and the blow —
Cut both the pipe and the life line, leaving the diver below!

Kanzo Makame, the diver, failing to quite understand,
Pulled the "haul up" on the life line, found it was slack in his hand;
Then, like a little brown stoic, lay down and died on the sand.

Joe Nagasaki, the "tender", smiling a sanctified smile,
Headed her straight for the gunboat — throwing out shells all the
    while —
Then went aboard and reported, "No makee dive in three mile!

"Dress no have got and no helmet — diver go shore on the spree;
Plenty wind come and break rudder — lugger get blown out to sea:
Take me to Japanee Consul, he help a poor Japanee!"

* * * *

So the Dutch let him go, and they watched him, as off from the
    Islands he ran,
Doubting him much, but what would you? You have to be sure of
    your man
Ere you wake up that nest full of hornets — the little brown men of
    Japan.

Down in the ooze and the coral, down where earth's wonders are
    spread,
Helmeted, ghastly, and swollen, Kanzo Makame lies dead:
Joe Nagasaki, his "tender", is owner and diver instead.

Wearer of pearls in your necklace, comfort yourself if you can,
These are the risks of the pearling — these are the ways of Japan,
"Plenty more Japanee diver, plenty more little brown man!"

THE CITY OF
DREADFUL THIRST

The stranger came from Narromine and made his little joke —
"They say we folks in Narromine are narrow-minded folk.
But all the smartest men down here are puzzled to define
A kind of new phenomenon that came to Narromine.

"Last summer up in Narromine 'twas gettin' rather warm —
Two hundred in the water bag, and lookin' like a storm —
We all were in the private bar, the coolest place in town,
When out across the stretch of plain a cloud came rollin' down,

"We don't respect the clouds up there, they fill us with disgust,
They mostly bring a Bogan shower — three raindrops and some
    dust;
But each man, simultaneous-like, to each man said, 'I think
That cloud suggests it's up to us to have another drink!'

"There's clouds of rain and clouds of dust — we'd heard of them
    before,
And sometimes in the daily press we read of 'clouds of war':
But — if this ain't the Gospel truth I hope that I may burst —
That cloud that came to Narromine was just a cloud of thirst.

"It wasn't like a common cloud, 'twas more a sort of haze;
It settled down about the streets, and stopped for days and days,
And not a drop of dew could fall and not a sunbeam shine
To pierce that dismal sort of mist that hung on Narromine.

"Oh, Lord! we had a dreadful time beneath that cloud of thirst!
We all chucked-up our daily work and went upon the burst.
The very blacks about the town that used to cadge for grub,
They made an organised attack and tried to loot the pub.

"We couldn't leave the private bar no matter how we tried;
Shearers and squatters, union men and blacklegs side by side
Were drinkin' there and dursn't move, for each was sure, he said,
Before he'd get a half a mile the thirst would strike him dead!

"We drank until the drink gave out, we searched from room to
    room,
And round the pub, like drunken ghosts, went howling through
    the gloom.
The shearers found some kerosene and settled down again,
But all the squatter chaps and I, we staggered to the train.

"And, once outside the cloud of thirst, we felt as right as pie,
But while we stopped about the town we had to drink or die.

But now I hear it's safe enough, I'm going back to work
Because they say the cloud of thirst has shifted on to Bourke.

"But when you see those clouds about — like this one over here —
All white and frothy at the top, just like a pint of beer,
It's time to go and have a drink, for if that cloud should burst
You'd find the drink would all be gone, for that's a cloud of thirst!"

* * * *

We stood the man from Narromine a pint of half-and-half;
He drank it off without a gasp in one tremendous quaff;
"I joined some friends last night," he said, "in what *they* called a
    spree;
But after Narromine 'twas just a holiday to me."

And now beyond the Western Range, where sunset skies are red,
And clouds of dust, and clouds of thirst, go drifting overhead,
The railway train is taking back, along the Western Line,
That narrow-minded person on his road to Narromine.

SALTBUSH BILL'S GAMECOCK

'Twas Saltbush Bill, with his travelling sheep, was making his way
    to town;
He crossed them over the Hard Times Run, and he came to the
    Take 'Em Down;
He counted through at the boundary gate, and camped at the
    drafting yard:
For Stingy Smith, of the Hard Times Run, had hunted him rather
    hard.
He bore no malice to Stingy Smith — 'twas simply the hand of fate
That caused his waggon to swerve aside and shatter old Stingy's
    gate;
And, being only the hand of fate, it follows, without a doubt,
It wasn't the fault of Saltbush Bill that Stingy's sheep got out.
So Saltbush Bill, with an easy heart, prepared for what might
    befall,
Commenced his stages on Take 'Em Down, the station of Rooster
    Hall.

'Tis strange how often the men outback will take to some curious
    craft,
Some ruling passion to keep their thoughts away from the
    overdraft;
And Rooster Hall, of the Take 'Em Down, was widely known to
    fame
As breeder of champion fighting cocks — his *forte* was the British
    Game.
The passing stranger within his gates that camped with old Rooster
    Hall
Was forced to talk about fowls all night, or else not talk at all.
Though droughts should come, and though sheep should die, his
    fowls were his sole delight;
He left his shed in the flood of work to watch two gamecocks fight.
He held in scorn the Australian Game, that long-legged child of
    sin;
In a desperate fight, with the steel-tipped spurs, the British Game
    must win!
The Australian bird was a mongrel bird, with a touch of the jungle
    cock;
The want of breeding must find him out, when facing the English
    stock;
For British breeding, and British pluck, must triumph it over all —
And that was the root of the simple creed that governed old
    Rooster Hall.

'Twas Saltbush Bill to the station rode ahead of his travelling sheep,
And sent a message to Rooster Hall that wakened him out of his
    sleep —
A crafty message that fetched him out, and hurried him as he
    came —
"A drover has an Australian Bird to match with your British
    Game."
'Twas done, and done in half a trice; a five-pound note aside;
Old Rooster Hall, with his champion bird, and the drover's bird
    untried.
"Steel spurs, of course?" said old Rooster Hall; "you'll need 'em,
    without a doubt!"
"You stick the spurs on your bird," said Bill, "but mine fights best
    without."

"Fights best without?" said old Rooster Hall; "he can't fight best
    unspurred!
You must be crazy!" But Saltbush Bill said, "Wait till you see my
    bird!"

So Rooster Hall to his fowl yard went, and quickly back he came,
Bearing a clipt and a shaven cock, the pride of his English Game.
With an eye as fierce as an eaglehawk, and a crow like a trumpet
    call,
He strutted about on the garden walk, and cackled at Rooster Hall.
Then Rooster Hall sent off a boy with word to his cronies two,
McCrae (the boss of the Black Police) and Father Donahoo.
Full many a cockfight old McCrae had held in his empty Court,
With Father D. as a picker-up — a regular all-round Sport!

They got the message of Rooster Hall, and down to his run they
    came,
Prepared to scoff at the drover's bird, and to bet on the English
    Game;
They hied them off to the drover's camp, while Saltbush rode
    before —
Old Rooster Hall was a blithesome man, when he thought of the
    treat in store.
They reached the camp, where the drover's cook, with countenance
    all serene,
Was boiling beef in an iron pot, but never a fowl was seen.

"Take off the beef from the fire," said Bill, "and wait till you see the
    fight;
There's something fresh for the bill-of-fare — there's game-fowl stew
    to-night!

For Mister Hall has a fighting cock, all feathered and clipped and
    spurred;
And he's fetched him here, for a bit of sport, to fight our
    Australian bird.
I've made a match that our pet will win, though he's hardly a
    fighting cock,
But he's game enough, and it's many a mile that he's tramped with
    the travelling stock."
The cook he banged on a saucepan lid; and, soon as the sound was
    heard,
Under the dray, in the shadows hid, a something moved and
    stirred:
A great tame Emu strutted out. Said Saltbush, "Here's our bird!"
But Rooster Hall, and his cronies two, drove home without a word.

The passing stranger within his gates that camps with old Rooster
    Hall
Must talk about something else than fowls, if he wishes to talk at
    all.
For the record lies in the local Court, and filed in its deepest vault,
That Peter Hall, of the Take 'Em Down, was tried for a fierce
    assault
On a stranger man, who, in all good faith, and prompted by what
    he heard,
Had asked old Hall if a British Game could beat an Australian
    bird;
And old McCrae, who was on the Bench, as soon as the case was
    tried,
Remarked, "Discharged with a clean discharge — the assault was
    justified!"

Hay and Hell
and Booligal

"You come and see me, boys," he said;
"You'll find a welcome and a bed
   And whisky any time you call;
Although our township hasn't got
The name of quite a lively spot —
   You see, I live in Booligal.

"And people have an awful down
Upon the district and the town —
   Which worse than hell itself they call;
In fact, the saying far and wide
Along the Riverina side
   Is 'Hay and Hell and Booligal'.

"No doubt it suits 'em very well
To say it's worse than Hay or Hell,
   But don't you heed their talk at all;
Of course, there's heat — no one denies —
And sand and dust and stacks of flies,
   And rabbits, too, at Booligal.

"But such a pleasant, quiet place,
You never see a stranger's face —
   They hardly ever care to call;
The drovers mostly pass it by;
They reckon that they'd rather die
   Than spend a night in Booligal.

"The big mosquitoes frighten some —
You'll lie awake to hear 'em hum —
   And snakes about the township crawl;
But shearers, when they get their cheque,
They never come along and wreck
   The blessed town of Booligal.

"But down in Hay the shearers come
And fill themselves with fighting rum,
   And chase blue devils up the wall,
And fight the snaggers every day,
Until there is the deuce to pay —
   There's none of that in Booligal.

"Of course, there isn't much to see —
The billiard table used to be
   The great attraction for us all,

Until some careless, drunken curs
Got sleeping on it in their spurs,
  And ruined it, in Booligal.

"Just now there is a howling drought
That pretty near has starved us out —
  It never seems to rain at all;
But, if there *should* come any rain,
You couldn't cross the black soil plain —
  You'd have to stop in Booligal."

* * * *

"*We'd have to stop!*" With bated breath
We prayed that both in life and death
  Our fate in other lines might fall:
"Oh, send us to our just reward
In Hay or Hell, but, gracious Lord,
  Deliver us from Booligal!"

A WALGETT EPISODE

The sun strikes down with a blinding glare,
  The skies are blue and the plains are wide,
The saltbush plains that are burnt and bare
  By Walgett out on the Barwon side —
The Barwon River that wanders down
In a leisurely manner by Walgett Town.

There came a stranger — a "cockatoo" —
  The word means farmer, as all men know
Who dwell in the land where the kangaroo
  Barks loud at dawn, and the white-eyed crow
Uplifts his song on the stockyard fence
As he watches the lambkins passing hence.

The sunburnt stranger was gaunt and brown,
  But it soon appeared that he meant to flout
The iron law of the country town,
  Which is — that the stranger has got to shout:
"If he will not shout we must take him down,"
Remarked the yokels of Walgett Town.

They baited a trap with a crafty bait,
  With a crafty bait, for they held discourse
Concerning a new chum who of late
  Had bought such a thoroughly lazy horse;
They would wager that no one could ride him down
The length of the city of Walgett Town.

The stranger was born on a horse's hide;
  So he took the wagers, and made them good
With his hard-earned cash — but his hopes they died,
  For the horse was a clothes-horse, made of wood!
'Twas a well-known horse that had taken down
Full many a stranger in Walgett Town.

The stranger smiled with a sickly smile —
  'Tis a sickly smile that the loser grins —
And he said he had travelled for quite a while
  In trying to sell some marsupial skins.
"And I thought that perhaps, as you've took me down,
You would buy them from me, in Walgett Town!"

He said that his home was at Wingadee,
  At Wingadee where he had for sale
Some fifty skins and would guarantee
  They were full-sized skins, with the ears and tail

Complete, and he sold them for money down
To a venturesome buyer in Walgett Town.

Then he smiled a smile as he pouched the pelf,
  "I'm glad that I'm quit of them, win or lose:
You can fetch them in when it suits yourself,
  And you'll find the skins — on the kangaroos!"
Then he left — and the silence settled down
Like a tangible thing upon Walgett Town.

FATHER RILEY'S HORSE

'Twas the horse thief, Andy Regan, that was hunted like a dog
  By the troopers of the upper Murray side,
They had searched in every gully — they had looked in every log,
  But never sight or track of him they spied,
Till the priest at Kiley's Crossing heard a knocking very late
  And a whisper "Father Riley — come across!"
So his Rev'rence in pyjamas trotted softly to the gate
  And admitted Andy Regan — and a horse!

"Now, it's listen, Father Riley, to the words I've got to say,
  For it's close upon my death I am tonight.
With the troopers hard behind me I've been hiding all the day
  In the gullies keeping close and out of sight.
But they're watching all the ranges till there's not a bird could fly,
  And I'm fairly worn to pieces with the strife,
So I'm taking no more trouble, but I'm going home to die,
  'Tis the only way I see to save my life.

"Yes, I'm making home to mother's, and I'll die o' Tuesday next
  An' be buried on the Thursday — and, of course,
I'm prepared to meet my penance, but with one thing I'm perplexed
  And it's — Father, it's this jewel of a horse!
He was never bought nor paid for, and there's not a man can swear
  To his owner or his breeder, but I know,
That his sire was by Pedantic from the Old Pretender mare
  And his dam was close related to The Roe.

"And there's nothing in the district that can race him for a step,
  He could canter while they're going at their top:
He's the king of all the leppers that was ever seen to lep,
  A five-foot fence — he'd clear it in a hop!
So I'll leave him with you, Father, till the dead shall rise again,
  'Tis yourself that knows a good 'un; and, of course,
You can say he's got by Moonlight out of Paddy Murphy's plain
  If you're ever asked the breeding of the horse!

"But it's getting on to daylight and it's time to say goodbye,
  For the stars above the east are growing pale.
And I'm making home to mother — and it's hard for me to die!
  But it's harder still, is keeping out of gaol!
You can ride the old horse over to my grave across the dip
  Where the wattle bloom is waving overhead.
Sure he'll jump them fences easy — you must never raise the whip
  Or he'll rush 'em! — now, goodbye!" and he had fled!

So they buried Andy Regan, and they buried him to rights,
  In the graveyard at the back of Kiley's Hill;
There were five-and-twenty mourners who had five-and-twenty
    fights
  Till the very boldest fighters had their fill.
There were fifty horses racing from the graveyard to the pub,
  And their riders flogged each other all the while.
And the lashin's of the liquor! And the lavin's of the grub!
  Oh, poor Andy went to rest in proper style.

Then the races came to Kiley's — with a steeplechase and all,
  For the folk were mostly Irish round about,
And it takes an Irish rider to be fearless of a fall,
  They were training morning in and morning out.
But they never started training till the sun was on the course
  For a superstitious story kept 'em back,
That the ghost of Andy Regan on a slashing chestnut horse,
  Had been training by the starlight on the track.

And they read the nominations for the races with surprise
  And amusement at the Father's little joke,
For a novice had been entered for the steeplechasing prize,
  And they found that it was Father Riley's moke!
He was neat enough to gallop, he was strong enough to stay!
  But his owner's views of training were immense,
For the Reverend Father Riley used to ride him every day,
  And he never saw a hurdle nor a fence.

And the priest would join the laughter: "Oh," said he, "I put him
    in,
  For there's five-and-twenty sovereigns to be won.
And the poor would find it useful, if the chestnut chanced to win,
  And he'll maybe win when all is said and done!"
He had called him Faugh-a-ballagh, which is French for "clear the
    course",
  And his colours were a vivid shade of green:
All the Dooleys and O'Donnells were on Father Riley's horse,
  While the Orangemen were backing Mandarin!

It was Hogan, the dog poisoner — aged man and very wise,
  Who was camping in the racecourse with his swag,
And who ventured the opinion, to the township's great surprise,
  That the race would go to Father Riley's nag.
"You can talk about your riders — and the horse has not been
    schooled,
  And the fences is terrific, and the rest!
When the field is fairly going, then ye'll see ye've all been fooled,
  And the chestnut horse will battle with the best.

"For there's some has got condition, and they think the race is
    sure,
  And the chestnut horse will fall beneath the weight,
But the hopes of all the helpless, and the prayers of all the poor,
  Will be running by his side to keep him straight.
And it's what's the need of schoolin' or of workin' on the track,
  Whin the saints are there to guide him round the course!
I've prayed him over every fence — I've prayed him out and back!
  And I'll bet my cash on Father Riley's horse!"

* * * *

Oh, the steeple was a caution! They went tearin' round and round,
  And the fences rang and rattled where they struck.
There was some that cleared the water — there was more fell in
    and drowned,
  Some blamed the men and others blamed the luck!
But the whips were flying freely when the field came into view,
  For the finish down the long green stretch of course,
And in front of all the flyers — jumpin' like a kangaroo,
  Came the rank outsider — Father Riley's horse!

Oh, the shouting and the cheering as he rattled past the post!
  For he left the others standing, in the straight;
And the rider — well they reckoned it was Andy Regan's ghost,
  And it beat 'em how a ghost would draw the weight!
But he weighed in, nine stone seven, then he laughed and
    disappeared,
  Like a banshee (which is Spanish for an elf),
And old Hogan muttered sagely, "If it wasn't for the beard
  They'd be thinking it was Andy Regan's self!"

And the poor of Kiley's Crossing drank the health at Christmastide
  Of the chestnut and his rider dressed in green.
There was never such a rider, not since Andy Regan died,
  And they wondered who on earth he could have been.
But they settled it among 'em, for the story got about,
  'Mongst the bushmen and the people on the course,
That the Devil had been ordered to let Andy Regan out
  For the steeplechase on Father Riley's horse!

THE SCOTCH ENGINEER

With eyes that searched in the dark,
Peering along the line,
Stood the grim Scotchman, Hector Clark,
Driver of "Forty-nine",
And the veldt fire flamed on the hills ahead,
Like a blood-red beacon sign.

There was word of a fight to the north,
And a column hard-pressed,
So they started the Highlanders forth,
Without food, without rest.

But the pipers gaily played,
Chanting their fierce delight,
And the armoured carriages rocked and swayed,
Laden with men of the Scotch Brigade,
Hurrying up to the fight,
And the grim, grey Highland engineer,
Driving them into the night.

Then a signal light glowed red,
And a picket came to the track.
"Enemy holding the line ahead,
Three of our mates we have left for dead,
Only we two got back."
And far to the north through the still night air,
They heard the rifles crack.

And the boom of a gun rang out,
Like the sound of a deep appeal,
And the picket stood in doubt
By the side of the driving wheel.

But the Engineer looked down,
With his hand on the starting-bar,
"Ride ye back to the town,
Ye know what my orders are,
Maybe they're wanting the Scotch Brigade
Up on those hills afar.

"I am no soldier at all,
Only an engineer,
But I could not bear that the folk should say,
Over in Scotland — Glasgow way —
That Hector Clark stayed here
With the Scotch Brigade till the foe were gone,

With ever a rail to run her on.
Ready behind! Stand clear!

"Fireman, get you gone
Into the armoured train,
I will drive her alone;
One more trip — and perhaps the last —
With a well-raked fire and an open blast —
Hark to the rifles again."

* * * *

On through the choking dark,
Never a lamp nor a light,
Never an engine spark,
Showing her hurried flight.
Over the lonely plain
Rushed the great armoured-train,
Hurrying up to the fight.

Then with her living freight
On to the foe she came,
And the rifles snapped their hate,
And the darkness spouted flame.

Over the roar of the fray
The hungry bullets whined,
As she dashed through the foe that lay
Loading and firing blind,
Till the glare of the furnace burning clear
Showed them the form of the engineer,
Sharply and well defined.

Through! They were safely through!
Hark to the column's cheer!
Surely the driver knew
He was to halt her here;
But he took no heed of the signals red,
And the fireman found, when he climbed ahead,
There on the floor of his engine — dead,
Lay the Scotch Engineer!

Song of the Future

'Tis strange that in a land so strong,
So strong and bold in mighty youth,
We have no poet's voice of truth
To sing for us a wondrous song.

Our chiefest singer yet has sung
In wild, sweet notes a passing strain,
All carelessly and sadly flung
To that dull world he thought so vain.

"I care for nothing, good nor bad,
My hopes are gone, my pleasures fled,
I am but sifting sand," he said:
What wonder Gordon's songs were sad!

And yet, not always sad and hard;
In cheerful mood and light of heart
He told the tale of Britomarte,
And wrote the Rhyme of Joyous Guard.

And some have said that Nature's face
To us is always sad; but these
Have never felt the smiling grace
Of waving grass and forest trees
On sunlit plains as wide as seas.

"A land where dull Despair is king
O'er scentless flower and songless bird!"
But we have heard the bellbirds ring
Their silver bells at eventide,
Like fairies on the mountain side,
The sweetest note man ever heard.

The wild thrush lifts a note of mirth;
The bronzewing pigeons call and coo
Beside their nests the long day through;
The magpie warbles clear and strong
A joyous, glad, thanksgiving song,
For all God's mercies upon earth.

And many voices such as these
Are joyful sounds for those to tell,
Who know the Bush and love it well,
With all its hidden mysteries.

We cannot love the restless sea,
That rolls and tosses to and fro
Like some fierce creature in its glee;

For human weal or human woe
It has no touch of sympathy.

For us the bush is never sad:
Its myriad voices whisper low,
In tones the bushmen only know,
Its sympathy and welcome glad.

For us the roving breezes bring
From many a blossom-tufted tree —
Where wild bees murmur dreamily —
The honey-laden breath of Spring.

* * * *

We have no tales of other days,
No bygone history to tell;
Our tales are told where campfires blaze
At midnight, when the solemn hush
Of that vast wonderland, the Bush,
Hath laid on every heart its spell.

Although we have no songs of strife,
Of bloodshed reddening the land,
We yet may find achievements grand
Within the bushman's quiet life.

Lift ye your faces to the sky
Ye far blue mountains of the west,
Who lie so peacefully at rest
Enshrouded in a haze of blue;
'Tis hard to feel that years went by
Before the pioneers broke through
Your rocky heights and walls of stone,
And made your secrets all their own.

For years the fertile Western plains
Were hid behind your sullen walls,
Your cliffs and crags and waterfalls
All weatherworn with tropic rains.

Between the mountains and the sea,
Like Israelites with staff in hand,
The people waited restlessly:
They looked towards the mountains old
And saw the sunsets come and go
With gorgeous golden afterglow,
That made the West a fairyland,
And marvelled what that West might be
Of which such wondrous tales were told.

For tales were told of inland seas
Like sullen oceans, salt and dead,
And sandy deserts, white and wan,
Where never trod the foot of man,
Nor bird went winging overhead,
Nor ever stirred a gracious breeze
To wake the silence with its breath —
A land of loneliness and death.

At length the hardy pioneers
By rock and crag found out the way,
And woke with voices of today,
A silence kept for years and years.

Upon the Western slope they stood
And saw — a wide expanse of plain
As far as eye could stretch or see
Go rolling westward endlessly.
The native grasses, tall as grain,
Were waved and rippled in the breeze;
From boughs of blossom-laden trees
The parrots answered back again.
They saw the land that it was good,
A land of fatness all untrod,
And gave their silent thanks to God.

The way is won! The way is won!
And straightway from the barren coast
There came a westward-marching host,
That aye and ever onward prest
With eager faces to the West,
Along the pathway of the sun.

The mountains saw them marching by:
They faced the all-consuming drought,
They would not rest in settled land:
But, taking each his life in hand,
Their faces ever westward bent
Beyond the farthest settlement,
Responding to the challenge cry
Of "better country further out".

And lo a miracle! the land
But yesterday was all unknown,
The wild man's boomerang was thrown
Where now great busy cities stand.

It was not much, you say, that these
Should win their way where none withstood;

In sooth there was not much of blood —
No war was fought between the seas.

It was not much! but we who know
The strange capricious land they trod —
At times a stricken, parching sod,
At times with raging floods beset —
Through which they found their lonely way,
Are quite content that you should say
It was not much, while we can feel
That nothing in the ages old,
In song or story written yet
On Grecian urn or Roman arch,
Though it should ring with clash of steel,
Could braver histories unfold
Than this bush story, yet untold —
The story of their westward march.

* * * *

But times are changed, and changes rung
From old to new — the olden days,
The old bush life and all its ways
Are passing from us all unsung.

The freedom, and the hopeful sense
Of toil that brought due recompense,
Of room for all, has passed away,
And lies forgotten with the dead.
Within our streets men cry for bread
In cities built but yesterday.

About us stretches wealth of land,
A boundless wealth of virgin soil
As yet unfruitful and untilled!
Our willing workmen, strong and skilled
Within our cities idle stand,
And cry aloud for leave to toil.

The stunted children come and go
In squalid lanes and alleys black;
We follow but the beaten track
Of other nations, and we grow
In wealth for some — for many, woe.

And it may be that we who live
In this new land apart, beyond
The hard old world grown fierce and fond
And bound by precedent and bond,

May read the riddle right and give
New hope to those who dimly see
That all things may be yet for good,
And teach the world at length to be
One vast united brotherhood.

* * * *

So may it be, and he who sings
In accents hopeful, clear, and strong,
The glories which that future brings
Shall sing, indeed, a wondrous song.

ANTHONY CONSIDINE

Out in the wastes of the West countrie,
  Out where the white stars shine,
Grim and silent as such men be,
Rideth a man with a history —
  Anthony Considine.

For the ways of men they are manifold
  As their differing views in life;
For some are sold for the lust of gold
  And some for the lust of strife:
But this man counted the world well lost
  For the love of his neighbour's wife.

They fled together, as those must flee
  Whom all men hold in blame;
Each to the other must all things be
Who cross the gulf of iniquity
  And live in the land of shame.

But a light-o'-love, if she sins with one,
  She sinneth with ninety-nine:
The rule holds good since the world begun —
Since ever the streams began to run
  And the stars began to shine.
The rule holds true, and he found it true —
  Anthony Considine.

A nobler spirit had turned in scorn
  From a love that was stained with mire;
A weaker being might mourn and mourn
  For the loss of his Heart's Desire:
But the anger of Anthony Considine
  Blazed up like a flaming fire.

And she, with her new love, presently
  Came past with her eyes ashine;
And God so willed it, and God knows why,
She turned and laughed as they passed him by —
  Anthony Considine.

Her laughter stung as a whip might sting;
  And mad with his wounded pride
He turned and sprang with a panther's spring
  And struck at his rival's side:
And only the woman, shuddering,
  Could tell how the dead man died!

She dared not speak — and the mystery
  Is buried in auld lang syne,
But out on the wastes of the West countrie,
Grim and silent as such men be,
Rideth a man with a history —
  Anthony Considine.

Song of the Artesian Water

Now the stock have started dying, for the Lord has sent a drought;
But we're sick of prayers and Providence — we're going to do
   without;
With the derricks up above us and the solid earth below,
We are waiting at the lever for the word to let her go.
  Sinking down, deeper down,
  Oh, we'll sink it deeper down:
As the drill is plugging downward at a thousand feet of level,
If the Lord won't send us water, oh, we'll get it from the devil;
  Yes, we'll get it from the devil deeper down.

Now, our engine's built in Glasgow by a very canny Scot,
And he marked it twenty horsepower, but he don't know what is
   what:
When Canadian Bill is firing with the sun-dried gidgee logs,
She can equal thirty horses and a score or so of dogs.
  Sinking down, deeper down,
  Oh, we're going deeper down:
If we fail to get the water then it's ruin to the squatter,
For the drought is on the station and the weather's growing hotter,
  But we're bound to get the water deeper down.

But the shaft has started caving and the sinking's very slow,
And the yellow rods are bending in the water down below,
And the tubes are always jamming and they can't be made to shift
Till we nearly burst the engine with a forty horsepower lift.
  Sinking down, deeper down,
  Oh, we're going deeper down:
Though the shaft is always caving, and the tubes are always
   jamming,
Yet we'll fight our way to water while the stubborn drill is
   ramming —
  While the stubborn drill is ramming deeper down.

But there's no artesian water, though we've passed three thousand
   feet,
And the contract price is growing and the boss is nearly beat.
But it must be down beneath us, and it's down we've got to go,
Though she's bumping on the solid rock four thousand feet below.
  Sinking down, deeper down,
  Oh, we're going deeper down:
And it's time they heard us knocking on the roof of Satan's
   dwellin';

But we'll get artesian water if we cave the roof of Hell in —
   Oh! we'll get artesian water deeper down.

But it's hark! the whistle's blowing with a wild, exultant blast,
And the boys are madly cheering, for they've struck the flow at
    last,
And it's rushing up the tubing from four thousand feet below
Till it spouts above the casing in a million-gallon flow.
   And it's down, deeper down —
   Oh, it comes from deeper down;
It is flowing, ever flowing, in a free, unstinted measure
From the silent hidden places where the old earth hides her
    treasure —
   Where the old earth hides her treasure deeper down.

And it's clear away the timber, and it's let the water run:
How it glimmers in the shadow, how it flashes in the sun!
By the silent belts of timber, by the miles of blazing plain
It is bringing hope and comfort to the thirsty land again.
   Flowing down, further down;
   It is flowing further down
To the tortured thirsty cattle, bringing gladness in its going;
Through the droughty days of summer it is flowing, ever flowing —
   It is flowing, ever flowing, further down.

A Disqualified
Jockey's Story

You see, the thing was this way — there was me,
That rode Panoppoly, the Splendour mare,
And Ikey Chambers on the Iron Dook,
And Smith, the half-caste rider, on Regret,
And that long bloke from Wagga — him what rode
Veronikew, the Snowy River horse.
Well, none of them had chances — not a chance
Among the lot, unless the rest fell dead
Or wasn't trying — for a blind man's dog
Could see Enchantress was a certain cop,
And all the books was layin' six to four.

They brought her out to show our lot the road,
Or so they said; but, then, Gord's truth! you know,
You can't believe 'em, though they took an oath
On forty Bibles that they'd tell the truth.
But anyhow, an amateur was up
On this Enchantress, and so Ike and me,
We thought that we might frighten him a bit
By asking if he minded riding rough —
"Oh, not at all," says he, "oh, not at all!
I learnt at Robbo Park, and if it comes
To bumping I'm your Moses! Strike me blue!"
Says he, "I'll bump you over either rail,
The inside rail or outside — which you choose
Is good enough for me" — which settled Ike;
For he was shaky since he near got killed
From being sent a buster on the rail,
When some chap bumped his horse and fetched him down
At Stony Bridge, so Ikey thought it best
To leave this bloke alone, and I agreed.

So all the books was layin' six to four
Against the favourite, and the amateur
Was walking this Enchantress up and down,
And me and Smithy backed him; for we thought
We might as well get something for ourselves,
Because we knew our horses couldn't win.
But Ikey wouldn't back him for a bob;
Because he said he reckoned he was stiff,
And all the books was layin' six to four.

Well, anyhow, before the start, the news
Got round that this here amateur was stiff,

And our good stuff was blued, and all the books
Was in it, and the prices lengthened out,
And every book was bustin' of his throat,
And layin' five to one the favourite.
So there was we that couldn't win ourselves,
And this here amateur that wouldn't try,
And all the books was layin' five to one.

So Smithy says to me, "You take a hold
Of that there moke of yours, and round the turn
Come up behind Enchantress with the whip
And let her have it; that long bloke and me
Will wait ahead, and when she comes to us
We'll pass her on and belt her down the straight,
And Ikey'll flog her home, because his boss
Is judge and steward and the Lord knows what,
And so he won't be touched — and, as for us,
We'll swear we only hit her by mistake!"
And all the books was layin' five to one.

Well, off we went, and comin' to the turn
I saw the amateur was holding back
And poking into every hole he could
To get her blocked, and so I pulled behind
And drew the whip and dropped it on the mare —
I let her have it twice, and then she shot
Ahead of me, and Smithy opened out
And let her up beside him on the rails,
And kept her there a-beltin' her like smoke
Until she struggled past him pullin' hard
And came to Ike; but Ikey drew his whip
And hit her on the nose and sent her back
And won the race himself — for, after all,
It seems he had a fiver on the Dook
And never told us — so our stuff was lost.
And then they had us up for ridin' foul,
And warned us off the tracks for twelve months each,
To get our livin' any way we could;
But Ikey wasn't touched, because his boss
Was judge and steward and the Lord knows what.

But Mister — if you'll lend us half-a-crown,
I know three certain winners at the Park —
Three certain cops as no one knows but me;
And — thank you, Mister, come an' have a beer
(I always like a beer about this time) ...
Well, so long, Mister, till we meet again.

THE ROAD TO GUNDAGAI

The mountain road goes up and down,
From Gundagai to Tumut town.

And branching off there runs a track,
Across the foothills grim and black,

Across the plains and ranges grey
To Sydney city far away.

* * * *

It came by chance one day that I
From Tumut rode to Gundagai.

And reached about the evening tide
The crossing where the roads divide;

And, waiting at the crossing place,
I saw a maiden fair of face,

With eyes of deepest violet blue,
And cheeks to match the rose in hue —

The fairest maids Australia knows
Are bred among the mountain snows.

Then, fearing I might go astray,
I asked if she could show the way.

Her voice might well a man bewitch —
Its tones so supple, deep, and rich.

"The tracks are clear," she made reply,
"And this goes down to Sydney town,
And that one goes to Gundagai."

Then slowly, looking coyly back,
She went along the Sydney track.

And I for one was well content
To go the road the lady went;

But round the turn a swain she met —
The kiss she gave him haunts me yet!

* * * *

I turned and travelled with a sigh
The lonely road to Gundagai.

SALTBUSH BILL'S SECOND FIGHT

The news came down on the Castlereagh, and went to the world at
  large,
That twenty thousand travelling sheep, with Saltbush Bill in
  charge,
Were drifting down from a dried-out run to ravage the Castlereagh;
And the squatters swore when they heard the news, and wished
  they were well away:
For the name and the fame of Saltbush Bill were over the
  countryside
For the wonderful way that he fed his sheep, and the dodges and
  tricks he tried.
He would lose his way on a Main Stock Route, and stray to the
  squatters' grass;
He would come to a run with the boss away, and swear he had
  leave to pass;
And back of all and behind it all, as well the squatters knew,
If he had to fight, he would fight all day, so long as his sheep got
  through:
But this is the story of Stingy Smith, the owner of Hard Times Hill,
And the way that he chanced on a fighting man to reckon with
  Saltbush Bill.

* * * *

'Twas Stingy Smith on his stockyard sat, and prayed for an early
  spring,
When he started at sight of a clean-shaved tramp, who walked with
  jaunty swing;
For a clean-shaved tramp with a jaunty walk a-swinging along the
  track
Is as rare a thing as a feathered frog on the desolate roads outback.
So the tramp he made for the travellers' hut, and asked could he
  camp the night;
But Stingy Smith had a bright idea, and he said to him, "Can you
  fight?"
"Why, what's the game?" said the clean-shaved tramp, as he looked
  at him up and down —
"If you want a battle, get off that fence, and I'll kill you for half-a-
  crown!
But, Boss, you'd better not fight with me, it wouldn't be fair nor
  right;
I'm Stiffener Joe, from the Rocks Brigade, and I killed a man in a
  fight:
I served two years for it, fair and square, and now I'm a trampin'
  back,

To look for a peaceful quiet life away on the outside track —"

"Oh, it's not myself, but a drover chap," said Stingy Smith with
  glee;

"A bullying fellow, called Saltbush Bill — and you are the man for
  me.

He's on the road with his hungry sheep, and he's certain to raise a
  row,

For he's bullied the whole of the Castlereagh till he's got them
  under cow —

Just pick a quarrel and raise a fight, and leather him good and
  hard,

And I'll take good care that his wretched sheep don't wander a half
  a yard.

It's a five-pound job if you belt him well — do anything short of kill,

For there isn't a beak on the Castlereagh will fine you for Saltbush
  Bill."

"I'll take the job," said the fighting man, "and hot as this cove
  appears,

He'll stand no chance with a bloke like me, what's lived on the
  game for years;

For he's maybe learnt in a boxing school, and sparred for a round
  or so,

But I've fought all hands in a ten foot ring each night in a
  travelling show;

They earnt a pound if they stayed three rounds, and they tried for
  it every night —

In a ten foot ring! Oh, that's the game that teaches a bloke to fight,

For they'd rush and clinch, it was Dublin Rules, and we drew no
  colour line;

And they all tried hard for to earn the pound, but they got no
  pound of mine:

If I saw no chance in the opening round I'd slog at their wind, and
  wait

Till an opening came — and it *always* came — and I settled 'em,
  sure as fate;

Left on the ribs and right on the jaw — and, when the chance
  comes, *make sure*!

And it's there a professional bloke like me gets home on an
  amateur:

"For it's my experience every day, and I make no doubt it's yours,

That a third-class pro is an over-match for the best of the
  amateurs —"

"Oh, take your swag to the travellers' hut," said Smith, "for you
  waste your breath;

You've a first-class chance, if you lose the fight, of talking your
    man to death.
I'll tell the cook you're to have your grub, and see that you eat
    your fill,
And come to the scratch all fit and well to leather this Saltbush
    Bill."

* * * *

'Twas Saltbush Bill, and his travelling sheep were wending their
    weary way
On the Main Stock Route, through the Hard Times Run, on their
    six-mile stage a day;
And he strayed a mile from the Main Stock Route, and started to
    feed along,
And, when Stingy Smith came up, Bill said that the Route was
    surveyed wrong;
And he tried to prove that the sheep had rushed and strayed from
    their camp at night,
But the fighting man he kicked Bill's dog, and of course that meant
    a fight:

So they sparred and fought, and they shifted ground and never a
    sound was heard
But the thudding fists on their brawny ribs, and the seconds'
    muttered word,
Till the fighting man shot home his left on the ribs with a mighty
    clout,
And his right flashed up with a half-arm blow — and Saltbush Bill
    "went out".
He fell face down, and towards the blow; and their hearts with fear
    were filled,
For he lay as still as a fallen tree, and they thought that he must be
    killed.

So Stingy Smith and the fighting man, they lifted him from the
    ground,
And sent to home for a brandy flask, and they slowly fetched him
    round;
But his head was bad, and his jaw was hurt — in fact, he could
    scarcely speak —
So they let him spell till he got his wits, and he camped on the run
    a week,
While the travelling sheep went here and there, wherever they liked
    to stray,
Till Saltbush Bill was fit once more for the track to the Castlereagh.

* * * *

Then Stingy Smith he wrote a note, and gave to the fighting man:
'Twas writ to the boss of the neighbouring run, and thus the
    missive ran:
"The man with this is a fighting man, one Stiffener Joe by name;
He came near murdering Saltbush Bill, and I found it a costly
    game:
But it's worth your while to employ the chap, for there isn't the
    slightest doubt
You'll have no trouble from Saltbush Bill while this man hangs
    about —"
But an answer came by the next week's mail, with news that might
    well appal:
"The man you sent with a note is not a fighting man at all!
He has shaved his beard, and has cut his hair, but I spotted him at
    a look;
He is Tom Devine, who has worked for years for Saltbush Bill as
    cook.
Bill coached him up in the fighting yarn, and taught him the tale
    by rote,
And they shammed to fight, and they got your grass and divided
    your five-pound note.
'Twas a clean take-in, and you'll find it wise — 'twill save you a lot
    of pelf —
When next you're hiring a fighting man, just fight him a round
    yourself."

* * * *

And the teamsters out on the Castlereagh, when they meet with a
    week of rain,
And the waggon sinks to its axle-tree, deep down in the black soil
    plain,
When the bullocks wade in a sea of mud, and strain at the load of
    wool,
And the cattle dogs at the bullocks' heels are biting to make them
    pull,
When the offside driver flays the team, and curses them while he
    flogs,
And the air is thick with the language used, and the clamour of
    men and dogs —
The teamsters say, as they pause to rest and moisten each hairy
    throat,
They wish they could swear like Stingy Smith when he read that
    neighbour's note.

Hard Luck

I left the course, and by my side
   There walked a ruined tout —
A hungry creature evil-eyed,
   Who poured this story out.

"You see," he said, "there came a swell
   To Kensington today,
And if I picked the winners well,
   A crown at least he'd pay.

"I picked three winners straight, I did,
   I filled his purse with pelf,
And then he gave me half a quid,
   To back one for myself.

"A half a quid to me he cast,
   I wanted it indeed.
So help me Bob, for two days past
   I haven't had a feed.

"But still I thought my luck was in,
   I couldn't go astray,
I put it all on Little Min,
   And lost it straightaway.

"I haven't got a bite or bed,
   I'm absolutely stuck,
So keep this lesson in your head:
   Don't over-trust your luck!"

The folks went homeward, near and far,
   The tout, Oh! where was he?
Ask where the empty boilers are,
   Beside the Circular Quay.

Song of the Federation

As the nations sat together, grimly waiting —
  The fierce old nations battle-scarred —
Grown grey in their lusting and their hating,
  Ever armed and ever ready keeping guard,
Through the tumult of their warlike preparation
  And the half-stilled clamour of the drums
Came a voice crying, "Lo! a new-made nation,
  To her place in the sisterhood she comes!"

And she came — she was beautiful as morning,
  With the bloom of the roses in her mouth,
Like a young queen lavishly adorning
  Her charms with the splendours of the South.
And the fierce old nations, looking on her,
  Said, "Nay, surely she were quickly overthrown,
Hath she strength for the burden laid upon her,
  Hath she power to protect and guard her own?"

Then she spoke, and her voice was clear and ringing
  In the ears of the nations old and grey,
Saying, "Hark, and ye shall see my children singing
  Their war song in countries far away.
They are strangers to the tumult of the battle,
  They are few but their hearts are very strong,
'Twas but yesterday they called unto the cattle,
  But they now sing Australia's marching song."

SONG OF THE AUSTRALIANS IN ACTION
For the honour of Australia, our mother,
  Side by side with our kin from over sea,
We have fought and we have tested one another,
  And enrolled among the brotherhood are we.

There was never post of danger but we sought it
  In the fighting, through the fire, and through the flood.
There was never prize so costly but we bought it,
  Though we paid for its purchase with our blood.

Was there any road too rough for us to travel?
  Was there any path too far for us to tread?
You can track us by the blood drops on the gravel
  On the roads that we milestoned with our dead!

And for you, oh our young and anxious mother,
  O'er your great gains keeping watch and ward,
Neither fearing nor despising any other,
  We will hold your possessions with the sword.

* * * *

Then they passed to the place of world-long sleeping,
   The grey-clad figures with their dead,
To the sound of their women softly weeping
   And the Dead March moaning at their head:
And the Nations, as the grim procession ended,
   Whispered, "Child! But ye have seen the price we pay,
From War may we ever be defended,
   Kneel ye down, new-made Sister — Let us Pray!"

THE OLD
AUSTRALIAN WAYS

The London lights are far abeam
  Behind a bank of cloud,
Along the shore the gas lights gleam,
  The gale is piping loud;
And down the Channel, groping blind,
  We drive her through the haze
Towards the land we left behind —
The good old land of "never mind",
  And old Australian ways.

The narrow ways of English folk
  Are not for such as we;
They bear the long-accustomed yoke
  Of staid conservancy:
But all our roads are new and strange
  And through our blood there runs
The vagabonding love of change
That drove us westward of the range
  And westward of the suns.

The city folk go to and fro
  Behind a prison's bars,
They never feel the breezes blow
  And never see the stars;
They never hear in blossomed trees
  The music low and sweet
Of wild birds making melodies,
Nor catch the little laughing breeze
  That whispers in the wheat.

Our fathers came of roving stock
  That could not fixed abide:
And we have followed field and flock
  Since e'er we learnt to ride;
By miner's camp and shearing shed,
  In land of heat and drought,
We followed where our fortunes led,
With fortune always on ahead
  And always further out.

The wind is in the barley grass,
  The wattles are in bloom;
The breezes greet us as they pass
  With honey-sweet perfume;

The parakeets go screaming by
   With flash of golden wing,
And from the swamp the wild ducks cry
Their long-drawn note of revelry,
   Rejoicing at the spring.

So throw the weary pen aside
   And let the papers rest,
For we must saddle up and ride
   Towards the blue hill's breast;
And we must travel far and fast
   Across their rugged maze,
To find the Spring of Youth at last,
And call back from the buried past
   The old Australian ways.

When Clancy took the drover's track
   In years of long ago,
He drifted to the outer back
   Beyond the Overflow;
By rolling plain and rocky shelf,
   With stockwhip in his hand,
He reached at last, oh lucky elf,
The Town of Come-and-Help-Yourself
   In Rough-and-Ready Land.

And if it be that you would know
   The tracks he used to ride,
Then you must saddle up and go
   Beyond the Queensland side —
Beyond the reach of rule or law,
   To ride the long day through,
In Nature's homestead — filled with awe:
You then might see what Clancy saw
   And know what Clancy knew.

The Ballad
of the Calliope

By the far Samoan shore,
Where the league-long rollers pour
All the wash of the Pacific on the coral-guarded bay,
Riding lightly at their ease,
In the calm of tropic seas,
The three great nations' warships at their anchors proudly lay.

Riding lightly, head to wind,
With the coral reefs behind,
Three German and three Yankee ships were mirrored in the blue;
And on one ship unfurled
Was the flag that rules the world —
For on the old *Calliope* the flag of England flew.

When the gentle offshore breeze,
That had scarcely stirred the trees,
Dropped down to utter stillness, and the glass began to fall,
Away across the main
Lowered the coming hurricane,
And far away to seaward hung the cloud wrack like a pall.

If the word had passed around,
"Let us move to safer ground;
Let us steam away to seaward" — then this tale were not to tell!
But each Captain seemed to say
"If the others stay, I stay!"
And they lingered at their moorings till the shades of evening fell.

Then the cloud wrack neared them fast,
And there came a sudden blast,
And the hurricane came leaping down a thousand miles of main!
Like a lion on its prey,
Leapt the storm fiend on the bay,
And the vessels shook and shivered as their cables felt the strain.

As the surging seas came by,
That were running mountains high,
The vessels started dragging, drifting slowly to the lee;
And the darkness of the night
Hid the coral reefs from sight,
And the Captains dared not risk the chance to grope their way to
    sea.

In the dark they dared not shift!
They were forced to wait and drift;

All hands stood by uncertain would the anchors hold or no.
  But the men on deck could see
  If a chance of hope might be —
There was little chance of safety for the men who were below.

  Through that long, long night of dread,
  While the storm raged overhead,
They were waiting by their engines, with the furnace fires aroar.
  So they waited, staunch and true,
  Though they knew, and well they knew,
They must drown like rats imprisoned if the vessel touched the
    shore.

  When the grey dawn broke at last,
  And the long, long night was past,
While the hurricane redoubled, lest its prey should steal away,
  On the rocks, all smashed and strewn,
  Were the German vessels thrown,
While the Yankees, swamped and helpless, drifted shorewards down
    the bay.

  Then at last spoke Captain Kane,
  "All our anchors are in vain,
And the Germans and the Yankees they have drifted to the lee!
  Cut the cables at the bow!
  We must trust the engines now!
Give her steam, and let her have it, lads, we'll fight her out to sea!"

  And the answer came with cheers
  From the stalwart engineers,
From the grim and grimy firemen at the furnaces below;
  And above the sullen roar
  Of the breakers on the shore
Came the throbbing of the engines as they laboured to and fro.

  If the strain should find a flaw,
  Should a bolt or rivet draw,
Then — God help them! for the vessel were a plaything in the tide!
  With a face of honest cheer,
  Quoth an English engineer,
"I will answer for the engines that were built on old Thames side!

  "For the stays and stanchions taut,
  For the rivets truly wrought,
For the valves that fit their faces as a glove should fit the hand.
  Give her every ounce of power,
  If we make a knot an hour
Then it's way enough to steer her and we'll drive her from the
    land."

Like a foam-flake tossed and thrown,
  She could barely hold her own,
While the other ships all helplessly were drifting to the lee.
  Through the smother and the rout
  The *Calliope* steamed out —
And they cheered her from the *Trenton* that was foundering in the
    sea.

  Aye! drifting shoreward there,
  All helpless as they were,
Their vessel hurled upon the reefs as weed ashore is hurled.
  Without a thought of fear
  The Yankees raised a cheer —
A cheer that English-speaking folk should echo round the world.

DO THEY KNOW?

Do they know? At the turn to the straight
  Where the favourites fail,
And every atom of weight
  Is telling its tale;
As some grim old stayer hard-pressed
  Runs true to his breed,
And with head just in front of the rest
  Fights on in the lead;
When the jockeys are out with the whips,
  With a furlong to go;
And the backers grow white to the lips —
  Do you think *they* don't know?

Do they know? As they come back to weigh
  In a whirlwind of cheers,
Though the spurs have left marks of the fray,
  Though the sweat on the ears
Gathers cold, and they sob with distress
  As they roll up the track,
They know just as well their success
  As the man on their back.
As they walk through a dense human lane,
  That sways to and fro,
And cheers them again and again,
  Do you think *they* don't know?

THE PASSING OF GUNDAGAI

"I'll introdooce a friend!" he said,
  "And if you've got a vacant pen
You'd better take him in the shed
And start him shearing straight ahead,
  He's one of these here quiet men.

"He never strikes — that ain't his game;
  No matter what the others try
He goes on shearing just the same.
I never rightly knew his name —
  We always call him 'Gundagai!'"

Our flashest shearer then had gone
  To train a racehorse for a race,
And while his sporting fit was on
He couldn't be relied upon,
  So "Gundagai" shore in his place.

Alas for man's veracity!
  For reputations false and true!
This "Gundagai" turned out to be,
For strife and all-round villainy,
  The very worst I ever knew!

He started racing Jack Devine,
  And grumbled when I made him stop.
The pace he showed was extra fine,
But all those pure-bred ewes of mine
  Were bleeding like a butcher's shop.

He cursed the sheep, he cursed the shed,
  From roof to rafter, floor to shelf;
As for my mongrel ewes, he said,
I ought to get a razor blade
  And shave the blooming things myself.

On Sundays he controlled a "school",
  And played "two-up" the livelong day;
And many a young confiding fool
He shore of his financial wool;
  And when he lost he would not pay.

He organised a shearers' race,
  And "touched" me to provide the prize.
His packhorse showed surprising pace
And won hands down — he was The Ace,
  A well-known racehorse in disguise.

Next day the bruiser of the shed
  Displayed an opal-tinted eye,
With large contusions on his head.
He smiled a sickly smile, and said
  He'd "had a cut at 'Gundagai!'"

But just as we were getting full
  Of "Gundagai" and all his ways,
A telegram for "Henry Bull"
Arrived. Said he, "That's me — all wool!
  Let's see what this here message says."

He opened it, his face grew white,
  He dropped the shears and turned away.
It ran, "Your wife took bad last night;
Come home at once — no time to write,
  We fear she may not last the day."

He got his cheque — I didn't care
  To dock him for my mangled ewes;
His store account — we "called it square".
Poor wretch! he had enough to bear,
  Confronted by such dreadful news.

The shearers raised a little purse
  To help a mate, as shearers will,
"To pay the doctor and the nurse,
And if there should be something worse —
  To pay the undertaker's bill."

They wrung his hand in sympathy,
  He rode away without a word,
His head hung down in misery.
A wandering hawker passing by
  Was told of what had just occurred.

"Well! that's a curious thing," he said,
  "I've known that feller all his life —
He's had the loan of this here shed!
I know his wife ain't nearly dead,
  Because he *hasn't got a wife*!"

                    * * * *

You should have heard the whipcord crack
  As angry shearers galloped by,
In vain they tried to fetch him back.
A little dust along the track
  Was all they saw of "Gundagai".

THE WARGEILAH HANDICAP

Wargeilah town is very small,
  There's no cathedral nor a club,
In fact the township, all in all,
  Is just one unpretentious pub;
And there, from all the stations round,
The local sportsmen can be found.

The sportsmen of Wargeilah side
  Are very few but very fit:
There's scarcely any sport been tried
  But what they held their own at it
In fact, to search their records o'er,
They held their own and something more.

'Twas round about Wargeilah town
  An English new chum did infest:
He used to wander up and down
  In baggy English breeches drest —
His mental aspect seemed to be
Just stolid self-sufficiency.

The local sportsmen vainly sought
  His tranquil calm to counteract,
By urging that he should be brought
  Within the Noxious Creatures Act.
"Nay, harm him not," said one more wise,
"He is a blessing in disguise!

"You see, he wants to buy a horse,
  To ride, and hunt, and steeplechase,
And carry ladies, too, of course,
  And pull a cart and win a race.
Good gracious! he must be a flat
To think he'll get a horse like that!

"But since he has so little sense
  And such a lot of cash to burn,
We'll sell him some experience
  By which alone a fool can learn.
Suppose we let him have The Trap
To win Wargeilah Handicap!"

And here, I must explain to you
  That, round about Wargeilah run,
There lived a very aged screw
  Whose days of brilliancy were done:

A grand old warrior in his prime —
But age will beat us all in time.

A trooper's horse in seasons past
    He did his share to keep the peace,
But took to falling, and at last
    Was cast for age from the Police.
A publican at Conroy's Gap
Then bought and christened him The Trap.

When grass was good, and horses dear,
    He changed his owner now and then
At prices ranging somewhere near
    The neighbourhood of two pound ten:
And manfully he earned his keep
By yarding cows and ration sheep.

They brought him in from off the grass
    And fed and groomed the old horse up;
His coat began to shine like glass —
    You'd think he'd win the Melbourne Cup.
And when they'd got him fat and flash
They asked the new chum — fifty — cash!

And when he said the price was high,
    Their indignation knew no bounds.
They said, "It's seldom you can buy
    A horse like that for fifty pounds!
We'll refund twenty if The Trap
Should fail to win the handicap!"

The deed was done, the price was paid,
    The new chum put the horse in train:
The local sports were much afraid
    That he would sad experience gain,
By racing with some shearer's hack,
Who'd beat him halfway round the track.

So, on this guileless English spark
    They did most fervently impress
That he must keep the matter dark,
    And not let any person guess
That he was purchasing The Trap
To win Wargeilah Handicap.

They spoke of "spielers from the Bland",
    And "champions from the Castlereagh",
And gave the youth to understand
    That all of these would stop away,

And spoil the race, if they should hear
That they had got The Trap to fear.

"Keep dark! They'll muster thick as flies
  When once the news gets sent around
We're giving such a splendid prize —
  A Snowdon horse worth fifty pound!
They'll come right in from Dandaloo,
And find — that it's a gift to you!"

The race came on — with no display,
  Nor any calling of the card,
But round about the pub all day
  A crowd of shearers, drinking hard,
And using language in a strain
'Twere flattery to call profane.

Our hero, dressed in silk attire —
  Blue jacket and a scarlet cap —
With boots that shone like flames of fire,
  Now did his canter on The Trap,
And walked him up and round about,
Until the other steeds came out.

He eyed them with a haughty look,
  But saw a sight that caught his breath!
It was! Ah John! The Chinee cook!
  In boots and breeches! Pale as death!
Tied with a rope, like any sack,
Upon a piebald pony's back!

The next, a colt — all mud and burrs!
  Half-broken, with a black boy up,
Who said, "You gim'me pair o' spurs,
  I win the bloomin' Melbourne Cup!"
These two were to oppose The Trap
For the Wargeilah Handicap!

They're off! The colt whipped down his head,
  And humped his back and gave a squeal,
And bucked into the drinking shed,
  Revolving like a Cath'rine wheel!
Men ran like rats! The atmosphere
Was filled with oaths and pints of beer!

But up the course the bold Ah John
  Beside The Trap raced neck and neck:
The boys had tied him firmly on,
  Which ultimately proved his wreck,

The saddle turned, and, like a clown,
He rode some distance upside down.

His legs around the horse were tied,
  His feet towards the heavens were spread,
He swung and bumped at every stride
  And ploughed the ground up with his head!
And when they rescued him, The Trap
Had won Wargeilah Handicap!

And no enquiries we could make
  Could tell by what false statements swayed
Ah John was led to undertake
  A task so foreign to his trade!
He only smiled and said, "Hoo Ki!
I stop topside, I win all 'li!"

But never, in Wargeilah Town,
  Was heard so eloquent a cheer
As when the President came down,
  And toasted, in Colonial Beer,
"The finest rider on the course!
The winner of the Snowdon Horse!"

"You go and get your prize," he said,
  "He's with a wild mob, somewhere round
The mountains near The Watershed;
  He's honestly worth fifty pound,
A noble horse, indeed, to win,
But none of *us* can run him in!

"We've chased him poor, we've chased him fat,
  We've run him till our horses dropped,
But by such obstacles as that
  A man like you will not be stopped,
You'll go and yard him any day,
So here's your health! Hooray! Hooray!"

* * * *

The day wound up with booze and blow
  And fights till all were well content,
But of the new chum, all I know
  Is shown by this advertisement —
"For Sale, the well-known racehorse Trap,
He won Wargeilah Handicap!"

ANY OTHER TIME

All of us play our very best game —
  Any other time.
Golf or billiards, it's all the same —
  Any other time.
Lose a match and you always say,
"Just my luck! I was 'off' to-day!
I could have beaten him quite halfway —
  Any other time!"

After a fiver you ought to go —
  Any other time.
Every man that you ask says "Oh,
  Any *other* time.
Lend you a fiver! I'd lend you two,
But I'm overdrawn and my bills are due,
Wish you'd ask me — now, mind you do —
  Any other time!"

Fellows will ask you out to dine —
  Any other time.
"Not tonight, for we're twenty-nine —
  Any other time.
Not tomorrow, for cook's on strike —
Not next day, I'll be out on the bike —
Just drop in whenever you like —
  Any other time!"

Seasick passengers like the sea —
  Any other time.
"Something...I ate...disagreed...with me!
  Any other time
Ocean-trav'lling is...simply bliss,
Must be my...liver...has gone amiss...
Why, I would laugh...at a sea...like this —
  Any other time."

Most of us mean to be better men —
  Any other time:
Regular upright characters then —
  Any other time.
Yet somehow as the years go by
Still we gamble and drink and lie,
When it comes to the last we'll want to die —
  Any other time!

THE LAST TRUMP

"You led the trump," the old man said
  With fury in his eye,
"And yet you hope my girl to wed!
Young man! your hopes of love are fled,
  'Twere better she should die!

"My sweet young daughter sitting there,
  So innocent and plump!
You don't suppose that she would care
To wed an outlawed man who'd dare
  To lead the thirteenth trump!

"If you had drawn their leading spade
  It meant a certain win!
But no! By Pembroke's mighty shade
The thirteenth trump you went and played
  And let their diamonds in!

"My girl! Return at my command
  His presents in a lump!
Return his ring! For understand
No man is fit to hold your hand
  Who leads a thirteenth trump!

"But hold! Give every man his due
  And every dog his day.
Speak up and say what made you do
This dreadful thing — that is, if you
  Have anything to say!"

He spoke. "I meant at first," said he,
  "To give their spades a bump:
Or lead the hearts, but then you see
I thought against us there might be,
  Perhaps, a fourteenth trump!"

                * * * *

They buried him at dawn of day
  Beside a ruined stump:
And there he sleeps the hours away
And waits for Gabriel to play
  The last — the fourteenth — trump.

TAR AND FEATHERS

Oh, the circus swooped down
  On the Narrabri town,
For the Narrabri populace moneyed are;
  And the circus man smiled
  At the folk he beguiled
To come all the distance from Gunnedah.

But a juvenile smart,
  Who objected to "part",
Went in "on the nod", and to do it he
  Crawled in through a crack
  In the tent at the back,
For the boy had no slight ingenuity.

Says he, with a grin,
  "*That's* the way to get in,
But I reckon I'd better be quiet, or
  They'll spiflicate me" —
  And he chuckled, for he
Had the loan of the circus proprietor.

But the showman astute
  On that wily galoot,
Soon dropped, and you'll say that he leathered him.
  Not he! With a grim
  Sort of humorous whim
He took him and tarred him and feathered him.

Says he, "You can go
  As a star with Jo-Jo,
And knock ev'ry Injun and Arab wry,
  With your name and your trade
  On the posters displayed,
'The Feathered What Is It from Narrabri!'"

Next day for his freak
  By a Narrabri beak
He was jawed with a deal of verbosity.
  For his only appeal
  Was "professional zeal" —
"He wanted another monstrosity."

Said his worship, "Begob!
  You are fined for-r-r-ty bob!
An' six shillin's costs to the *clurk*," he says;
  Yet the Narrabri Joy,
  Half-bird and half-boy,
Has a "down" on himself and on circuses.

It's Grand

It's grand to be a squatter
  And sit upon a post,
And watch your little ewes and lambs
  A-giving up the ghost.

It's grand to be a "cockie"
  With wife and kids to keep,
And find an all-wise Providence
  Has mustered all your sheep.

It's grand to be a western man,
  With shovel in your hand,
To dig your little homestead out
  From underneath the sand.

It's grand to be a shearer,
  Along the Darling side,
And pluck the wool from stinking sheep
  That some days since have died.

It's grand to be a rabbit
  And breed till all is blue,
And then to die in heaps because
  There's nothing left to chew.

It's grand to be a Minister
  And travel like a swell,
And tell the central district folk
  To go to — Inverell.

It's grand to be a Socialist
  And lead the bold array
That marches to prosperity
  At seven bob a day.

It's grand to be an unemployed
  And lie in the Domain,
And wake up every second day
  And go to sleep again.

It's grand to borrow English tin
  To pay for wharves and Rocks,
And then to find it isn't in
  The little money-box.

It's grand to be a democrat
  And toady to the mob,
For fear that if you told the truth
  They'd hunt you from your job.

It's grand to be a lot of things
    In this fair southern land,
But if the Lord would send us rain,
    That would, indeed, be grand!

OUT OF SIGHT

They held a polo meeting at a little country town,
And all the local sportsmen came to win themselves renown.
There came two strangers with a horse, and I am much afraid
They both belonged to what is called "the take-you-down brigade".

They said their horse could jump like fun, and asked an amateur
To ride him in the steeplechase, and told him they were sure,
The last time round, he'd sail away with such a swallow's flight
The rest would never see him go — he'd finish out of sight.

So out he went; and, when folk saw the amateur was up,
Some local genius called the race "the dude-in-danger cup".
The horse was known as "Who's Afraid", by "Panic" from "The
    Fright",
But still his owners told the jock he'd finish out of sight.

And so he did; for "Who's Afraid", without the least pretence,
Disposed of him by rushing through the very second fence;
And when they ran the last time round the prophecy was right —
For he was in the ambulance, and safely "out of sight".

THE ROAD TO OLD MAN'S TOWN

The fields of youth are filled with flowers,
  The wine of youth is strong:
What need have we to count the hours?
  The summer days are long.

But soon we find to our dismay
  That we are drifting down
The barren slopes that fall away
Towards the foothills grim and grey
  That lead to Old Man's Town.

And marching with us on the track
  Full many friends we find:
We see them looking sadly back
  For those that dropped behind.

But God forbid a fate so dread —
  Alone to travel down
The dreary road we all must tread,
With faltering steps and whitening head,
  The road to Old Man's Town!

THE OLD TIMER'S STEEPLECHASE

The sheep were shorn and the wool went down
  At the time of our local racing:
And I'd earned a spell — I was burnt and brown —
So I rolled my swag for a trip to town
  And a look at the steeplechasing.

'Twas rough and ready — an uncleared course
  As rough as the blacks had found it;
With barbed wire fences, topped with gorse,
And a water jump that would drown a horse,
  And the steeple three times round it.

There was never a fence the tracks to guard —
  Some straggling posts defined 'em:
And the day was hot, and the drinking hard,
Till none of the stewards could see a yard
  Before nor yet behind 'em!

But the bell was rung and the nags were out,
  Excepting an old outsider
Whose trainer started an awful rout,
For his boy had gone on a drinking bout
  And left him without a rider.

"Is there not one man in the crowd," he cried,
  "In the whole of the crowd so clever,
Is there not one man that will take a ride
On the old white horse from the northern side
  That was bred on the Mooki River?"

'Twas an old white horse that they called The Cow,
  And a cow would look well beside him;
But I was pluckier then than now
(And I wanted excitement anyhow),
  So at last I agreed to ride him.

And the trainer said, "Well, he's dreadful slow,
  And he hasn't a chance whatever;
But I'm stony broke, so it's time to show
A trick or two that the trainers know
  Who train by the Mooki River.

"The first time round at the further side,
  With the trees and the scrub about you,
Just pull behind them and run out wide
And then dodge into the scrub and hide,
  And let them go round without you.

"At the third time round, for the final spin
   With the pace, and the dust to blind 'em,
They'll never notice if you chip in
For the last half-mile — you'll be sure to win,
   And they'll think you raced behind 'em.

"At the water jump you may have to swim —
   He hasn't a hope to clear it —
Unless he skims like the swallows skim
At full speed over, but not for him!
   He'll never go next or near it.

"But don't you worry — just plunge across,
   For he swims like a well-trained setter.
Then hide away in the scrub and gorse
The rest will be far ahead of course —
   The further ahead the better.

"You must rush the jumps in the last half-round
   For fear that he might refuse 'em;
He'll try to baulk with you, I'll be bound,
Take whip and spurs on the mean old hound,
   And don't be afraid to use 'em.

"At the final round, when the field are slow
   And you are quite fresh to meet 'em,
Sit down, and hustle him all you know
With the whip and spurs, and he'll have to go —
   Remember, you've *got* to beat 'em!"

* * * *

The flag went down and we seemed to fly,
   And we made the timbers shiver
Of the first big fence, as the stand flashed by,
And I caught the ring of the trainer's cry:
   "Go on! For the Mooki River!"

I jammed him in with a well-packed crush,
   And recklessly — out for slaughter —
Like a living wave over fence and brush
We swept and swung with a flying rush,
   Till we came to the dreaded water.

Ha, ha! I laugh at it now to think
   Of the way I contrived to work it.
Shut in amongst them, before you'd wink,
He found himself on the water's brink,
   With never a chance to shirk it!

The thought of the horror he felt beguiles
   The heart of this grizzled rover!
He gave a snort you could hear for miles,
And a spring would have cleared the Channel Isles
   And carried me safely over!

Then we neared the scrub, and I pulled him back
   In the shade where the gum leaves quiver:
And I waited there in the shadows black
While the rest of the horses, round the track,
   Went on like a rushing river!

At the second round, as the field swept by,
   I saw that the pace was telling;
But on they thundered, and by and by
As they passed the stand I could hear the cry
   Of the folk in the distance, yelling!

Then the last time round! And the hoofbeats rang!
   And I said, "Well, it's now or never!"
And out on the heels of the throng I sprang,
And the spurs bit deep and the whipcord sang
   As I rode! For the Mooki River!

We raced for home in a cloud of dust
   And the curses rose in chorus.
'Twas flog, and hustle, and jump you must!
And The Cow ran well — but to my disgust
   There was one got home before us.

'Twas a big black horse, that I had not seen
   In the part of the race I'd ridden;
And his coat was cool and his rider clean,
And I thought that perhaps I had not been
   The only one that had hidden.

And the trainer came with a visage blue
   With rage, when the race concluded:
Said he, "I thought you'd have pulled us through,
But the man on the black horse planted too,
   And nearer to home than you did!"

* * * *

Alas to think that those times so gay
   Have vanished and passed forever!
You don't believe in the yarn you say?
Why, man! 'Twas a matter of every day
   When we raced on the Mooki River!

IN THE STABLE

What! You don't like him; well, maybe — we all have our fancies,
    of course:
Brumby to look at you reckon? Well, no: he's a thoroughbred
    horse;
Sired by a son of old Panic — look at his ears and his head —
Lop-eared and Roman-nosed, ain't he? — well, that's how the
    Panics are bred.
Gluttonous, ugly and lazy, rough as a tip-cart to ride,
Yet if you offered a sovereign apiece for the hairs on his hide
That wouldn't buy him, nor twice that; while I've a pound to the
    good,
This here old stager stays by me and lives like a thoroughbred
    should:
Hunt him away from his bedding, and sit yourself down by the
    wall,
Till you hear how the old fellow saved me from Gilbert, O'Maley
    and Hall.

* * * *

Gilbert and Hall and O'Maley, back in the bushranging days,
Made themselves kings of the district — ruled it in old-fashioned
    ways —
Robbing the coach and the escort, stealing our horses at night,
Calling sometimes at the homesteads and giving the women a
    fright:
Came to the station one morning — and why they did this no one
    knows —
Took a brood mare from the paddock — wanting some fun, I
    suppose —
Fastened a bucket beneath her, hung by a strap round her flank,
Then turned her loose in the timber back of the seven-mile tank.

Go! She went mad! She went tearing and screaming with fear
    through the trees,
While the curst bucket beneath her was banging her flanks and her
    knees.
Bucking and racing and screaming she ran to the back of the run,
Killed herself there in a gully; by God, but they paid for their fun!
Paid for it dear, for the black boys found tracks, and the bucket,
    and all,
And I swore that I'd live to get even with Gilbert, O'Maley and
    Hall.

Day after day then I chased them — 'course they had friends on the
 sly,
Friends who were willing to sell them to those who were willing to
 buy.
Early one morning we found them in camp at the Cockatoo Farm
One of us shot at O'Maley and wounded him under the arm:
Ran them for miles in the ranges, till Hall, with his horse fairly
 beat,
Took to the rocks and we lost him — the others made good their
 retreat.
It was war to the knife then, I tell you, and once, on the door of
 my shed,
They nailed up a notice that offered a hundred reward for my head!

Then we heard they were gone from the district, they stuck up a
 coach in the West,
And I rode by myself in the paddocks, taking a bit of a rest,
Riding this colt as a youngster — awkward, half-broken and shy,
He wheeled round one day on a sudden; I looked, but I couldn't
 see why,
But I soon found out why, for before me, the hillside rose up like a
 wall,
And there on the top with their rifles were Gilbert, O'Maley and
 Hall!

'Twas a good three-mile run to the homestead — bad going, with
 plenty of trees —
So I gathered the youngster together, and gripped at his ribs with
 my knees.
'Twas a mighty poor chance to escape them! It puts a man's nerve
 to the test
On a half-broken colt to be hunted by the best mounted men in
 the West.
But the half-broken colt was a racehorse! He lay down to work
 with a will,
Flashed through the scrub like a clean-skin — by Heavens we *flew*
 down the hill!
Over a twenty-foot gully he swept with the spring of a deer
And they fired as we jumped, but they missed me — a bullet sang
 close to my ear —
And the jump gained us ground, for they shirked it: but I saw as
 we raced through the gap
That the rails at the homestead were fastened — I was caught like a
 rat in a trap.
Fenced with barbed wire was the paddock — barbed wire that
 would cut like a knife —
How was a youngster to clear it that never had jumped in his life?

Bang went a rifle behind me — the colt gave a spring, he was hit;
Straight at the sliprails I rode him — I felt him take hold of the bit;
Never a foot to the right or the left did he swerve in his stride,
Awkward and frightened, but honest, the sort it's a pleasure to ride!
Straight at the rails, where they'd fastened barbed wire on the top of the post,
Rose like a stag and went over, with hardly a scratch at the most;
Into the homestead I darted, and snatched down my gun from the wall,
And I tell you I made them step lively, Gilbert, O'Maley and Hall!

Yes! There's the mark of the bullet — he's got it inside of him yet
Mixed up somehow with his victuals, but bless you he don't seem to fret!
Gluttonous, ugly, and lazy — eats any thing he can bite;
Now, let us shut up the stable, and bid the old fellow goodnight:
Ah! We can't breed 'em, the sort that were bred when we old 'uns were young.
Yes, I was saying, these bushrangers, none of 'em lived to be hung,
Gilbert was shot by the troopers, Hall was betrayed by his friend,
Campbell disposed of O'Maley, bringing the lot to an end.

But you can talk about riding — I've ridden a lot in the past —
Wait till there's rifles behind you, you'll know what it means to go fast!
I've steeplechased, raced, and "run horses", but I think the most dashing of all
Was the ride when the old fellow saved me from Gilbert, O'Maley and Hall!

"He Giveth His Beloved Sleep"

The long day passes with its load of sorrow:
  In slumber deep
I lay me down to rest until tomorrow —
  Thank God for sleep.

Thank God for all respite from weary toiling,
  From cares that creep
Across our lives like evil shadows, spoiling
  God's kindly sleep.

We plough and sow, and, as the hours grow later,
  We strive to reap,
And build our barns, and hope to build them greater
  Before we sleep.

We toil and strain and strive with one another
  In hopes to heap
Some greater share of profit than our brother
  Before we sleep.

What will it profit that with tears or laughter
  Our watch we keep?
Beyond it all there lies the Great Hereafter!
  Thank God for sleep!

For, at the last, beseeching Christ to save us,
  We turn with deep
Heartfelt thanksgiving unto God, who gave us
  The Gift of Sleep.

DRIVER SMITH

'Twas Driver Smith of Battery A was anxious to see a fight;
He thought of the Transvaal all the day, he thought of it all the
    night —
"Well, if the battery's left behind, I'll go to the war," says he,
"I'll go a-driving an ambulance in the ranks of the A.M.C.

"I'm fairly sick of these here parades, it's want of a change that kills
A-charging the Randwick Rifle Range and aiming at Surry Hills.
And I think if I go with the ambulance I'm certain to find a show,
For they have to send the medical men wherever the troops can go.

"Wherever the rifle bullets flash and the Maxims raise a din,
It's there you'll find the medical men a-raking the wounded in —
A-raking 'em in like human flies — and a driver smart like me
Will find some scope for his extra skill in the ranks of the A.M.C."

So Driver Smith he went to the war a-cracking his driver's whip,
From ambulance to collecting base they showed him his regular
    trip.
And he said to the boys that were marching past, as he gave his
    whip a crack,
"You'll walk yourselves to the fight," says he — "Lord spare me, I'll
    drive you back."

Now, the fight went on in the Transvaal hills for the half of a day
    or more,
And Driver Smith he worked his trip — all aboard for the seat of
    war!
He took his load from the stretcher men and hurried 'em
    homeward fast
Till he heard a sound that he knew full well — a battery rolling
    past.

He heard the clink of the leading chains and the roll of the guns
    behind —
He heard the crack of the drivers' whips, and he says to 'em,
    "Strike me blind,
I'll miss me trip with this ambulance, although I don't care to shirk,
But I'll take the car off the line to-day and follow the guns at
    work."

Then up the Battery Colonel came a-cursing 'em black in the face.
"Sit down and shift 'em, you drivers there, and gallop 'em into
    place."
So off the Battery rolled and swung, a-going a merry dance,
And holding his own with the leading gun goes Smith with his
    ambulance.

They opened fire on the mountainside, a-peppering by and large,
When over the hill above their flank the Boers came down at the
    charge;
They rushed the guns with a daring rush, a-volleying left and right,
And Driver Smith with his ambulance moved up to the edge of the
    fight.

The gunners stuck to their guns like men, and fought like the wild
    cats fight,
For a Battery man don't leave his gun with ever a hope in sight;
But the bullets sang and the Mausers cracked and the Battery men
    gave way,
Till Driver Smith with his ambulance drove into the thick of the
    fray.

He saw the head of the Transvaal troop a-thundering to and fro,
A hard old face with a monkey beard — a face that he seemed to
    know;
"Now, who's that leader," said Driver Smith, "I've seen him before
    today.
Why, bless my heart, but it's Kruger's self," and he jumped for him
    straight away.

He collared old Kruger round the waist and hustled him into the
    van.
It wasn't according to stretcher drill for raising a wounded man;
But he forced him in and said: "All aboard, we're off for a little
    ride,
And you'll have the car to yourself," says he, "I reckon we're full
    inside."

He wheeled his team on the mountainside and set 'em a merry
    pace,
A-galloping over the rocks and stones, and a lot of the Boers gave
    chase;
But Driver Smith had a fairish start, and he said to the Boers,
    "Good day,
You have Buckley's chance for to catch a man that was trained in
    Battery A."

He drove his team to the hospital and said to the P.M.O.,
"Beg pardon, sir, but I missed a trip, mistaking the way to go;
And Kruger came to the ambulance and asked could we spare a
    bed,
So I fetched him here, and we'll take him home to show for a bob
    a head."

So the word went round to the English troops to say they need
    fight no more,

For Driver Smith with his ambulance had ended the blooming war:
And in London now at the music halls he's starring it every night,
And drawing a hundred pounds a week to tell how he won the
    fight.

THERE'S ANOTHER
BLESSED HORSE FELL DOWN

When you're lying in your hammock, sleeping soft and sleeping
    sound,
  Without a care or trouble on your mind,
And there's nothing to disturb you but the engines going round,
  And you're dreaming of the girl you left behind;
In the middle of your joys you'll be wakened by a noise,
  And a clatter on the deck above your crown,
And you'll hear the corporal shout as he turns the picket out,
  "There's another blessed horse fell down."

You can see 'em in the morning, when you're cleaning out the stall,
  A-leaning on the railings nearly dead,
And you reckon by the evening they'll be pretty sure to fall,
  And you curse them as you tumble into bed.
Oh, you'll hear it pretty soon, "Pass the word for Denny Moon,
  There's a horse here throwing handsprings like a clown";
And it's "Shove the others back or he'll cripple half the pack,
  There's another blessed horse fell down."

And when the war is over and the fighting all is done,
  And you're all at home with medals on your chest,
And you've learnt to sleep so soundly that the firing of a gun
  At your bedside wouldn't rob you of your rest;
As you lie in slumber deep, if your wife walks in her sleep,
  And tumbles down the stairs and breaks her crown,
Oh, it won't awaken you, for you'll say, "It's nothing new,
  It's another blessed horse fell down."

ON THE TREK

Oh, the weary, weary journey on the trek, day after day,
    With sun above and silent veldt below;
And our hearts keep turning homeward to the youngsters far away,
    And the homestead where the climbing roses grow.
Shall we see the flats grow golden with the ripening of the grain?
    Shall we hear the parrots calling on the bough?
Ah! the weary months of marching ere we hear them call again,
    For we're going on a long job now.

In the drowsy days on escort, riding slowly half asleep,
    With the endless line of waggons stretching back,
While the khaki soldiers travel like a mob of travelling sheep,
    Plodding silent on the never-ending track,
While the constant snap and sniping of the foe you never see
    Makes you wonder will your turn come — when and how?
As the Mauser ball hums past you like a vicious kind of bee —
    Oh! we're going on a long job now.

When the dash and the excitement and the novelty are dead,
    And you've seen a load of wounded once or twice,
Or you've watched your old mate dying — with the vultures
      overhead,
    Well, you wonder if the war is worth the price.
And down along Monaro now they're starting out to shear,
    I can picture the excitement and the row;
But they'll miss me on the Lachlan when they call the roll this
      year,
    For we're going on a long job now.

THE LAST PARADE

With never a sound of trumpet,
  With never a flag displayed,
The last of the old campaigners
  Lined up for the last parade.

Weary they were and battered,
  Shoeless, and knocked about;
From under their ragged forelocks
  Their hungry eyes looked out.

And they watched as the old commander
  Read out, to the cheering men,
The Nation's thanks and the orders
  To carry them home again.

And the last of the old campaigners,
  Sinewy, lean, and spare —
He spoke for his hungry comrades:
  "Have we not done our share?

"Starving and tired and thirsty
  We limped on the blazing plain;
And after a long night's picket
  You saddled us up again.

"We froze on the windswept kopjes
  When the frost lay snowy white.
Never a halt in the daytime,
  Never a rest at night!

"We knew when the rifles rattled
  From the hillside bare and brown,
And over our weary shoulders
  We felt warm blood run down.

"As we turned for the stretching gallop,
  Crushed to the earth with weight;
But we carried our riders through it —
  Carried them p'raps too late.

"Steel! We were steel to stand it —
  We that have lasted through,
We that are old campaigners
  Pitiful, poor, and few.

"Over the sea you brought us,
  Over the leagues of foam:

Now we have served you fairly
   Will you not take us home?

"Home to the Hunter River,
   To the flats where the lucerne grows;
Home where the Murrumbidgee
   Runs white with the melted snows.

"This is a small thing, surely!
   Will not you give command
That the last of the old campaigners
   Go back to their native land?"

* * * *

They looked at the grim commander,
   But never a sign he made.
"Dismiss!" and the old campaigners
   Moved off from their last parade.

Johnny Boer

Men fight all shapes and sizes as the racing horses run,
And no man knows his courage till he stands before a gun.
At mixed-up fighting, hand to hand, and clawing men about
They reckon Fuzzy-wuzzy is the hottest fighter out.
But Fuzzy gives himself away — his style is out of date,
He charges like a driven grouse that rushes on its fate;
You've nothing in the world to do but pump him full of lead:
But when you're fighting Johnny Boer you have to use your head;
He don't believe in front attacks or charging at the run,
He fights you from a kopje with his little Maxim gun.

For when the Lord He made the earth, it seems uncommon clear,
He gave the job of Africa to some good engineer,
Who started building fortresses on fashions of his own —
Lunettes, redoubts, and counterscarps all made of rock and stone.
The Boer needs only bring a gun, for ready to his hand
He finds these heaven-built fortresses all scattered through the land;
And there he sits and winks his eye and wheels his gun about,
And we must charge across the plain to hunt the beggar out.
It ain't a game that grows on us, there's lots of better fun
Than charging at old Johnny with his little Maxim gun.

On rocks a goat could scarcely climb, steep as the walls of Troy,
He wheels a four-point-seven about as easy as a toy;
With bullocks yoked and drag ropes manned, he lifts her up the
    rocks
And shifts her every now and then, as cunning as a fox.
At night you mark her right ahead, you see her clean and clear,
Next day at dawn — "What, ho! she bumps" — from somewhere in
    the rear.
Or else the keenest-eyed patrol will miss him with the glass —
He's lying hidden in the rocks to let the leaders pass;
But when the main guard comes along he opens up the fun,
There's lots of ammunition for the little Maxim gun.

But after all the job is sure, although the job is slow,
We have to see the business through, the Boer has got to go.
With Nordenfeldt and lyddite shell it's certain, soon or late,
We'll hunt him from his kopjes and across the Orange State;
And then across those open flats you'll see the beggar run,
And we'll be running after with *our* little Maxim gun.

RIGHT IN FRONT OF THE ARMY

"Where 'ave you been this week or more,
'Aven't seen you about the war?
Thought perhaps you was at the rear
Guarding the waggons." "What, us? No fear!
Where have we been? Why, bless my heart,
Where have we been since the bloomin' start?
    Right in the front of the army,
      Battling day and night!
    Right in the front of the army,
      Teaching 'em how to fight!"
    Every separate man you see,
    Sapper, gunner, and C.I.V.,
    Every one of 'em seems to be
    Right in the front of the army!

Most of the troops to the camp had gone,
When we met with a cow gun toiling on;
And we said to the boys, as they walked her past,
"Well, thank goodness, you're here at last!"
"Here at last! Why, what d'yer mean?
Ain't we just where we've always been?
    Right in the front of the army,
      Battling day and night!
    Right in the front of the army,
      Teaching 'em how to fight!"
    Correspondents and vets in force,
    Mounted foot and dismounted horse,
    All of them were, as a matter of course,
    Right in the front of the army.

Old Lord Roberts will have to mind
If ever the enemy get behind;
For they'll smash him up with a rear attack,
Because his army has got no back!
Think of the horrors that might befall
An army without any rear at all!
    Right in the front of the army,
      Battling day and night!
    Right in the front of the army,
      Teaching 'em how to fight!
    Swede attachés and German counts,
    Yeomen (known as De Wet's remounts),
    All of them were by their own accounts
    Right in the front of the army!

THAT V.C.

'Twas in the days of front attack,
  This glorious truth we'd yet to learn it —
That every "front" had got a back,
  And French was just the man to turn it.

A wounded soldier on the ground
  Was lying hid behind a hummock;
He proved the good old proverb sound —
  An army travels on its stomach.

He lay as flat as any fish,
  His nose had worn a little furrow;
He only had one frantic wish,
  That like an ant-bear he could burrow.

The bullets whistled into space,
  The pom-pom gun kept up its braying,
The four-point-seven supplied the bass —
  You'd think the devil's band was playing.

A valiant comrade, crawling near,
  Observed his most supine behaviour,
And crept towards him, "Hey! what cheer?
  Buck up," said he, "I've come to save yer.

"You get up on my shoulders, mate,
  And if we live beyond the firing,
I'll get the V.C. sure as fate,
  Because our blokes is all retiring.

"It's fifty pounds a year," says he,
  "I'll stand you lots of beer and whisky."
"No," says the wounded man, "not me,
  I'll not be saved, it's far too risky.

"I'm fairly safe behind this mound,
  I've worn a hole that seems to fit me;
But if you lift me off the ground,
  It's fifty pounds to one they'll hit me."

So back towards the firing line
  Our friend crept slowly to the rear, oh!
Remarking, "What a selfish swine!
  He might have let me be a hero."

JOCK

There's a soldier that's been doing of his share
In the fighting up and down and round about.
He's continually marching here and there
And he's fighting, morning in and morning out.

The Boer, you see, he generally runs;
But sometimes when he hides behind a rock,
And we can't make no impression with the guns,
Oh, then you'll hear the order, "Send for Jock!"

Yes, it's Jock — Scotch Jock.
He's the fellow that can give or take a knock.
For he's hairy and he's hard,
And his feet are by the yard,
And his face is like the face what's on a clock.
But when the bullets fly you will mostly hear the cry —
"Send for Jock!"

The Cavalry have gun and sword and lance,
Before they choose their weapon, why, they're dead.
The Mounted Fut are hampered in advance
By holding of their helmets on their head.

And when the Boer has dug himself a trench
And placed his Maxim gun behind a rock,
These mounted heroes — pets of Johnny French —
They have to sit and wait and send for Jock!

Yes, the Jocks — Scotch Jocks,
With their music that'd terrify an ox!
When the bullets kick the sand
You can hear the sharp command —
"Forty-Second! At the double! Charge the rocks!"
And the charge is like a flood
When they've warmed the Highland blood
Of the Jocks!

Santa Claus

Halt! Who goes there? The sentry's call
Rose on the midnight air
Above the noises of the camp,
The roll of wheels, the horses' tramp.
The challenge echoed over all —
Halt! Who goes there?

A quaint old figure clothed in white,
He bore a staff of pine,
An ivy wreath was on his head.
"Advance, oh friend," the sentry said,
"Advance, for this is Christmas night,
And give the countersign."

"No sign nor countersign have I,
Through many lands I roam
The whole world over far and wide,
To exiles all at Christmastide,
From those who love them tenderly
I bring a thought of home.

"From English brook and Scottish burn,
From cold Canadian snows,
From those far lands ye hold most dear
I bring you all a greeting here,
A frond of a New Zealand fern,
A bloom of English rose.

"From faithful wife and loving lass
I bring a wish divine,
For Christmas blessings on your head."
"I wish you well," the sentry said,
"But here, alas! you may not pass
Without the countersign."

He vanished — and the sentry's tramp
Re-echoed down the line.
It was not till the morning light
The soldiers knew that in the night
Old Santa Claus had come to camp
Without the countersign.

III

SALTBUSH BILL J.P.,
AND OTHER VERSES

Song of the Wheat

We have sung the song of the droving days,
   Of the march of the travelling sheep;
By silent stages and lonely ways
   Thin, white battalions creep.
But the man who now by the land would thrive
   Must his spurs to a ploughshare beat.
Is there ever a man in the world alive
   To sing the song of the Wheat!

It's west by south of the Great Divide
   The grim grey plains run out,
Where the old flock masters lived and died
   In a ceaseless fight with drought.
Weary with waiting and hope deferred
   They were ready to own defeat,
Till at last they heard the master-word
   And the master-word was Wheat.

Yarran and Myall and Box and Pine —
   'Twas axe and fire for all;
They scarce could tarry to blaze the line
   Or wait for the trees to fall,
Ere the team was yoked and the gates flung wide,
   And the dust of the horses' feet
Rose up like a pillar of smoke to guide
   The wonderful march of Wheat.

Furrow by furrow, and fold by fold,
   The soil is turned on the plain;
Better than silver and better than gold
   Is the surface-mine of the grain.
Better than cattle and better than sheep
   In the fight with the drought and heat.
For a streak of stubbornness wide and deep
   Lies hid in a grain of Wheat.

When the stock is swept by the hand of fate,
   Deep down in his bed of clay
The brave brown Wheat will lie and wait
   For the resurrection day:
Lie hid while the whole world thinks him dead;
   But the spring rain, soft and sweet,
Will over the steaming paddocks spread
   The first green flush of the Wheat.

Green and amber and gold it grows
  When the sun sinks late in the West
And the breeze sweeps over the rippling rows
  Where the quail and the skylark nest.
Mountain or river or shining star,
  There's never a sight can beat —
Away to the skyline stretching far —
  A sea of the ripening Wheat.

When the burning harvest sun sinks low,
  And the shadows stretch on the plain,
The roaring strippers come and go
  Like ships on a sea of grain;
Till the lurching, groaning waggons bear
  Their tale of the load complete.
Of the world's great work he has done his share
  Who has gathered a crop of wheat.

Princes and Potentates and Czars,
  They travel in regal state,
But old King Wheat has a thousand cars
  For his trip to the water-gate;
And his thousand steamships breast the tide
  And plough thro' the wind and sleet
To the lands where the teeming millions bide
  That say, "Thank God for Wheat!"

BRUMBY'S RUN

The Aboriginal term for a wild horse is "brumby".
At a recent trial in Sydney a Supreme Court Judge,
hearing of "brumby horses", asked "Who is Brumby, and where is his run?"

It lies beyond the Western Pines
   Towards the sinking sun,
And not a survey mark defines
   The bounds of "Brumby's run".

On odds and ends of mountain land
   On tracks of range and rock,
Where no one else can make a stand,
   Old Brumby rears his stock —

A wild, unhandled lot they are
   Of every shape and breed,
They venture out 'neath moon and star
   Along the flats to feed.

But when the dawn makes pink the sky
   And steals along the plain,
The Brumby horses turn and fly
   Towards the hills again.

The traveller by the mountain track
   May hear their hoofbeats pass,
And catch a glimpse of brown and black,
   Dim shadows on the grass.

The eager stock horse pricks his ears
   And lifts his head on high
In wild excitement when he hears
   The Brumby mob go by.

Old Brumby asks no price or fee
   O'er all his wide domains:
The man who yards his stock is free
   To keep them for his pains.

So, off to scour the mountainside
   With eager eyes aglow,
To strongholds where the wild mobs hide
   The gully-rakers go.

A rush of horses through the trees,
   A red shirt making play;
A sound of stockwhips on the breeze,
   They vanish far away!

* * * *

Ah, me! before our day is done
  We long with bitter pain
To ride once more on Brumby's run
  And yard his mob again.

SALTBUSH BILL
ON THE PATRIARCHS

Come all ye little rouseabouts and climb upon my knee;
To-day, ye see, is Christmas Day, and so it's up to me
To give you some instruction like — a kind of Christmas tale —
So name your yarn, and off she goes. What, "Jonah and the
    Whale"?

Well, whales is sheep I've never shore; I've never been to sea,
So all them great Leviathans is mysteries to me;
But there's a tale the Bible tells I fully understand,
About the time the Patriarchs were settling on the land.

Those Patriarchs of olden time, when all is said and done,
They lived the same as far-out men on many a Queensland run —
A lot of roving, droving men that drifted to and fro,
The same we did out Queensland way a score of years ago.

Now Isaac was a squatter man, and Jacob was his son,
And when the boy grew up, you see, he wearied of the run.
You know the way that boys grow up — there's some that stick at
    home.
But any boy that's worth his salt will roll his swag and roam;

So Jacob caught the roving fit and took the drovers' track
To where his uncle had a run, beyond the outer back;
You see they made for outback runs for room to stretch and grow,
The same we did out Queensland way, a score of years ago.

Now, Jacob knew the ways of stock — that's most uncommon
    clear —
For when he got to Laban's Run, they made him overseer.
He didn't ask a pound a week, but bargained for his pay,
To take the roan and strawberry calves — the same we'd take
    today.

The duns and blacks and "Goulburn roans" (that's brindles), coarse
    and hard,
He branded them with Laban's brand, in Old Man Laban's yard;
So, when he'd done the station work for close on seven year,
Why, all the choicest stock belonged to Laban's overseer.

It's often so with overseers — I've seen the same thing done
By many a Queensland overseer on many a Queensland run —
But when the mustering time came on old Laban acted straight.
He gave him country of his own outside the bound'ry gate.

He gave him stock, and offered him his daughter's hand in troth;
And Jacob first he married one, and then he married both.
You see, they weren't particular about a wife or so;
No more were we up Queensland way a score of years ago.

But when the stock were strong and fat with grass and lots of rain,
Then Jacob felt the call to take the homeward road again.
It's strange in every creed and clime, no matter where you roam,
There comes a day when every man would like to make for home.

So off he set, with sheep and goats — a mighty moving band —
To battle down the homeward track along the Overland.
It's droving mixed-up mobs like that, that makes men cut their
    throats.
I've travelled rams, which Lord forget, but never travelled goats.

But Jacob knew the ways of stock, for, so the story goes,
When battlin' through the Philistines — selectors, I suppose —
He thought he'd have to fight his way, an awkward sort of job;
So what did Old Man Jacob do — of course, he split the mob.

He sent the strong stock on ahead to battle out the way;
He couldn't hurry lambing ewes — no more you could today —
And down the road, from run to run, his hand 'gainst every hand,
He moved that mighty mob of stock across the Overland.

The thing is made so clear and plain, so solid in and out,
There isn't any room at all for any kind of doubt.
It's just a plain straightforward tale — a tale that lets you know
The way they lived in Palestine three thousand years ago.

It's strange to read it all today, the shifting of the stock;
You'd think you see the caravans that loaf behind the flock.
The little donkeys and the mules, the sheep that slowly spread,
And maybe Dan or Naphthali a-ridin' on ahead;

The long, dry, dusty summer days, the smouldering fires at night;
The stir and bustle of the camp at break of morning light;
The little kids that skipped about, the camels' dead-slow tramp —
I wish I'd done a week or two in Old Man Jacob's camp!

But if I keep the narrer path, some day, perhaps, I'll know
How Jacob bred them strawberry calves three thousand years ago.

THE REVEREND MULLINEUX

I'd reckon his weight at eight-stun-eight,
  And his height at five-foot-two,
With a face as plain as an eight-day clock
And a walk as brisk as a bantam-cock —
  Game as a bantam, too,
Hard and wiry and full of steam,
That's the boss of the English team,
  The Reverend Mullineux.

Makes no row when the game gets rough —
  None of your "Strike me blue!
You's want smacking across the snout!"
Plays like a gentleman out-and-out —
  Such as he ought to do.
"Kindly remove from off my face!"
That's the way that he states his case —
  Reverend Mullineux.

Kick! He can kick like an army mule —
  Runs like a kangaroo!
Hard to get by as a lawyer plant,
Tackles his man like a bulldog ant —
  Fetches him over too!
Didn't the public cheer and shout
Watchin' him chuckin' big blokes about —
  Reverend Mullineux.

Scrimmage was packed on his prostrate form.
  Somehow the ball got through.
Who was it tackled our big half-back,
Flinging him down like an empty sack,
  Right on our goal line too?
Who but the man that we thought was dead,
Down with a score of 'em on his head —
  Reverend Mullineux.

WISDOM OF HAFIZ:
THE PHILOSOPHER TAKES TO RACING

My son, if you go to the races to battle with Ikey and Mo,
Remember, it's seldom the pigeon can pick out the eye of the crow;
Remember, they live by the business; remember, my son, and go
    slow!

If ever an owner should tell you, "Back mine" — don't you be such
    a flat.
He knows his own cunning no doubt — does he know what the
    others are at?
Find out what he's frightened of most, and invest a few dollars on
    that.

Walk not in the track of the trainer, nor hang round the rails at
    his stall.
His wisdom belongs to his patron — shall he give it to one and to
    all?
When the stable is served he may tell you — and his words are like
    jewels let fall.

Run wide of the tipster, who whispers that Borak is sure to be first,
He tells the next mug that he meets with a tale with the placings
    reversed;
And, remember, of judges of racing, the jockey's the absolute worst.

When they lay three to one on the field, and the runners are
    twenty-and-two,
Take a pull at yourself; take a pull — it's a mighty big field to get
    through.
Is the club handicapper a fool? If a fool is about, perhaps it's you!

Beware of the critic who tells you the handicap's absolute rot,
For this is chucked in, and that's hopeless, and somebody ought to
    be shot.
How is it he can't make a fortune himself when he knows such a
    lot?

From tipsters, and jockeys, and trials, and gallops, the glory has
    gone,
For this is the wisdom of Hafiz that sages have pondered upon,
"The very best tip in the world is to see the commission go on!"

SALTBUSH BILL, J.P.

Beyond the land where Leichhardt went,
  Beyond Sturt's western track,
The rolling tide of change has sent
  Some strange J.P.s out back.

And Saltbush Bill, grown old and grey,
  And worn with want of sleep,
Received the news in camp one day
  Behind the travelling sheep,

That Edward Rex, confiding in
  His known integrity,
By hand and seal on parchment skin
  Had made him a J.P.

He read the news with eager face
  But found no word of pay.
"I'd like to see my sister's place
  And kids on Christmas Day.

"I'd like to see green grass again,
  And watch clear water run,
Away from this unholy plain,
  And flies, and dust, and sun."

At last one little clause he found
  That might some hope inspire,
"A magistrate may charge a pound
  For inquest on a fire."

A big blacks' camp was built close by
  And Saltbush Bill, says he,
"I think that camp might well supply
  A job for a J.P."

That night, by strange coincidence,
  A most disastrous fire
Destroyed the country residence
  Of Jacky Jack, Esquire.

'Twas mostly leaves, and bark, and dirt;
  The party most concerned
Appeared to think it wouldn't hurt
  If forty such were burned.

Quite otherwise thought Saltbush Bill,
  Who watched the leaping flame.

"The home is small", said he, "but still
  The principle's the same.

"'Midst palaces though you should roam,
  Or follow pleasure's tracks,
You'll find", he said, "no place like home,
  At least like Jacky Jack's.

"Tell every man in camp 'Come quick',
  Tell every black Maria,
I give tobacco half a stick —
  Hold inquest long-a fire."

Each juryman received a name
  Well suited to a Court.
"Long Jack" and "Stumpy Bill" became
  "John Long" and "William Short".

While such as "Tarpot", "Bullock Dray",
  And "Tommy Wait-a-While",
Became, for ever and a day,
  "Scott", "Dickens", and "Carlyle".

And twelve good sable men and true
  Were soon engaged upon
The conflagration that o'erthrew
  The home of John A. John.

Their verdict, "Burnt by act of fate",
  They scarcely had returned
When, just behind the magistrate,
  Another humpy burned!

The jury sat again and drew
  Another stick of plug.
Said Saltbush Bill, "It's up to you
  Put some one long-a jug."

"I'll camp the sheep", he said, "and sift
  The evidence about."
For quite a week he couldn't shift,
  The way the fires broke out.

The jury thought the whole concern
  As good as any play.
They used to "take him oath" and earn
  Three sticks of plug a day.

At last the tribe lay down to sleep
  Homeless, beneath a tree;

And onward with his travelling sheep
  Went Saltbush Bill, J.P.

The sheep delivered, safe and sound,
  His horse to town he turned,
And drew some five-and-twenty pound
  For fees that he had earned.

And where Monaro's ranges hide
  Their little farms away,
His sister's children by his side,
  He spent his Christmas Day.

The next J.P. that went outback
  Was shocked, or pained, or both
At hearing every pagan black
  Repeat the juror's oath.

No matter though he turned and fled
  They followed faster still,
"You make it inkwich, boss," they said
  "All same like Saltbush Bill."

They even said they'd let him see
  The fires originate.
When he refused they said that he
  Was "No good magistrate".

And out beyond Sturt's Western track,
  And Leichhardt's furthest tree,
They wait till fate shall send them back
  Their Saltbush Bill, J.P.

THE RIDERS IN THE STAND

There's some that ride the Robbo style, and bump at every stride;
While others sit a long way back, to get a longer ride.
There's some that ride like sailors do, with legs, and arms, and
    teeth;
And some ride on the horse's neck, and some ride underneath.

But all the finest horsemen out — the men to beat the band —
You'll find amongst the crowd that ride their races in the stand.
They'll say, "He had the race in hand, and lost it in the straight".
They'll show how Godby came too soon, and Barden came too
    late.

They'll say Chevalley lost his nerve, and Regan lost his head;
They'll tell how one was "livened up" and something else was
    "dead" —
In fact, the race was never run on sea, or sky, or land,
But what you'd get it better done by riders in the stand.

The rule holds good in everything in life's uncertain fight:
You'll find the winner can't go wrong, the loser can't go right.
You ride a slashing race, and lose — by one and all you're banned!
Ride like a bag of flour, and win — they'll cheer you in the stand.

Waltzing Matilda

Carrying a Swag

Oh there once was a swagman camped in the billabongs,
  Under the shade of a Coolibah tree;
And he sang as he looked at the old billy boiling,
  "Who'll come a-waltzing Matilda with me."

  Who'll come a-waltzing Matilda, my darling,
    Who'll come a-waltzing Matilda with me.
  Waltzing Matilda and leading a water-bag,
    Who'll come a-waltzing Matilda with me.

Up came the jumbuck to drink at the waterhole,
  Up jumped the swagman and grabbed him in glee;
And he sang as he put him away in his tucker-bag,
  "You'll come a-waltzing Matilda with me."

  Who'll come a-waltzing Matilda, my darling,
    Who'll come a-waltzing Matilda with me.
  Waltzing Matilda and leading a water-bag,
    Who'll come a-waltzing Matilda with me.

Up came the squatter a-riding his thoroughbred;
  Up came policemen — one, two, and three.
"Whose is the jumbuck you've got in the tucker-bag?
  You'll come a-waltzing Matilda with we."

  Who'll come a-waltzing Matilda, my darling,
    Who'll come a-waltzing Matilda with me.
  Waltzing Matilda and leading a water-bag,
    Who'll come a-waltzing Matilda with me.

Up sprang the swagman and jumped in the waterhole,
  Drowning himself by the Coolibah tree;
And his voice can be heard as it sings in the billabongs,
  "Who'll come a-waltzing Matilda with me."

  Who'll come a-waltzing Matilda, my darling,
    Who'll come a-waltzing Matilda with me.
  Waltzing Matilda and leading a water-bag,
    Who'll come a-waltzing Matilda with me.

AN ANSWER TO VARIOUS BARDS

Well, I've waited mighty patient while they all came rolling in,
Mister Lawson, Mister Dyson, and the others of their kin,
With their dreadful, dismal stories of the overlander's camp,
How his fire is always smoky, and his boots are always damp;
And they paint it so terrific it would fill one's soul with gloom,
But you know they're fond of writing about "corpses" and "the tomb".
So, before they curse the bushland they should let their fancy range,
And take something for their livers, and be cheerful for a change.

Now, for instance, Mister Lawson — well, of course, we almost cried
At the sorrowful description how his "little 'Arvie" died.
And we wept in silent sorrow when "His Father's Mate" was slain;
Then he went and killed the father, and we had to weep again.
Ben Duggan and Jack Denver, too, he caused them to expire,
And he went and cooked the gander of Jack Dunn, of Nevertire;
And he spoke in terms prophetic of a revolution's beat,
When the world should hear the clamour of those people in the street;
But the shearer chaps who start it — why, he rounds on them in blame,
And he calls 'em "agitators" who are living on the game.
So, no doubt, the bush is wretched if you judge it by the groan
Of the sad and soulful poet with a graveyard of his own.

But I "over-write" the bushmen! Well, I own without a doubt
That I always see a hero in the "man from furthest out".
I could never contemplate him through an atmosphere of gloom,
And a bushman never struck me as a subject for "the tomb".
If it ain't all "golden sunshine" where the "wattle branches wave",
Well, it ain't all damp and dismal, and it ain't all "lonely grave".
And, of course, there's no denying that the bushman's life is rough,
But a man can easy stand it if he's built of sterling stuff;
Tho' it's seldom that the drover gets a bed of eiderdown,
Yet the man who's born a bushman, he gets mighty sick of town,
For he's jotting down the figures, and he's adding up the bills
While his heart is simply aching for a sight of southern hills.
Then he hears a wool team passing with a rumble and a lurch,
And although the work is pressing yet it brings him off his perch.
For it stirs him like a message from his station friends afar
And he seems to sniff the ranges in the scent of wool and tar;
And it takes him back in fancy, half in laughter, half in tears,
To a sound of other voices and a thought of other years,

194

When the woolshed rang with bustle from the dawning of the day,
And the shear blades were a-clicking to the cry of "wool away!"
When his face was somewhat browner and his frame was firmer set,
And he feels his flabby muscles with a feeling of regret.
Then the wool team slowly passes and his eyes go sadly back
To the dusty little table and the papers in the rack,
And his thoughts go to the terrace where his sickly children squall,
And he thinks there's something healthy in the bush life after all.

But we'll go no more a-droving in the wind or in the sun,
For our fathers' hearts have failed us and the droving days are
    done.
There's a nasty dash of danger where the long-horned bullock
    wheels,
And we like to live in comfort and to get our reg'lar meals.
And to hang about the townships suits us better, you'll agree,
For a job at washing bottles is the job for such as we.
Let us herd into the cities, let us crush and crowd and push
Till we lose the love of roving and we learn to hate the bush;
And we'll turn our aspirations to a city life and beer,
And we'll sneak across to England — it's a nicer place than here;
For there's not much risk of hardship where all comforts are in
    store,
And the theatres are plenty and the pubs are more and more.

But that ends it, Mister Lawson, and it's time to say good-bye,
We must agree to differ in all friendship, you and I;
And our personal opinions — well, they're scarcely worth a rush,
For there's some that like the city and there's some that like the
    bush;
And there's no one quite contented, as I've always heard it said,
Except one favoured person, and *he* turned out to be dead.
So we'll work our own salvation with the stoutest hearts we may,
And if fortune only favours we will take the road some day,
And go droving down the river 'neath the sunshine and the stars,
And then we'll come to Sydney and vermilionise the bars.

T.Y.S.O.N.

'Across the Queensland border line
  The mobs of cattle go;
They travel down in sun and shine
  On dusty stage, and slow.
The drovers, riding slowly on
  To let the cattle spread,
Will say, "Here's one old landmark gone,
  For old man Tyson's dead."

What tales there'll be in every camp
  By men that Tyson knew;
The swagmen, meeting on the tramp,
  Will yarn the long day through,
And tell of how he passed as "Brown",
  And fooled the local men.
"But not for me — I struck the town,
And passed the message further down;
  That's T.Y.S.O.N.!"

There stands a little country town
  Beyond the border line,
Where dusty roads go up and down,
  And banks with pubs combine.
A stranger came to cash a cheque,
  Few were the words he said;
A handkerchief about his neck,
  An old hat on his head.

A long, grey stranger, eagle-eyed,
  "You know me? Of course you do."
"It's not my work," the boss replied,
  "To know such tramps as you."
"Well, look here, Mister, don't be flash,"
  Replied the stranger then,
"I never care to make a splash,
I'm simple — but I've got the cash,
  I'm T.Y.S.O.N."

But in that last great drafting yard,
  Where Peter keeps the gate,
And souls of sinners find it barred,
  And go to meet their fate;
There's one who ought to enter in,
  For good deeds done on earth;
Such deeds as merit ought to win,
  Kind deeds of sterling worth.

Not by the straight and narrow gate,
   Reserved for wealthy men,
But through the big gate, opened wide,
The grizzled figure, eagle-eyed,
   Will travel through — and then
Old Peter'll say, "We pass him through,
There's many a thing he used to do,
Good-hearted things that no one knew;
   That's T.Y.S.O.N."

As Long As
Your Eyes Are Blue

Wilt thou love me, sweet, when my hair is grey,
　And my cheeks shall have lost their hue?
When the charms of youth shall have passed away,
　Will your love as of old prove true?
For the looks may change, and the heart may range,
　And the love be no longer fond;
Wilt thou love with truth in the years of youth
　And away to the years beyond?

Oh, I love you, sweet, for your locks of brown
　And the blush on your cheek that lies —
But I love you most for the kindly heart
　That I see in your sweet blue eyes —
For the eyes are signs of the soul within,
　Of the heart that is leal and true,
And mine own sweetheart, I shall love you still,
　Just as long as your eyes are blue.

For the locks may bleach, and the cheeks of peach
　May be reft of their golden hue;
But mine own sweetheart, I shall love you still,
　Just as long as your eyes are blue.

THE "BOTTLE-OH" MAN

I ain't the kind of bloke as takes to any steady job —
   I drives a bottle cart around the town.
A man what keeps his eye about need never want a bob —
   I couldn't bear to work for every brown.
There's lots of 'andy things about in everybody's yard,
   There's cocks and 'ens a-running to and fro,
And little dorgs what comes and barks — we takes 'em off their guard;
   And we puts 'em with the Empty Bottle, oh!

   So it's "Any empty bottles, any empty bottles, oh!"
   You can hear us shout for half a mile or so;
   You can see the women rushing
   To take in the Monday's washing
   When they hear the cry of "Empty Bottle, oh!"

I'm driving down by Wexford Street, and up a window goes —
   A girl puts out 'er 'ead and looks at me,
An all right tart with ginger hair and freckles on 'er nose —
   I stops the cart and walks across to see.
"There ain't no bottles 'ere," says she, "since father took the pledge."
   "No bottles 'ere?" says I. "I'd like to know
Wot right you 'ave to stick your 'ead outside the winder-ledge,
   If you 'aven't got no Empty Bottle, oh!"

I sometimes gives the 'orse a spell, and then the push and me
   We takes a little trip to Chowder Bay;
Oh, ain't it nice the 'ole day long a-gazing at the sea
   And a-hiding of the tanglefoot away!
But when the booze gets 'old of us and fellers starts to "scrap",
   There's some what likes blue metal for to throw!
But as for me, I always says, for laying out a trap,
   Oh, there's nothing like an Empty Bottle, oh!

THE STORY OF MONGREL GREY

This is the story the stockman told,
  On the cattle camp, when the stars were bright;
The moon rose up like a globe of gold
  And flooded the plain with her mellow light.
We watched the cattle till dawn of day
And he told me the story of Mongrel Grey.

"He was a knock-about station hack,
  Spurred and walloped, and banged and beat;
Ridden all day with a sore on his back,
  Left all night with nothing to eat.
That was a matter of everyday —
Common occurrence to Mongrel Grey.

"Pr'aps we'd have sold him, but someone heard
  He was bred out back on a flooded run,
Where he learnt to swim like a water bird,
  Midnight or midday were all as one.
In the flooded ground he could find his way,
Nothing could puzzle old Mongrel Grey.

"'Tis a special gift that some horses learn,
  When the floods are out they will splash along
In girth-deep water, and twist and turn
  From hidden channel and billabong.
Never mistaking the road to go,
For a man may guess — but the horses *know*.

"I was camping out with my youngest son
  — Bit of a nipper just learnt to speak —
In an empty hut on the lower run,
  Shooting and fishing in Conroy's Creek.
The youngster toddled about all day,
And with our horses was Mongrel Grey.

"All of a sudden the flood came down
  Fresh from the hills with the mountain rain,
Roaring and eddying, rank and brown,
  Over the flats and across the plain.
Rising and falling — fall of night —
Nothing but water appeared in sight!

"'Tis a nasty place when the floods are out,
  Even in daylight, for all around

Channels and billabongs twist about,
    Stretching for miles in the flooded ground.
And to move was a hopeless thing to try
In the dark, with the water just racing by.

"I had to try it. I heard a roar,
    And the wind swept down with the blinding rain;
And the water rose till it reached the floor
    Of our highest room, and 'twas very plain
The way the water was sweeping down
We must shift for the highlands at once, or drown.

"Off to the stable I splashed, and found
    The horses shaking with cold and fright;
I led them down to the lower ground,
    But never a yard would they swim that night!
They reared and snorted and turned away,
And none would face it but Mongrel Grey.

"I bound the child on the horse's back,
    And we started off with a prayer to Heaven,
Through the rain and the wind and the pitchy black,
    For I knew that the instinct God has given
To guide His creatures by night and day
Would lead the footsteps of Mongrel Grey.

"He struck deep water at once and swam —
    I swam beside him and held his mane —
Till we touched the bank of the broken dam
    In shallow water — then off again,
Swimming in darkness across the flood,
Rank with the smell of the drifting mud.

"He turned and twisted across and back,
    Choosing the places to wade or swim,
Picking the safest and shortest track,
    The pitchy darkness was clear to him.
Did he strike the crossing by sight or smell?
The Lord that led him alone could tell!

"He dodged the timber whene'er he could,
    But the timber brought us to grief at last;
I was partly stunned by a log of wood,
    That struck my head as it drifted past;
And I lost my grip of the brave old grey,
And in half a second he swept away.

"I reached a tree, where I had to stay,
    And did a perish for two days hard;

And lived on water — but Mongrel Grey,
  He walked right into the homestead yard
At dawn next morning, and grazed around,
With the child on top of him safe and sound.

"We keep him now for the wife to ride,
  Nothing too good for him now of course;
Never a whip on his fat old hide,
  For she owes the child to that old grey horse.
And not Old Tyson himself could pay,
The purchase money of Mongrel Grey."

GILHOOLEY'S ESTATE

A ballad concerning the amalgamation of the legal profession

Oh, Mr Gilhooley he turned up his toes,
   As most of us do, soon or late;
And Jones was a lawyer, as everyone knows,
   So they took him Gilhooley's estate.

Gilhooley in life had been living so free
   'Twas thought his possessions were great,
So Jones, with a smile, says, "There's many a fee
   For me in Gilhooley's estate."

They made out a list of his property fine,
   It totalled a thousand and eight;
But the debts were nine hundred and ninety and nine —
   The debts of Gilhooley's estate.

So Mrs Gilhooley says, "Jones, my dear man,
   My childer have little to ait:
Just keep the expenses as low as you can
   Against poor Gilhooley's estate."

But Jones says, "The will isn't clear in its terms,
   I fear it will need some debate,
And the law won't allow me (attorneys are worms)
   To appear in Gilhooley's estate."

So a barrister man, with a wig on his head,
   And a brief in his hand quite elate,
Went up to the Court where they bury the dead,
   Just to move in Gilhooley's estate.

But His Honour the Judge said, "I think that the joint
   Legatees must be called to pro*bate* —
Ex parte Pokehorney is clear on the point —
   The point of Gilhooley's estate.

"I order a suit to be brought just to try
   If this is correct that I state —
A nice friendly suit, and the costs, by and by,
   Must be borne by Gilhooley's estate."

So Mrs Gilhooley says, "Jones, you'll appear!
   Thim barristers' fees is too great;
The suit is but friendly." "Attorneys, my dear,
   Can't be heard in Gilhooley's estate."

From Barristers' Court there's a mighty hurrah
   Arises both early and late:
It's only the whoop of the Junior Bar
   Dividing Gilhooley's estate.

THE ROAD
TO HOGAN'S GAP

Now look, y' see, it's this way like,
  Y' cross the broken bridge
And run the crick down till y' strike
  The second right-hand ridge.

The track is hard to see in parts,
  But still it's pretty clear;
There's been two Injin hawkers' carts
  Along that road this year.

Well, run that right-hand ridge along,
  It ain't, to say, too steep.
There's two fresh tracks might put y' wrong
  Where blokes went out with sheep.

But keep the crick upon your right,
  And follow pretty straight
Along the spur, until y' sight
  A wire and sapling gate.

Well, that's where Hogan's old grey mare
  Fell off and broke her back;
You'll see her carcase layin' there,
  Jist down below the track.

And then you drop two mile, or three,
  It's pretty steep and blind;
You want to go and fall a tree
  And tie it on behind.

And then you'll pass a broken cart
  Below a granite bluff;
And that is where you strike the part
  They reckon pretty rough.

But by the time you've got that far
  It's either cure or kill,
So turn your horses round the spur
  And face 'em up the hill.

For, look, if you should miss the slope
  And get below the track,
You haven't got the whitest hope
  Of ever gettin' back.

An' halfway up you'll see the hide
  Of Hogan's brindled bull;

Well, mind and keep the right-hand side,
　　The left's too steep a pull.

And both the banks is full of cracks;
　　An' just about at dark
You'll see the last year's bullock tracks
　　Where Hogan drew the bark.

The marks is old and pretty faint
　　And grown with scrub and such;
Of course the track to Hogan's ain't
　　A road that's travelled much.

But turn and run the tracks along
　　For half a mile or more,
And then, of course, you can't go wrong —
　　You're right at Hogan's door.

When first you come to Hogan's gate
　　He mightn't show, perhaps;
He's pretty sure to plant and wait
　　To see it ain't the traps.

I wouldn't call it good enough
　　To let your horses out;
There's some that's pretty extra rough
　　Is livin' round about.

It's likely if your horses did
　　Get feedin' near the track,
It's goin' to cost at least a quid
　　Or more to get them back.

So, if you find they're off the place,
　　It's up to you to go
And flash a quid in Hogan's face —
　　He'll know the blokes that know.

But, listen, if you're feelin' dry,
　　Just see there's no one near,
And go and wink the other eye
　　And ask for ginger beer.

The blokes come in from near and far
　　To sample Hogan's pop;
They reckon once they breast the bar
　　They stay there till they drop.

On Sundays you can see them spread
　　Like flies around the tap.

It's like that song "The Livin' Dead"
   Up there at Hogan's Gap.

They like to make it pretty strong
   Whenever there's a charnce;
So when a stranger comes along
   They always holds a darnce.

There's recitations, songs, and fights,
   They do the thing a treat.
There's one long bloke up there recites
   As well as e'er you'd meet.

They're lively blokes all right up there,
   It's never dull a day.
I'd go meself if I could spare
   The time to get away.

* * * *

The stranger turned his horses, quick,
   He didn't cross the bridge.
He didn't go along the crick
   To strike the second ridge.

He didn't make the trip, because
   He wasn't feeling fit.
His business up at Hogan's was
   To serve him with a writ.

He reckoned if he faced the pull
   And climbed the rocky stair,
The next to come might find his hide
A landmark on the mountain side,
Along with Hogan's brindled bull
   And Hogan's old grey mare!

A Singer of the Bush

There is waving of grass in the breeze
   And a song in the air,
And a murmur of myriad bees
   That toil everywhere.
There is scent in the blossom and bough,
   And the breath of the spring
Is as soft as a kiss on a brow —
   And springtime I sing.

There is drought on the land, and the stock
   Tumble down in their tracks
Or follow — a tottering flock —
   The scrub-cutter's axe.
While ever a creature survives
   The axes shall swing;
We are fighting with fate for their lives —
   And the combat I sing.

"Shouting" for a Camel

It was over at Coolgardie that a mining speculator,
  Who was going down the township just to make a bit o' chink,
Went off to hire a camel from a camel propagator,
  And the Afghan said he'd lend it if he'd stand the beast a drink.
Yes, the only price he asked him was to stand the beast a drink.
He was cheap, very cheap, as the dromedaries go.

So the mining speculator made the bargain, proudly thinking
  He had bested old Mahomet, he had done him in the eye.
Then he clambered on the camel, and the while the beast was
    drinking
  He explained the situation to the miners standing by.
That 'twas cheap, very cheap, as the dromedaries go.

But the camel kept on drinking and he filled his hold with water,
  And the more he had inside him yet the more he seemed to
    need,
For he drank it by the gallon, and his girths grew taut and tauter,
  And the miners muttered softly, "Yes, he's very dry indeed!
But he's cheap, very cheap, as the dromedaries go."

So he drank up twenty buckets — it was weird to watch him suck
    it,
  And the market price for water was per bucket half a crown.
Then the speculator stopped him, saying, "Not another bucket —
  If I give him any more there'll be a famine in the town.
Take him back to old Mahomet and I'll tramp it through the
    town."
He was cheap, very cheap, as the speculators go.

There's a moral to this story — in your hat you ought to paste it —
  Be careful whom you shout for when a camel is about,
And there's plenty human camels who, before they'll see you waste
    it,
  Will drink up all you'll pay for if you're fool enough to shout:
If you chance to strike a camel when you're fool enough to shout,
You'll be cheap, very cheap, as the speculators go.

MULLIGAN'S MARE

Oh, Mulligan's bar was the deuce of a place
To drink and to fight, and to gamble and race;
The height of choice spirits from near and from far
Were all concentrated on Mulligan's bar.

There was "Jerry the Swell", and the jockey boy Ned,
"Dog-bite-me" — so called from the shape of his head —
And a man whom the boys, in their musical slang,
Designed as the "Gaffer of Mulligan's Gang".

Now, Mulligan's Gang had a racer to show,
A bad 'un to look at, a good 'un to go;
Whenever they backed her you safely might swear
She'd walk in a winner, would Mulligan's mare.

But Mulligan, having some radical views,
Neglected his business and got "on the booze";
He took up with runners — a treacherous troop —
Who gave him away and he "fell in the soup".

And so it turned out on a fine summer day,
A bailiff turned up with a writ of "*fi fa*";
He walked to the bar with a manner serene,
"I levy," said he, "in the name of the Queen."

Then Mulligan wanted, in spite of the law,
To pay out the bailiff with "*one* in the jaw";
He drew out to hit him, but, ere you could wink,
He changed his intentions and stood him a drink.

A great consultation there straightway befell
'Twixt jockey boy Neddy and Jerry the Swell,
And the man with the head, who remarked, "Why, you bet!
Dog-bite-me!" said he, "but we'll diddle 'em yet.

"We'll slip out the mare from her stall in a crack,
And put in her place the old broken-down hack;
The hack is so like her, I'm ready to swear
The bailiff will think he has Mulligan's mare.

"So out with the racer and in with the screw,
We'll show him what Mulligan's talent can do;
And if he gets nasty and dares to say much
I'll knock him as stiff as my grandmother's crutch."

Then off to the town went the mare and the lad;
The bailiff came out, never dream't he was "had";

But marched to the stall with a confident air —
"I levy," said he, "upon Mulligan's mare."

He never would let her go out of his sight,
He watched her by day and he watched her by night,
For races were coming away in the West
And Mulligan's mare had a chance with the best.

And, thinking to quietly serve his own ends,
He sent off a wire to some bookmaking friends:
"Get all you can borrow, beg, snavel, or snare
And lay the whole lot against Mulligan's mare."

The races came round, and a crowd on the course
Were laying the mare till they made themselves hoarse,
And Mulligan's party, with ardour intense,
They backed her for pounds and for shillings and pence.

And think of the grief of the bookmaking host
At sound of the summons to go to the post —
For down to the start with her thoroughbred air
As fit as a fiddle pranced Mulligan's mare!

They started, and off went the boy to the front,
He cleared out at once, and he made it a hunt;
He steadied as rounding the corner they wheeled,
Then gave her her head and she smothered the field.

The race put her owner right clear of his debts,
He landed a fortune in stakes and in bets,
He paid the old bailiff the whole of his pelf,
And gave him a hiding to keep for himself.

So all you bold sportsmen take warning, I pray,
Keep clear of the running, you'll find it don't pay;
For the very best rule that you'll hear in a week —
Is never to bet on a thing that can speak.

And whether you're lucky or whether you lose,
Keep clear of the cards and keep clear of the booze,
And fortune in season will answer your prayer,
And send you a flyer like Mulligan's mare.

THE MOUNTAIN SQUATTER

Here in my mountain home,
  On rugged hills and steep,
I sit and watch you come,
  Oh Riverina Sheep!

You come from fertile plains
  Where saltbush (sometimes) grows,
And flats that (when it rains)
  Will blossom like the rose.

But when the summer sun
  Gleams down like burnished brass
You have to leave your run
  And hustle off for grass.

'Tis then that — forced to roam —
  You come to where I keep,
Here in my mountain home,
  A boarding-house for sheep.

Around me where I sit
  The wary wombat goes,
A beast of little wit
  But what he knows, he *knows*.

The very same remark
  Applies to me also,
I don't give out a spark,
  But what I know, I *know*.

My brain perhaps would show
  No convolutions deep;
But anyhow I know
  The way to handle sheep.

These Riverina cracks,
  They do not care to ride
The half-inch hanging tracks
  Along the mountain side.

Their horses shake with fear
  When loosened boulders go,
With leaps, like startled deer,
  Down to the gulfs below.

Their very dogs will shirk,
  And drop their tails in fright
When asked to go and work
  A mob that's out of sight.

My little collie pup
  Works silently and wide,
You'll see her climbing up
  Along the mountain side.

As silent as a fox
  You'll see her come and go
A shadow through the rocks
  Where ash and messmate grow.

Then, lost to sight and sound
  Behind some rugged steep,
She works her way around
  And gathers up the sheep.

And working wide and shy,
  She holds them rounded up.
The cash ain't coined to buy
  That little collie pup.

And so I draw a screw
  For self and dog and keep
To boundary ride for you,
  Oh Riverina Sheep!

And when the autumn rain
  Has made the herbage grow,
You travel off again,
  And glad — no doubt — to go!

But some are left behind
  Around the mountain's spread,
For those we cannot find
  We put them down as dead.

But when we say *adieu*
  And close the boarding job,
I always find a few
  Fresh earmarks in my mob.

So what with those I sell,
  And what with those I keep,
You pay me pretty well,
  Oh Riverina Sheep!

It's up to me to shout
  Before we say goodbye —
"Here's to a howlin' drought
  All west of Gundagai!"

Pioneers

They came of bold and roving stock that would not fixed abide;
They were the sons of field and flock since e'er they learned to ride;
We may not hope to see such men in these degenerate years
As those explorers of the bush — the brave old pioneers.

'Twas they who rode the trackless bush in heat and storm and
    drought;
'Twas they that heard the master-word that called them further
    out;
'Twas they that followed up the trail the mountain cattle made
And pressed across the mighty range where now their bones are
    laid.

But now the times are dull and slow, the brave old days are dead
When hardy bushmen started out, and forced their way ahead
By tangled scrub and forests grim towards the unknown west,
And spied the far-off promised land from off the ranges' crest.

Oh! ye, that sleep in lonely graves by far-off ridge and plain,
We drink to you in silence now as Christmas comes again,
The men who fought the wilderness through rough, unsettled
    years —
The founders of our nation's life, the brave old pioneers.

SANTA CLAUS IN THE BUSH

It chanced out back at the Christmas time,
  When the wheat was ripe and tall,
A stranger rode to the farmer's gate,
  A sturdy man, and a small.

"Run down, run down, my little son Jack,
  And bid the stranger stay;
And we'll hae a crack for the 'Auld Lang Syne',
  For tomorrow is Christmas Day."

"Nay now, nay now," said the dour gude wife,
  "But ye should let him be;
He's maybe only a drover chap
  From the land o' the Darling Pea.

"Wi' a drover's tales, and a drover's thirst
  To swiggle the whole night through;
Or he's maybe a life assurance carle,
  To talk ye black and blue."

"Gude wife, he's never a drover chap,
  For their swags are neat and thin;
And he's never a life assurance carle,
  Wi' the brick dust burnt in his skin.

"Gude wife, gude wife, be not so dour,
  For the wheat stands ripe and tall,
And we shore wi' a seven-pound fleece this year,
  Ewes and weaners and all.

"There is grass to spare, and the stock are fat,
  When they whiles are gaunt and thin,
And we owe a tithe to the travelling poor,
  So we must ask him in.

"You can set him a chair to the table side,
  And give him a bite to eat;
An omelette made of a new-laid egg,
  Or a tasty piece of meat."

"But the native cats have taken the fowls,
  They have na' left a leg;
And he'll get no omelette here at all
  Till the emu lays an egg!"

"Run down, run down, my little son Jack,
  To where the emus bide,

Ye shall find the old hen on the nest,
 While the old cock sits beside.

"But speak them fair, and speak them soft,
 Lest they kick ye a fearsome jolt,
Ye can give them a feed of thae half-inch nails,
 Or a rusty carriage bolt."

So little son Jack ran blithely down,
 With the rusty nails in hand,
Till he came where the emus fluffed and scratched,
 By their nest in the open sand.

And there he has gathered the new-laid egg,
 Would feed three men or four,
And the emus came for the half-inch nails,
 Right up to the settler's door.

"A waste of food," said the dour gude wife,
 As she took the egg, wi' a frown.
"But he gets no meat, unless ye run
 A paddymelon down."

"Gae oot, gae oot, my little son Jack,
 Wi' your twa-three doggies small;
Gin ye come not back wi' a paddymelon,
 Then come not back at all."

So little son Jack he raced and he ran,
 And he was bare o' the feet,
And soon he captured the paddymelon,
 Was gorged wi' the stolen wheat.

"Sit down, sit down, my bonny wee man,
 To the best that the house can do —
An omelette made of the emu egg
 And a paddymelon stew."

"'Tis well, 'tis well," said the bonny wee man;
 "I have eaten the wide world's meat,
But the food that is given wi' a right good will
 Is the sweetest food to eat.

"But the night draws on to the Christmas Day
 And I must rise and go,
For I have a mighty way to ride
 To the land of the Esquimaux.

"And it's there I must load my sledges up
 With the reindeers four-in-hand,

That go to the North, South, East, and West,
  To every Christian land."

"To the Esquimaux," said the dour gude wife,
  "Ye suit my husband well!
For when he gets up on his journey horse
  He's a bit of a liar himsel'."

Then out wi' a laugh went the bonny wee man
  To his old horse grazing nigh,
And away like a meteor flash they went
  Far off to the Northern sky.

* * * *

When the children woke on the Christmas morn
  They chattered might and main —
Wi' a sword and gun for little son Jack,
  And a braw new doll for Jane,
And a packet o' nails for the twa emus;
  But the dour gude wife got nane.

"In re a Gentleman, One"

*When an attorney is called before the Full Court to answer for any alleged
misconduct it is not usual to publish his name until he is found guilty; until
then the matter appears in the papers as, "In re a Gentleman, One of the
Attorneys of the Supreme Court," or, more shortly,
"In re a Gentleman, One."*

We see it each day in the paper,
   And know that there's mischief in store;
That some unprofessional caper
   Has landed a shark on the shore.
We know there'll be plenty of trouble
   Before they get through with the fun,
Because he's been coming the double
   On clients, has "Gentleman, One."

Alas! for the gallant attorney,
   Intent upon cutting a dash,
Sets out on life's perilous journey
   With rather more cunning than cash.
And fortune at first is inviting —
   He struts his brief hour in the sun —
But, lo! on the wall is the writing
   Of Nemesis, "Gentleman, One."

For soon he runs short of the dollars,
   He fears he must go to the wall;
So Peter's trust-money he collars
   To pay off his creditor, Paul;
Then robs right and left — for he goes it
   In earnest when once he's begun.
Descensus averni — he knows it;
   It's easy for "Gentleman, One."

The crash comes as sure as the seasons;
   He loses his coin in a mine,
Or booming in land, or for reasons
   Connected with women and wine.
Or maybe the cards or the horses
   A share of the damage have done.
No matter; the end of the course is
   The same: "*Re* a Gentleman, One."

He struggles a while to keep going,
   To stave off detection and shame;
But creditors clamorous growing
   Ere long put an end to the game.

At length the poor soldier of Satan
  His course to a finish has run —
And just think of Windeyer waiting
  To deal with "a Gentleman, One!"

And some face it boldly, and brazen
  The shame and the utter disgrace;
While others, more sensitive, hasten
  Their names and their deeds to efface.
They snap the frail thread which the Furies
  And Fates have so cruelly spun.
May the Great Final Judge and His juries
  Have mercy on "Gentleman, One!"

AT THE
MELTING OF THE SNOW

There's a sunny Southern land,
  And it's there that I would be
Where the big hills stand,
  In the South Countrie!
When the wattles bloom again,
  Then it's time for us to go
To the old Monaro country
  At the melting of the snow.

To the East or to the West,
  Or wherever you may be,
You will find no place
  Like the South Countrie.
For the skies are blue above,
  And the grass is green below,
In the old Monaro country
  At the melting of the snow.

Now the team is in the plough,
  And the thrushes start to sing,
And the pigeons on the bough
  Are rejoicing at the Spring.
So come my comrades all,
  Let us saddle up and go
To the old Monaro country
  At the melting of the snow.

A DREAM OF
THE MELBOURNE CUP

A Long Way After Gordon

Bring me a quart of colonial beer
And some doughy damper to make good cheer,
   I must make a heavy dinner;
Heavily dine and heavily sup
Of indigestible things full-up,
Next month they run the Melbourne Cup,
   And I have to dream the winner.

Stoke it in, boys! the half-cooked ham,
The rich ragout and the charming cham,
   I've got to mix my liquor;
Give me a gander's gaunt hind leg,
Hard and tough as a wooden peg,
And I'll grease it down with a hard-boiled egg,
   'Twill make me dream the quicker.

Now I am full of fearful feed,
Now I may dream a race indeed,
   In my restless troubled slumber;
While the nightmares race through my heated brain
And their devil riders spur amain,
The tip for the Cup will reward my pain,
   And I'll spot the winning number.

Thousands and thousands and thousands more,
Like sands on the white Pacific shore,
   The crowding people cluster;
For evermore it's the story old,
While races are bought and backers are sold,
Drawn by the greed of the gain of gold,
   In their thousands still they muster.

        * * * *

And the bookies' cries grow fierce and hot,
"I'll lay the Cup! The double, if not!"
   "Five monkeys, Little John, sir!"
"Here's fives bar one, I lay, I lay!"
And so they shout through the live-long day,
And stick to the game that is sure to pay,
   While fools put money on, sir!

And now in my dream I seem to go
And bet with a "book" that I seem to know —

A Hebrew moneylender;
A million to five is the price I get —
Not bad! but before I book the bet
The horse's name I clean forget,
  His number and even gender.

Now for the start, and here they come,
And the hoof-strokes roar like a mighty drum
  Beat by a hand unsteady;
They come like a rushing, roaring flood,
Hurrah for the speed of the Chester blood!
For Acme is making the pace so good
  There are some of 'em done already.

But round the back she begins to tire,
And a mighty shout goes up: "Crossfire!"
  The magpie jacket's leading;
And Crossfire challenges fierce and bold,
And the lead she'll have and the lead she'll hold,
But at length gives way to the black and gold,
  Which away to the front is speeding.

Carry them on and keep it up —
A flying race is the Melbourne Cup,
  You must race and stay to win it;
And old Commotion, Victoria's pride,
Now takes the lead with his raking stride,
And a mighty roar goes far and wide —
  "There's only Commotion in it!"

But one draws out from the beaten ruck,
And up on the rails by a piece of luck
  He comes in a style that's clever;
"It's Trident! Trident! Hurrah for Hales!
Go at 'em now while their courage fails";
"Trident! Trident! for New South Wales!"
  "The blue and white for ever!"

Under the whip! With the ears flat back,
Under the whip! Though the sinews crack,
  No sign of the base white feather;
Stick to it now for your breeding's sake,
Stick to it now though your hearts should break,
While the yells and roars make the grandstand shake,
  They come down the straight together.

Trident slowly forges ahead,
The fierce whips cut and the spurs are red,
  The pace is undiminished;

Now for the Panics that never fail!
But many a backer's face grows pale
As old Commotion swings his tail
   And swerves — and the Cup is finished.

* * * *

And now in my dream it all comes back:
I bet my coin on the Sydney crack,
   A million I've won, no question!
Give me my money, you hook-nosed hog!
Give me my money, bookmaking dog!
But he disappears in a kind of fog,
   And I wake with "the indigestion".

THE GUNDAROO BULLOCK

Oh, there's some that breeds the Devon that's as solid as a stone,
And there's some that breeds the brindle which they call the
  "Goulburn Roan";
But amongst the breeds of cattle there are very, very few
Like the hairy-whiskered bullock that they bred at Gundaroo.

Far away by Grabben Gullen, where the Murrumbidgee flows,
There's a block of broken countryside where no one ever goes;
For the banks have gripped the squatters, and the free selectors too,
And their stock are always stolen by the men of Gundaroo.

There came a low informer to the Grabben Gullen side,
And he said to Smith the squatter, "You must saddle up and ride,
For your bullock's in the harness-cask of Morgan Donahoo —
He's the greatest cattle-stealer that abides in Gundaroo."

"Oh, ho!" said Smith, the owner of the Grabben Gullen run,
"I'll go and get the troopers by the sinking of the sun,
And down into his homestead tonight we'll take a ride,
With warrants to identify the carcase and the hide."

That night rode down the troopers, the squatter at their head,
They rode into the homestead, and pulled Morgan out of bed.
"Now, show to us the carcase of the bullock that you slew —
The great marsupial bullock that you killed in Gundaroo."

They peered into the harness-cask, and found it wasn't full,
But down among the brine they saw some flesh and bits of wool.
"What's this?" exclaimed the trooper — "an infant, I declare."
Said Morgan, "'Tis the carcase of an old man native bear.
I heard that ye were coming, so an old man bear I slew,
Just to give you kindly welcome to my home in Gundaroo.

"The times is something awful, as you can plainly see,
The banks have broke the squatters, and they've broke the likes
  of me;
We can't afford a bullock — such expense would never do —
So an old man bear for breakfast is a treat in Gundaroo."

And along by Grabben Gullen where the rushing river flows,
In the block of broken country where there's no one ever goes,
On the Upper Murrumbidgee they're a hospitable crew,
But you mustn't ask for "bullock" when you go to Gundaroo.

LAY OF THE MOTOR CAR

We're away! and the wind whistles shrewd
  In our whiskers and teeth;
And the granite-like grey of the road
  Seems to slide underneath.
As an eagle might sweep through the sky,
  So we sweep through the land;
And the pallid pedestrians fly
  When they hear us at hand.

We outpace, we outlast, we outstrip!
  Not the fast-fleeing hare,
Nor the racehorses under the whip,
  Nor the birds of the air
Can compete with our swiftness sublime,
  Our ease and our grace.
We annihilate chickens and time
  And policemen and space.

Do you mind that fat grocer who crossed?
  How he dropped down to pray
In the road when he saw he was lost;
  How he melted away
Underneath, and there rang through the fog
  His earsplitting squeal
As he went — Is that he or a dog,
  That stuff on the wheel?

THE CORNER MAN

I dreamed a dream at the midnight deep,
  When fancies come and go
To vex a man in his soothing sleep
  With thoughts of awful woe —
I dreamed that I was the corner man
  Of a nigger minstrel show.

I cracked my jokes, and the building rang
  With laughter loud and long;
I hushed the house as I softly sang
  An old plantation song —
A tale of the wicked slavery days
  Of cruelty and wrong.

A small boy sat on the foremost seat —
  A mirthful youngster he,
He beat the time with his restless feet
  To each new melody,
And he picked me out as the brightest star
  Of the black fraternity.

"Oh, father," he said, "what *would* we do
  If the corner man should die?
I never saw such a man — did you?
  He makes the people cry,
And then, when he likes, he makes them laugh."
  The old man made reply:

"We each of us fill a very small space
  On the great creation's plan,
If a man don't keep his lead in the race
  There's plenty more that can;
The world can very soon fill the place
  Of even a corner man."

                    * * * *

I woke with a jump, rejoiced to find
  Myself at home in bed,
And I framed a moral in my mind
  From the words the old man said.
The world will jog along just the same
  When its corner men are dead.

When Dacey
Rode the Mule

'Twas in a small, up-country town,
  When we were boys at school,
There came a circus with a clown
  And with a bucking mule.
The clown announced a scheme they had —
  The mule was such a king —
They'd give a crown to any lad
  Who'd ride him round the ring.
And, gentle reader, do not scoff
  Nor think the man a fool,
To buck a porous plaster off
  Was pastime to that mule.

The boys got on — he bucked like sin —
  He threw them in the dirt,
And then the clown would raise a grin
  By asking, "Were they hurt?"
But Johnny Dacey came one night,
  The crack of all the school,
Said he, "I'll win the crown all right,
  Bring in your bucking mule."
The elephant went off his trunk,
  The monkey played the fool
And all the band got blazing drunk
  When Dacey rode the mule.

But soon there rose an awful shout
  Of laughter, when the clown,
From somewhere in his pants drew out
  A little paper crown.
He placed the crown on Dacey's head,
  While Dacey looked a fool,
"Now, there's your crown, my lad," he said,
  "For riding of the mule!"
The band struck up with "Killaloe",
  And "Rule Britannia, Rule",
And "Young Man from the Country", too,
  When Dacey rode the mule.

Then Dacey, in a furious rage,
  For vengeance on the show
Ascended to the monkeys' cage
  And let the monkeys go;
The blue-tailed ape and chimpanzee

He turned abroad to roam;
Good faith! It was a sight to see
  The people step for home.
For big baboons with canine snout
  Are spiteful, as a rule,
The people didn't sit it out
  When Dacey rode the mule.

And from the beasts that did escape
  The bushmen all declare
Were born some creatures partly ape
  And partly native bear.
They're rather few and far between;
  The race is nearly spent;
But some of them may still be seen
  In Sydney Parliament.
And when those legislators fight,
  And drink, and act the fool —
It all commenced that wretched night
  When Dacey rode the mule.

THE MYLORA ELOPEMENT

By the winding Wollondilly where the weeping willows weep,
And the shepherd with his billy half awake and half asleep
Folds his fleecy flocks that linger homewards in the setting sun,
Lived my hero, Jim the Ringer, "cocky" on Mylora Run.

Jimmy loved the super's daughter, Miss Amelia Jane McGrath,
Long and earnestly he sought her, but he feared her stern papa;
And Amelia loved him truly — but the course of love, if true,
Never yet ran smooth or duly, as it ought, I think, to do.

Watching with his slow affection once Jim saw McGrath the boss
Riding out by Jim's selection, looking for a station 'oss
That was running in the ranges with a mob of outlaws wild,
Old McGrath "Good day" exchanges — off goes Jim to see his
    child;

Says, "The old man's after Stager, which he'll find is no light job,
And tomorrow I will wager he will try and yard the mob.
Will you come with me tomorrow, I will let the parson know,
And for ever joy, or sorrow, he will join us here below!

"I will bring my nags so speedy, Crazy Jane and Tambourine,
One more kiss — don't think I'm greedy — goodbye, lass, before
    I'm seen —
Just one more — God bless you, dearie! Don't forget to meet me
    here,
Life without you is but weary! now, once more goodbye, my dear."

            The daylight shines on figures twain
            That ride across Mylora plain,
            Laughing and talking — Jim and Jane.
            "Steadily, darling. There's lots of time,
            Didn't we slip the old man prime!
            I knew he'd tackle that Bowneck mob,
            I reckon he'll find it too big a job.
            They've beaten us all. I had a try,
            But the warrigal devils seem to fly.
            That Sambo's a real good bit of stuff
            No doubt, but not quite good enough.
            He'll have to gallop the livelong day,
            To cut and come, to race and stay.

            I hope he yards 'em; 'twill do him good,
            To see us going I don't think would."
            A turn in the road, and fair and square,
            They meet the old man standing there.
            "What's up?" "Why, running away, of course,"

Says Jim, emboldened. The old man turned,
His eye with wild excitement burned.
"I've raced all day through the scorching heat
After old Bowneck: now I'm beat.
But over that range I think you'll find
The Bowneck mob all run stone-blind.
Will you go and leave the mob behind?
Which will you do? Take the girl away,
Or ride like a white man should today,
And yard old Bowneck? Go or stay?"
Says Jim, "I can't throw this away,
We can bolt some other day, of course,
Amelia Jane, get off that horse.
Up you get, old man. Whoop, halloo,
Here goes to put old Bowneck through!"
Two distant specks on the mountainside,
Two stockwhips echoing far and wide.
Amelia Jane sat down and cried.

"Sakes, Amelia, what's up now,
Leading old Sambo, too, I vow,
And him dead beat. Where have you been?
Bolted with Jim! What *do* you mean?
Met the old man with Sambo licked
From running old Bowneck. Well, I'm kicked.
Run 'em till Sambo nearly dropped?
What did Jim do when you were stopped?
Did you bolt from father across the plain?
Jim made you get off Crazy Jane!
And father got on, and away again.
The two of 'em went in the ranges grim.
Good boy, Jimmy! Well done, Jim!
They're sure to get them now, of course,
That Tambourine is a spanking horse.
And Crazy Jane is good as gold.
And Jim, they say, rides pretty bold;
Not like your father, but very fair.
Jim will have to follow the mare."
"It never was yet in father's hide
To best my Jim on the mountainside.
Jim can rally, and Jim can ride."
But here again Amelia cried.

The sound of a whip comes faint and far,
A rattle of hoofs, and here they are,
In all their tameless pride.
The fleet wild horses snort with fear,

And wheel and break as the yard draws near.
Now, Jim the Ringer, ride!
Wheel 'em! Wheel 'em! Wo back there, wo!
And the foam-flakes fly like the driven snow,
As under the whip the horses go
Adown the mountain side.

And Jim, hands down, and teeth firm set,
On a horse that never has failed him yet,
Is after them down the range.
Well ridden, well ridden, they wheel, wo back,
And long and loud the stockwhips crack.
Their flying course they change.
"Steadily does it — let Sambo go!
Open those sliprails down below.
Smart! or you'll be too late.
They'll follow old Sambo up — look out!
Wheel that black horse — give Sam a clout.
They're in! Make fast the gate."

The mob is safely in the yard;
The old man mounts delighted guard.
No eyes had he but for his prize.
Jim catches poor Amelia's eyes.
"Will you come with me after all I've done?
Here's Crazy Jane is fit to run
For a prince's life — now, don't say no;
Slip on while the old man's down below
At the inner yard, and away we'll go.
Will you come, my girl?" "I will, you bet,
We'll manage this here elopement yet."

By the winding Wollondilly stands the hut of Ringer Jim.
And his loving little Meely makes a perfect god of him.
He has stalwart sons and daughters, and, I think, before he's done,
There'll be numerous "six-fortys" taken on Mylora Run.

THE PANNIKIN POET

There's nothing here sublime,
But just a roving rhyme,
Run off to pass the time,
  With nought titanic in
The theme that it supports
And, though it treats of quarts,
It's bare of golden thoughts —
  It's just a pannikin.

I think it's rather hard
That each Australian bard —
Each wan, poetic card —
  With thoughts galvanic in
His fiery soul alight,
In wild aerial flight,
Will sit him down and write
  About a pannikin.

He makes some new chum fare
From out his English lair
To hunt the native bear,
  That curious mannikin;
And then when times get bad
That wand'ring English lad
Writes out a message sad
  Upon his pannikin:

"Oh, mother, think of me
Beneath the wattle tree."
(For you may bet that he
  Will drag the wattle in.)
"Oh, mother, here I think
That I shall have to sink
There ain't a single drink
  The water bottle in."

The dingo homeward hies,
The sooty crows uprise
And caw their fierce surprise
  A tone Satanic in;
And bearded bushmen tread
Around the sleeper's head —
"See here — the bloke is dead."
  "Now, where's his pannikin?"

They read his words and weep,
And lay him down to sleep
Where wattle branches sweep
   A style mechanic in;
And, reader, that's the way
The poets of today
Spin out their little lay
   About a pannikin.

The Protest

I say 'e *isn't* Remorse!
  'Ow do I know?
Saw 'im on Riccarton course
  Two year ago!
Think I'd forget any 'orse?
  Course 'e's The Crow!

Bumper Maginnis and I,
  After a "go",
Walkin' our 'orses to dry,
  I says, "Hello!
What's that old black goin' by?"
  Bumper says, "Oh!
That's an old cuddy of Flanagan's
  — Runs as The Crow!"

Now they make out 'e's Remorse.
  Well, but I *know*.
Soon as I came on the course
  I says, "'Ello!
'Ere's the old Crow."
Once a man's seen any 'orse,
  'Course 'e must know.
Sure as there's wood in this table,
  I say 'e's The Crow.

(Cross-examined by the Committee)

'Ow do I know the moke
  After one sight?
S'posin' you met a bloke
  Down town at night,
Wouldn't you know 'im again when you met 'im?
  That's *'im* all right!

What was the brand on 'is 'ide?
  I couldn't say.
Brands can be transmogrified.
  That ain't the way —
It's the *look* of a 'orse and the way that 'e moves
  That I'd know any day.

What was the boy on 'is back?
  Why, 'e went past
All of a minute, and off down the track.
  — "The 'orse went as fast?"

True, so 'e did! But, my eyes, what a treat!
 'Ow can I notice the 'ands and the seat
Of each bumble-faced kid of a boy that I meet?
 Lor'! What a question to ast!

(Protest dismissed)

An Evening
in Dandaloo

It was while we held our races —
Hurdles, sprints and steeplechases —
    Up in Dandaloo,
That a crowd of Sydney stealers,
Jockeys, pugilists and spielers
Brought some horses, real heelers,
    Came and put us through.

Beat our nags and won our money,
Made the game by no means funny,
    Made us rather blue;
When the racing was concluded,
Of our hard-earned coin denuded
Dandaloonies sat and brooded
    There in Dandaloo.

                * * * *

Night came down on Johnson's shanty
Where the grog was no means scanty,
    And a tumult grew
Till some wild, excited person
Galloped down the township cursing,
"Sydney push have mobbed Macpherson,
    Roll up, Dandaloo!"

Great St Denis! what commotion!
Like the rush of stormy ocean
    Fiery horsemen flew.
Dust and smoke and din and rattle,
Down the street they spurred their cattle
To the war-cry of the battle,
    "Wade in, Dandaloo!"

So the boys might have their fight out,
Johnson blew the bar-room light out,
    Then, in haste, withdrew.
And in darkness and in doubting
Raged the conflict and the shouting,
"Give the Sydney push a clouting,
    Go it, Dandaloo!"

Jack Macpherson seized a bucket,
Every head he saw, he struck it —
    Struck in earnest, too;

And a man from Lower Wattle,
Whom a shearer tried to throttle,
Hit out freely with a bottle,
　　There in Dandaloo.

Skin and hair were flying thickly,
When a light was fetched, and quickly
　　Brought a fact to view —
On the scene of the diversion
Every single, solid person
Came along to help Macpherson —
　　All were Dandaloo!

When the list of slain was tabled,
Some were drunk and some disabled,
　　Still we found it true.
In the darkness and the smother
We'd been belting one another;
Jack Macpherson bashed his brother
　　There in Dandaloo.

So we drank, and all departed —
How the "mobbing" yarn was started
　　No one ever knew —
And the stockmen tell the story
Of that conflict fierce and gory,
How we fought for love and glory
　　Up in Dandaloo.

It's a proverb now, or near it —
At the races you can hear it,
　　At the dog fights, too;
Every shrieking, dancing drover,
As the canines topple over,
Yells applause to Grip or Rover,
　　"Give him 'Dandaloo'!"

And the teamster slowly toiling
Through the deep black country soiling
　　Wheels and axles, too,
Lays the whip on Spot and Banker,
Rouses Tarboy with a flanker —
"Redman! Ginger! Heave there! Yank her!
　　Wade in, Dandaloo!"

A Ballad of Ducks

The railway rattled and roared and swung
With jolting carriage and bumping trucks.
The sun, like a billiard red ball, hung
In the Western sky: and the tireless tongue
Of the wild-eyed man in the corner told
This terrible tale of the days of old,
And the party that ought to have kept the ducks.

"Well, it ain't all joy bein' on the land
With an overdraft that'd knock you flat;
And the rabbits have pretty well took command;
But the hardest thing for a man to stand
Is the feller who says, 'Well, I told you so!
You should ha' done this way, don't you know!'
I could lay a bait for a man like that.

"The grasshoppers struck us in ninety-one
And what they leave — well, it ain't *de luxe*.
But a growlin' fault-findin' son of a gun
Who'd lent some money to stock our run —
I said they'd eaten what grass we had —
Says he, 'Your management's very bad,
You had a right to have kept some ducks!'

"To have kept some ducks! And the place was white!
Wherever you went you had to tread
On grasshoppers guzzlin' day and night;
And when with a swoosh they rose in flight,
If you didn't look out for yourself they'd fly
Like bullets into your open eye
And knock it out of the back of your head.

"There isn't a turkey or goose or swan,
Or a duck that quacks, or a hen that clucks,
Can make a difference on a run
When a grasshopper plague has once begun;
'If you'd finance us,' I says, 'I'd buy
Ten thousand emus and have a try;
The job,' I says, 'is too big for ducks!

"'You must fetch a duck when you come to stay;
A great big duck — a Muscovy toff —
Ready and fit,' I says, 'for the fray;
And if the grasshoppers come our way
You turn your duck into the lucerne patch,

And I'd be ready to make a match
That the grasshoppers eats his feathers off!'

"He came to visit us by and by,
And it just so happened one day in spring
A kind of a cloud came over the sky —
A wall of grasshoppers nine miles high,
And nine miles thick, and nine hundred wide,
Flyin' in regiments, side by side,
And eatin' up every living thing.

"All day long, like a shower of rain,
You'd hear 'em smackin' against the wall,
Tap, tap, tap, on the window pane,
And they'd rise and jump at the house again
Till their crippled carcases piled outside.
But what did it matter if thousands died —
A million wouldn't be missed at all.

"We were drinkin' grasshoppers — so to speak —
Till we skimmed their carcases off the spring;
And they fell so thick in the station creek
They choked the waterholes all the week.
There was scarcely room for a trout to rise,
And they'd only take artificial flies —
They got so sick of the real thing.

"An Arctic snowstorm was beat to rags
When the hoppers rose for their morning flight
With a flapping noise like a million flags:
And the kitchen chimney was stuffed with bags
For they'd fall right into the fire, and fry
Till the cook sat down and began to cry —
And never a duck or a fowl in sight!

"We strolled across to the railroad track —
Under a cover, beneath some trucks,
I sees a feather and hears a quack;
I stoops and I pulls the tarpaulin back —
Every duck in the place was there,
No good to them was the open air.
'Mister', I says, 'There's your blanky ducks!'"

TOMMY CORRIGAN

Died August 13 1894

You talk of riders on the flat, of nerve and dash and pace!
Not one in fifty has the nerve to ride a steeplechase.
It's gay enough while horses pull and take their fences strong,
To rush a flyer to the front and bring the field along;
But what about the last half mile, with horses blown and beat —
When every jump means all you know to keep him on his feet!
When any slip means sudden death — with wife and child to keep,
It needs some pluck to draw the whip and flog him at the leap.
But Corrigan would ride them out by danger undismayed,
He never flinched from fence or wall, he never was afraid.

With easy seat and nerve of steel, light hand and cheery face,
He held the rushing horses back and made the sluggards race,
He gave the shirkers extra heart, he steadied down the rash,
He rode great clumsy, boring brutes and chanced the fatal smash,
He got the rushing Wymlet home that never jumped at all,
But clambered over every fence and clouted every wall;
But ah! you should have heard the cheers that shook the members'
    stand
Whenever Tommy Corrigan weighed out to ride Lone Hand!

They were, indeed, a splendid pair — the great upstanding horse,
The gamest jockey on his back that ever faced a course,
Though weight was big and pace was hot and jumps were stiff and
    tall,
"You follow Tommy Corrigan" was passed to one and all.
And every man in Ballarat raised all he could command
To put on Tommy Corrigan when riding old Lone Hand.

But now we'll keep his memory green while horsemen come and go,
We may not see his like again where silks and satins glow;
We'll drink to him in silence, boys, he's followed down the track
Where many a good man went before, but never one came back.
And let us hope in that far land, where shades of brave men reign,
That gallant Tommy Corrigan will ride Lone Hand again.

THE REVEILLE

Trumpets of the Lancer Corps
Sound a loud reveille;
Sound it over Sydney shore,
Send the message far and wide
Down the Richmond River side.
Boot and saddle, mount and ride,
Sound a loud reveille.

Whither go ye, Lancers gay,
With your bold reveille?
O'er the ocean far away
From your sunny southern home,
Over leagues of trackless foam
In a foreign land to roam,
With your bold reveille.

When we hear our brethren call,
Sound a clear reveille.
Then we answer, one and all,
Answer that the world may see,
Of the English stock are we,
At their side we still will be,
Sound a bold reveille.

English troops are buried deep.
Sound a soft reveille.
In this foreign land asleep,
Underneath Majuba Hill,
Lying sleeping very still,
Nevermore those squadrons will
Answer to reveille.

Onward without fear or doubt,
Sound a bold reveille.
'Till that shame is blotted out.
While our Empire's bounds are wide,
Britons all stand side by side,
Boot and saddle, mount and ride.
Hear the bold reveille.

THE MAORI'S WOOL

Now, this is just a simple tale to tell the reader how
They civilised the Maori tribe at Rooti-iti-au.

* * * *

The Maoris are a mighty race — the finest ever known;
Before the missionaries came they worshipped wood and stone;
They went to war and fought like fiends, and when the war was
    done
They pacified their conquered foes by eating every one.
But nowadays about the *pahs* in idleness they lurk,
Prepared to smoke or drink or talk — or anything but work.
Around the hills their flocks of sheep are fed on tribal lands —
A communistic ownership that no one understands.
The richest tribe in all the North in sheep and horse and cow
Were those who led their simple lives at Rooti-iti-au.

'Twas down to town at Wellington a noble Maori came,
A Rangatira of the best, Rerenga was his name —
(The word "Rerenga" means a "snag" — but until he was gone
This didn't strike the folk he met — it struck them later on,)
He stalked into the Bank they call the "Great Financial Hell",
And told the Chief Financial Fiend the tribe had wool to sell.
The Bold Bank Manager looked grave — the price of wool was
    high.
He said, "We'll lend you what you need — we're not disposed to
    buy.
You ship the wool to England, Chief! You'll find it's good advice,
And meanwhile you can draw from us the local market price."
The Chief he thanked him courteously and said he wished to state
In all the Rooti-iti tribe his *mana* would be great,
But still their tribe were simple folk who might not understand
This strange financial jugglery which gave them cash in hand
Before the wool was sold at all; and even after sale
Perhaps they mightn't get the price — the notion turned him pale!
So off he started home again, with trouble on his brow,
To lay the case before the tribe at Rooti-iti-au.

They held a great *korero* in the Rooti-iti clan,
With speeches lasting half a day from every leading man.
They called themselves poetic names — "lost children in a wood";
They said the Great Bank Manager was *"Kapai"* — extra good!
And so they sent Rerenga down, full-powered and well-equipped,
To draw as much as he could get, and let the wool be shipped,
And wedged into a "Cargo Tank", full up from stern to bow —
A mighty clip of wool went Home from Rooti-iti-au.

It was the Bold Bank Manager who drew a heavy cheque;
Rerenga cashed it thoughtfully, then clasped him round the neck.
A hug from him was not at all a thing you'd call a lark,
You see, he lived on mutton-birds and dried remains of shark.
But still it showed his gratitude, and, as he pouched the pelf,
"I'll *'haka'* for you, sir," he said. "In honour of yourself!"
The *haka* is a striking dance — the sort they don't allow
In any place more civilised than Rooti-iti-au.

He *"haka'd"* most effectively — then, with an airy grace
Rubbed noses with the Manager, and vanished into space.
But when the Wool-return came back, ah me, what sighs and
    groans!
For every bale of Maori wool was loaded up with stones!
Yes — thumping great New Zealand rocks among the wool they
    found;
On every rock the Bank had lent just seven pence a pound.
And now the Bold Bank Manager, with trouble on his brow,
Is searching vainly for the chief from Rooti-iti-au.

Sunrise on the Coast

Grey dawn on the sandhills — the night wind has drifted
   All night from the rollers a scent of the sea;
With the dawn the grey fog his battalions has lifted,
   At the scent of the morning they scatter and flee.

Like mariners calling the roll of their number
   The sea fowl put out to the infinite deep.
And far overhead — sinking softly to slumber —
   Worn out by their watching, the stars fall asleep.

To eastward where resteth the dome of the skies on
   The sea line stirs softly the curtain of night;
And far from behind the enshrouded horizon
   Comes the voice of a God saying, "Let there be light."

And lo, there is light! Evanescent and tender,
   It glows ruby-red where 'twas now ashen grey;
And purple and scarlet and gold in its splendour —
   Behold, 'tis that marvel, the birth of a day!

Song of the Pen

Not for the love of women toil we, we of the craft,
  Not for the people's praise.
Only because our Goddess made us her own, and laughed,
  Claiming us all our days.

Claiming our best endeavour, body and heart and brain,
  Given with no reserve.
Niggard is she towards us, granting us little gain,
  Still we are proud to serve.

Not unto us is given choice of the tasks we try —
  Gathering grain or chaff.
One of her favoured servants toils at an epic high,
  One — that a child may laugh.

Yet if we serve her truly in our appointed place,
  Freely she doth accord
Unto her faithful servants always this saving grace;
  Work is its own reward!

IV

A LATE
COLLECTION

THE BUSHFIRE

An Allegory

'Twas on the famous Empire run,
  Whose sun does never set,
Whose grass and water, so they say,
  Have never failed them yet —
They carry many million sheep,
  Through seasons dry and wet.

They call the homestead Albion House,
  And then, along with that,
There's Welshman's Gully, Scotchman's Hill,
  And Paddymelon Flat:
And all these places are renowned
  For making jumbucks fat.

And the out-paddocks — holy frost!
  There wouldn't be no sense
For me to try and tell you half —
  They really are immense;
A man might ride for days and weeks
  And never strike a fence.

But still for years they never had
  Been known a sheep to lose;
Old Billy Gladstone managed it,
  And you can bet your shoes
He'd scores of supers under him,
  And droves of jackaroos.

Old Billy had an eagle eye,
  And kept his wits about —
If any chaps got trespassing
  He quickly cleared 'em out;
And coves that used to "work a cross",
  They hated him, no doubt.

But still he managed it in style,
  Until the times got dry,
And Billy gave the supers word
  To see and mind their eye —
"If any paddocks gets a-fire
  I'll know the reason why."

Now on this point old Bill was sure,
  Because, for many a year,
Whenever times got dry at all,

As sure as you are here,
The Paddymelon Flat got burnt,
  Which Bill thought rather queer.

He sent his smartest supers there
  To try and keep things right.
No use! The grass was always dry —
  They'd go to sleep at night,
And when they woke they'd go and find
  The whole concern alight.

One morning it was very hot —
  The sun rose in a haze;
Old Bill was cutting down some trees
  (One of his little ways);
A black boy came hot-foot to say
  The Flat was in a blaze.

Old Bill he swears a fearful oath
  And lets the tommy fall —
Says he: "I'll take this business up,
  And fix it once for all;
If this goes on, the cursed run
  Will send us to the wall."

So he withdrew his trespass suits —
  He'd one with Dutchy's boss —
In prosecutions criminal
  He entered *nolle pros.*,
But these were neither here nor there —
  They always meant a loss.

And off to Paddymelon Flat
  He started double-quick
Drayloads of men with lots of grog
  Lest heat should make them sick,
And all the strangers came around
  To see him do the trick.

And there the fire was flaming bright,
  For miles and miles it spread,
And many a sheep and horse and cow
  Were numbered with the dead —
The super came to meet Old Bill,
  And this is what he said:

"No use, to try to beat it out,
  'Twill dry you up like toast,
I've done as much as man can do,

Although I never boast;
I think you'd better chuck it up,
    And let the jumbucks roast."

Then Bill said just two words: "You're sacked,"
    And pitches off his coat,
And wrenches down a blue-gum bough
    And clears his manly throat,
And into it like threshing wheat
    Right sturdily he smote

And beat the blazing grass until
    His shirt was dripping wet;
And all the people watched him there
    To see what luck he'd get,
"Gosh! don't he make the cinders fly,"
    And, "Golly, don't he sweat!"

But though they worked like Trojans all,
    The fire still went ahead
So far as you could see around;
    The very skies were red,
Sometimes the flames would start afresh,
    Just where they thought it dead.

His men, too, quarrelled 'mongst themselves,
    And some coves gave it best
And some said, "Light a fire in front,
    And burn from east to west" —
But Bill, he still kept sloggin' in,
    And never took no rest.

Then, through the crowd a cornstalk kid
    Come ridin' to the spot;
Says he to Bill, "Now take a spell,
    You're lookin' very 'ot,
And if you'll only listen, why,
    I'll tell you what is what.

"These coves as set your grass on fire,
    There ain't no mortal doubt,
I've seen 'em ridin' here and there,
    And pokin' round about;
It ain't no use your workin' here,
    Until you finds them out.

"See yonder, where you beat the fire —
    It's blazin' up again,
And fires are starting right and left

On Tipperary plain,
Beating them out is useless quite,
    Unless Heaven sends the rain."

Then Bill, he turns upon the boy,
    "Oh, hold your tongue, you pup!"
But a cinder blew across the creek
    While Bill stopped for a sup,
And fired the Albion paddocks, too —
    It was a bitter cup;
Old Bill's great heart was broke at last,
    He had to chuck it up.

Moral

The run is England's Empire great,
    The fire is the distress
That burns the stock they represent —
    Prosperity you'll guess.
And the blue-gum bough is the Home Rule Bill
    That's making such a mess.

And Ireland green, of course I mean
    By Paddymelon Flat;
All men can see the fire, of course,
    Spreads on at such a bat,
But who are setting it alight,
    I cannot tell you that.

But this I think all men will see,
    And hold it very true —
"Don't quarrel with effects until
    The *cause* is brought to view."
What is the cause? That cornstalk boy —
    He seemed to think he knew.

THE MAORI PIG MARKET

In distant New Zealand, whose tresses of gold
  The billows are ceaselessly combing,
Away in a village all tranquil and old
I came on a market where porkers were sold —
  A market for pigs in the gloaming.

And Maoris in plenty in picturesque rig
  The lands of their forefathers roaming,
Were weighing their swine, whether little or big,
For purchasers paid by the weight of the pig —
  The weight of the pig in the gloaming.

And one mighty chieftain, I grieve to relate,
  The while that his porker was foaming
And squealing like fifty — that Maori sedate,
He leant on the pig just to add to its weight —
  He leant on the pig in the gloaming.

Alas! For the buyer, an Irishman stout —
  O'Grady, I think, his cognomen —
Perceived all his doings, and, giving a shout,
With the butt of his whip laid him carefully out
  By the side of his pig in the gloaming.

A terrible scrimmage did straightway begin,
  And I thought it was time to be homing,
For Maoris and Irish were fighting like sin
'Midst war-cries of "Pakeha!" "Batherashin!"
While the pigs did their best to lend tone to the din
  As I fled from the spot in the gloaming.

BEHIND THE SCENES

The actor struts his little hour,
  Between the limelight and the band;
The public feel the actor's power,
  Yet nothing do they understand
Of all the touches here and there
  That make or mar the actor's part,
They never see, beneath the glare,
  The artist striving after art.

To them it seems a labour slight
  Where nought of study intervenes;
You see it in another light
  When once you've been behind the scenes.

For though the actor at his best
  Is, like a poet, born not made,
He still must study with a zest
  And practise hard to learn his trade.
So, whether on the actor's form
  The stately robes of Hamlet sit,
Or as Macbeth he rave and storm,
  Or plays burlesque to please the pit,

'Tis each and all a work of art,
  That constant care and practice means —
The actor who creates a part
  Has done his work behind the scenes.

Reconstruction

From a Farmer's Point of View

So, the bank has bust its boiler! And in six or seven year
  It will pay me all my money back — of course!
But the horse will perish waiting while the grass is germinating,
  And I reckon I'll be something like the horse.

There's the ploughing to be finished and the ploughmen want their
    pay,
  And I'd like to wire the fence and sink a tank;
But I own I'm fairly beat how I'm going to make ends meet
  With my money in a reconstructed bank.

"It's a safe and sure investment!" But it's one I can't afford,
  For I've got to meet my bills and pay the rent,
And the cash I had provided (so these meetings hàve decided)
  Shall be collared by the bank at three per cent.

I can draw out half my money, so they tell me, from the Crown;
  But — it's just enough to drive a fellow daft —
My landlord's quite distressed, by this very bank he's pressed,
  And he'll sell me up, to pay his overdraft.

There's my nearest neighbour, Johnson, owed this self-same bank a
    debt,
  Every feather off his poor old back they pluck't,
For they set to work to shove him, and they sold his house above
    him,
  Lord! They never gave *him* time to reconstruct.

And their profits from the business have been twenty-five per cent,
  Which, I reckon, is a pretty tidy whack,
And I think it's only proper, now the thing has come a cropper,
  That they ought to pay a little of it back.

I have read about "reserve funds", "banking freeholds", and the
    like,
  Till I thought the bank had thousands of as*sets*,
And it strikes me very funny that they take a fellow's money
  When they haven't got enough to pay their debts.

And they say they've lent my money, and they can't get paid it
    back,
  I know their rates per cent were tens and twelves;
And if now they've made a blunder after scooping all this plunder,
  Why, they ought to fork the money out themselves.

So all you bank shareholders, if you won't pay what you owe,
  You will find that on your bank will fall a blight;
And the reason is because it's simply certain that deposits
  Will be stopped, the bank will bust, and serve you right!

The Ghost
of the Murderer's Hut

My horse had been lamed in the foot
  In the rocks at the back of the run,
So I camped at the Murderer's Hut,
  At the place where the murder was done.

The walls were all spattered with gore,
  A terrible symbol of guilt;
And the bloodstains were fresh on the floor
  Where the blood of the victim was spilt.

The wind hurried past with a shout,
  The thunderstorm doubled its din
As I shrank from the danger without,
  And recoiled from the horror within.

When lo! at the window a shape,
  A creature of infinite dread;
A thing with the face of an ape,
  And with eyes like the eyes of the dead.

With the horns of a fiend, and a skin
  That was hairy as satyr or elf,
And a long, pointed beard on its chin —
  My God! 'twas the Devil himself.

In anguish I sank on the floor,
  With terror my features were stiff,
Till *the thing* gave a kind of a roar,
  Ending up with a resonant "Biff!"

Then a cheer burst aloud from my throat,
  For the thing that my spirit did vex
Was naught but an elderly goat —
  Just a goat of the masculine sex.

When his master was killed he had fled,
  And now, by the dingoes bereft,
The nannies were all of them dead,
  And only the billy was left.

So we had him brought in on a stage
  To the house where, in style, he can strut,
And he lives to a fragrant old age
  As the Ghost of the Murderer's Hut.

THE MATRIMONIAL STAKES

I wooed her with a steeplechase, I won her with a fall,
  I made her heartstrings quiver on the flat
When the pony missed his take-off, and we crashed into the wall;
  Well, she simply *had* to have me after that!

It awoke a thrill of int'rest when they pulled me out for dead
  From beneath the shattered ruins of a horse;
And although she *looked* indiff'rent when I landed — on my
    head —
  In the water, it appealed to her, of course!

When I won the Flappers' Flatrace it was "all Sir Garneo",
  For she praised the way I made my final run.
And she thought the riding won it — for how *could* the poor girl
    know
  That a monkey could have ridden it and won!

Then they "weighed me in" a winner — it's not often that occurs!
  So I didn't let my golden chances slip,
For I showed her all the blood-marks where I jabbed him with the
    spurs,
  And the whip-strokes where I hit him with the whip.

Then I asked her if she loved me, and she seemed inclined to shirk
  For a moment, so I took her by the head
(So to speak) and rushed her at it; and she seemed to like the work
  When she kissed me, though she blushed a rosy red.

She's a mouth as soft as velvet, and she plenty has of heart,
  I could worship every little step she takes;
And the saddling-bell is ringing, so we're going to the start,
  Certain winners for the Matrimonial Stakes!

SYDNEY CUP, 1899

An Outside Tip

Of course they all say if this Bobadil starts
   He'll settle 'em all in a flash:
For the pace he can go will be breaking their hearts,
   And he ends with the "Bobadil dash".
But there's one in the race is a fancy of mine
   Whenever the distance is far —
Crosslake! He's inbred to the Yattendon line,
   And we know what the Yattendons are.

His feet are his trouble: they're tender as gum!
   If only his feet are got straight,
If the field were all Bobadils — let 'em *all* come
   So long as they carry the weight.
For a three-year-old colt with nine-three on his back —
   Well, he needs to be rather a star!
And with seven stone ten we will trust the old black,
   For we know what the Yattendons are.

He is sired by Lochiel, which ensures that his pace
   Is enough, and a little to spare.
But the blood that will tell at the end of the race
   Is the blood of the Yattendon mare.
And this "Bobby" will find, when the whips are about,
   It's a very fast journey and far.
And there's just the least doubt — will he battle it out?
   But we *know* what the Yattendons are.

In the rest of the field there are some that can stay,
   And a few that can fly — while they last.
But the old black outsider will go all the way,
   And finish uncommonly fast.
If his feet last him out to the end of the trip —
   Bare-footed or shod with a bar —
If he once gets this Bobadil under the whip,
   Then he'll show what the Yattendons are.

The Federal Bus Conductor and the Old Lady

Now 'urry, Mrs New South Wales, and come along of us,
We're all a-goin' ridin' in the Federation 'bus.
A fam'ly party, don't you know — yes, Queensland's comin', too.
You can't afford it! Go along! We've kep' box seat for you.
The very one of all the lot that can afford it best,
You'll only have to pay your share the same as all the rest.

You say your sons is workin' men, and can't afford to ride!
Well, *all* our sons is workin' men, a-smokin' up outside.
You think you might be drove to smash by some unskilful bloke!
Well, ain't we all got necks ourselves? And we don't want 'em
    broke.
You bet your life we're not such fools but what we'll do our best
To keep from harm — for harm to one is harm to all the rest.

Now, don't go trudgin' on alone, but get aboard the trap;
That basket, labelled "Capital", you take it in your lap!
It's nearly time we made a start, so let's 'ave no more talk:
You 'urry up and get aboard, or else stop out and walk.
We've got a flag; we've got a band; our 'orses travels fast;
Ho! Right away, Bill! Let 'em go! The old 'un's come at last!

THE LOST LEICHHARDT

An English scientific society is fitting out a pioneering
party to search for traces of the lost explorer Leichhardt

Another search for Leichhardt's tomb,
   Though fifty years have fled
Since Leichhardt vanished in the gloom,
   Our one Illustrious Dead!

But daring men from Britain's shore,
   The fearless bulldog breed,
Renew the fearful task once more,
   Determined to succeed.

Rash men, that know not what they seek,
   Will find their courage tried.
For things have changed on Cooper's Creek
   Since Ludwig Leichhardt died.

Along where Leichhardt journeyed slow
   And toiled and starved in vain;
These rash excursionists must go
   Per Queensland railway train.

Out on those deserts lone and drear
   The fierce Australian black
Will say — "You show it pint o' beer,
   It show you Leichhardt track!"

And loud from every squatter's door
   Each pioneering swell
Will hear the wild pianos roar
   The strains of "Daisy Bell".

The watchers in those forests vast
   Will see, at fall of night,
Commercial travellers bounding past
   And darting out of sight.

About their path a fearful fate
   Will hover always near.
A dreadful scourge that lies in wait —
   The Longreach Horehound Beer!

And then, to crown this tale of guilt,
   They'll find some scurvy knave,
Regardless of their quest, has built
   A pub on Leichhardt's grave!

* * * *

Ah, yes! Those British pioneers
  Had best at home abide,
For things have changed in fifty years
  Since Ludwig Leichhardt died.

INVESTIGATING FLORA

'Twas in scientific circles
　　That the great Professor Brown
Had a world-wide reputation
　　As a writer of renown.
He had striven finer feelings
　　In our natures to implant
By his *Treatise on the Morals*
　　Of the Red-eyed Bulldog Ant.
He had hoisted an opponent
　　Who had trodden unawares
On his "*Reasons for Bare Patches*
　　On the Female Native Bears".
So they gave him an appointment
　　As instructor to a band
Of the most attractive females
　　To be gathered in the land.

'Twas a "Ladies' Science Circle" —
　　Just the latest social fad
For the Nicest People only,
　　And to make their rivals mad.
They were fond of "science rambles"
　　To the country from the town —
A parade of female beauty
　　In the leadership of Brown.
They would pick a place for luncheon
　　And catch beetles on their rugs;
The Professor called 'em "optera" —
　　They called 'em "nasty bugs".
Well, the thing was bound to perish
　　For no lovely woman can
Feel the slightest real interest
　　In a club without a Man —
The Professor hardly counted
　　He was crazy as a loon,
With a countenance suggestive
　　Of an elderly baboon.
But the breath of Fate blew on it
　　With a sharp and sudden blast,
And the "Ladies' Science Circle"
　　Is a memory of the past.

There were two-and-twenty members,
　　Mostly young and mostly fair,
Who had made a great excursion

To a place called Dontknowwhere,
At the crossing of Lost River,
  On the road to No Man's Land.
There they met an old selector,
  With a stockwhip in his hand,
And the sight of so much beauty
  Sent him slightly "off his nut";
So he asked them, smiling blandly,
  "Would they come down to the hut?"
"I am come," said the Professor,
  In his thin and reedy voice,
"To investigate your flora,
  Which I hear is very choice."
The selector stared dumbfounded,
  Till at last he found his tongue:
"To investigate my Flora!
  Oh, you howlin' Brigham Young!
Why, you've two-and-twenty wimmen —
  Reg'lar slap-up wimmen, too!
And you're after little Flora!
  And a crawlin' thing like you!
Oh, you Mormonite gorilla!
  Well, I've heard it from the first
That you wizened little fellers
  Is a hundred times the worst!
But a dried-up ape like you are,
  To be marchin' through the land
With a pack of lovely wimmen —
  Well, I cannot understand!"

"You mistake," said the Professor,
  In a most indignant tone —
While the ladies shrieked and jabbered
  In a fashion of their own —
"You mistake about these ladies,
  I'm a lecturer of theirs;
I am Brown, who wrote the *Treatise
  On the Female Native Bears*!
When I said we wanted flora,
  What I meant was native flowers."
"Well, you *said* you wanted *Flora*,
  And I'll swear you don't get ours!
But here's Flora's self a-comin',
  And it's time for you to skip,
Or I'll write a treatise on you,
  And I'll write it with the whip!
Now, I wants no explanations;

Just you hook it out of sight,
Or you'll charm the poor girl some'ow!"
  The Professor looked in fright:
She was six feet high and freckled,
  And her hair was turkey-red.
The Professor gave a whimper,
  And threw down his bag and fled,
And the Ladies' Science Circle,
  With a simultaneous rush,
Travelled after its Professor,
  And went screaming through the bush!

At the crossing of Lost River,
  On the road to No Man's Land,
Where the grim and ghostly gum trees
  Block the view on every hand,
There they weep and wail and wander,
  Always seeking for the track,
For the hapless old Professor
  Hasn't sense to guide 'em back;
And they clutch at one another,
  And they yell and scream in fright
As they see the gruesome creatures
  Of the grim Australian night;
And they hear the mopoke's hooting,
  And the dingo's howl so dread,
And the flying foxes' jabber
  From the gum trees overhead;
While the weird and wary wombats,
  In their subterranean caves,
Are a-digging, always digging,
  At those wretched people's graves;
And the pike-horned Queensland bullock,
  From his shelter in the scrub,
Has his eye on the proceedings
  Of the Ladies' Science Club.

Fed Up

I ain't a timid man at all, I'm just as brave as most,
I'll take my chance in open fight and die beside my post;
But riding round the 'ole day long as target for a Krupp,
A-drawing fire from Koppies — well, I'm fair fed up.

It's wonderful how few get hit, it's luck that pulls us through;
Their rifle fire's no class at all, it misses me and you;
But when they sprinkle shells around like water from a cup
From that there blooming pom-pom gun — well, I'm fed up.

We never get a chance to charge, to do a thrust and cut,
I'll have to chuck the Cavalry and join the Mounted Fut.
But after all — What's Mounted Fut? I saw them t'other day,
They occupied a koppie when the Boers had run away.
The Cavalry went riding on and seen a score of fights,
But there they kept them Mounted Fut three solid days and
    nights —
Three solid starving days and nights with scarce a bite or sup,
Well! after that on Mounted Fut I'm fair fed up.

And tramping with the Footies ain't as easy as it looks,
They scarcely ever see a Boer except in picture books.
They do a march of twenty mile that leaves 'em nearly dead,
And then they find the bloomin' Boers is twenty miles ahead.
Each Footy is as full of fight as any bulldog pup,
But walking forty miles to fight — well, I'm fed up!

So after all I think that when I leave the Cavalry
I'll either join the ambulance or else the A.S.C.;
They've always tucker in the plate and coffee in the cup,
But bully beef and biscuits — well! I'm fair fed up!

COMMANDEERING

Our hero was a Tommy with a conscience free from care,
And such an open countenance that when he breathed the air
He mopped up all the atmosphere — so little went to spare
You could hardly say he breathed, he "commandeered" it.

For nowadays you'll notice when a man is "on the make",
And other people's property is anxious for to take,
We never use such words as "steal", or "collar", "pinch", or
    "shake".
No, the fashion is to say we "commandeered" it.

And our simple-minded hero used to grumble at his lot,
Said he, "This commandeerin's just a little bit too hot,
A fellow has to carry every blooming thing he's got;
Whatever he puts down they'll commandeer it."

So after much anxiety our simple-minded elf
He thought he'd do a little commandeering for himself,
And the first thing that he noticed was a bottle on a shelf
In a cottage, so he thought he'd commandeer it.

"What ho!" says he, "a bottle, and, by George, it's full of beer,
And no commanding officer to come and interfere.
Here's my own blooming health," says he, "I'm on the
    commandeer."
And without another word he commandeered it.

* * * *

On his subsequent proceedings we must draw a little veil,
For the Boers had left some sheep dip in that bottle labelled "Ale";
But the doctor said he'd shift it — if all other methods fail,
We must use the stomach pump and commandeer it.

THE RUM PARADE

Tune: "Ballyhooley"

Now ye gallant Sydney boys, who have left your household joys
   To march across the sea in search of glory,
I am very much afraid that you do not love parade,
   But the rum parade is quite another story.
For the influenza came and to spoil its little game,
   They ordered we should drink a curious mixture;
Though at first it frightened some, when they found it mostly rum,
   Parade became a very pleasant fixture.

Chorus

So it's forward the Brigade, if they'll hold a rum parade
   At Pretoria there's nothing to alarm ye;
And it's easy to be seen if they leave out the quinine,
   Ye'll be there before the blessed British Army.

Then a corporal he come and he said I drank the rum,
   But the quinine never reached its destination;
For begob he up and swored that I threw it overboard,
   Sure my heart was filled with grief and indignation.
For I'm different to some, I prefer quinine to rum,
   And I only take the rum just as a favour,
And it's easy to be seen I'm so fond of the quinine,
   That I keep it lest the rum should spoil its flavour.

When we get to Africay we'll be landed straight away,
   And quartered with the troops of Queen Victoria;
And we hope they'll understand that the moment that we land
   We are ready for a march upon Pretoria.
And we'll pay off all the scores on old Kruger and his Boers,
   And just to prove our manners aren't a failure,
And to show we are not mean, shure we'll give them the quinine,
   And drink the rum in honour of Australia.

Now Listen To Me
And I'll Tell You My Views

Now listen to me and I'll tell you my views concerning the African war,
And the man who upholds any different views, the same is a rotten Pro-Boer!
(Though I'm getting a little bit doubtful myself, as it drags on week after week:
But it's better not ask any questions at all — let us silence all doubts with a shriek!)

And first let us shriek the unstinted abuse that the Tory Press prefer —
De Wet is a madman, and Steyn is a liar, and Kruger a pitiful cur!
(Though I think if Oom Paul — as old as he is — were to walk down the Strand with his gun,
A lot of these heroes would hide in the sewers or take to their heels and run!
For Paul he has fought like a man in his day, but now that he's feeble and weak
And tired, and lonely, and old and grey, of course it's quite safe to shriek!)

And next let us join in the bloodthirsty shriek, Hooray for Lord Kitchener's "bag"!
For the fireman's torch and the hangman's cord — they are hung on the English Flag!
In the front of our brave old army! Whoop! the farmhouse blazes bright.
And their women weep and their children die — how dare they presume to fight!
For none of them dress in a uniform, the same as by rights they ought.
They're fighting in rags and in naked feet, like Wallace's Scotchmen fought!
(And they clothe themselves from our captured troops — and they're catching them every week;
And they don't hang *them* — and the shame is ours, but we cover the shame with a shriek!)

And, lastly, we'll shriek the political shriek as we sit in the dark and doubt;
Where the Birmingham Judas led us in, and there's no one to lead us out.

And Rosebery — whom we depended upon! Would only the Oracle
    speak!
"You go to the Grocers," says he, "for your laws!" By heavens! it's
    time to shriek!

A NERVOUS
GOVERNOR-GENERAL

We read in the press that Lord Northcote is here
  To take up Lord Tennyson's mission.
'Tis pleasant to find they have sent us a Peer,
  And a man of exalted position.
It's his business to see that the Radical horde
  From loyalty's path does not swerve us;
But his tastes, and the task, don't seem quite in accord
  For they say that His Lordship is nervous.

Does he think that wild animals walk in the street,
  Where the wary marsupial is hopping?
Does he think that the snake and the platypus meet
  And "bail up" the folk who go shopping?
And that boomerangs fly round the scared passer-by
  Who has come all this way to observe us.
While the blackfellow launches a spear at his eye?
  — No wonder His Lordship is nervous.

Does he think that with callers he'll be overtasked,
  From a baronet down to a barber?
Does he dream of the number of times he'll be asked
  "What he thinks of our Beautiful Harbour?"
Does he sadly reflect on the sorrows that ding
  Round his task? (From such sorrows preserve us!)
He must hear John See speak and O'Sullivan sing,
  — It's enough to make any man nervous.

Does he think he'll be waked in the dead of the night
  From Melbourne to go willy-nilly,
To live at the Federal Capital site
  At Tumut or Wagra-go-billy?
Well, the Melbournites *may* let the Capital go
  (Here we wink with one eye, please observe us!)
But not in a hurry! By no means! Oh, no!
  He has not the least need to be nervous!

THE PREMIER
AND THE SOCIALIST

The Premier and the Socialist
  Were walking through the State:
They wept to see the Savings Bank
  Such funds accumulate.
"If these were only cleared away,"
  They said, "it would be great."

"If three financial amateurs
  Controlled them for a year,
Do you suppose," the Premier said,
  "That they would get them clear?"
"I think so," said the Socialist;
  "They would — or very near!"

"If we should try to raise some cash
  On assets of our own,
Do you suppose," the Premier said,
  "That we could float a loan?"
"I doubt it," said the Socialist,
  And groaned a doleful groan.

"Oh, Savings, come and walk with us!"
  The Premier did entreat;
"A little walk, a little talk,
  Away from Barrack Street;
My Socialistic friend will guide
  Your inexperienced feet."

"We do not think," the Savings said,
  "A Socialistic crank,
Although he chance just now to hold
  A legislative rank,
Can teach experienced Banking men
  The way to run a Bank."

The Premier and the Socialist
  They passed an Act or so
To take the little Savings out
  And let them have a blow.
"We'll teach the Banks," the Premier said,
  "The way to run the show.

"There's Tom Waddell — in Bank Finance
  Can show them what is what.
I used to prove not long ago

His Estimates were rot.
But that — like many other things —
  I've recently forgot.

"Advances on a dried-out farm
  Are what we chiefly need,
And loans to friends of Ms.L.A.
  Are very good, indeed,
See how the back-block Cockatoos
  Are rolling up to feed."

"But not on us," the Savings cried,
  Falling a little flat,
"We didn't think a man like you
  Would do a thing like that;
For most of us are very small,
  And none of us are fat."

"This haughty tone," the Premier said,
  "Is not the proper line;
Before I'd be dictated to
  My billet I'd resign!"
"How brightly," said the Socialist,
  "Those little sovereigns shine."

The Premier and the Socialist
  They had their bit of fun;
They tried to call the Savings back
  But answer came there none,
Because the back-block Cockatoos
  Had eaten every one.

THE MAN
FROM GOONDIWINDI, Q.

I

This is the sunburnt bushman who
Came down from Goondiwindi, Q.

II

This is the Push from Waterloo
That spotted the sunburnt bushman who
Came down from Goondiwindi, Q.

III

These are the wealthy uncles — two,
Part of the Push from Waterloo
That spotted the sunburnt bushman who
Came down from Goondiwindi, Q.

IV

This is the game, by no means new,
Played by the wealthy uncles — two,
Part of the Push from Waterloo
That spotted the sunburnt bushman who
Came down from Goondiwindi, Q.

V

This is the trooper dressed in blue
Who busted the game by no means new
Played by the wealthy uncles — two,
Part of the Push from Waterloo
That spotted the sunburnt bushman who
Came down from Goondiwindi, Q.

VI

This is the magistrate who knew
Not only the trooper dressed in blue,
But also the game by no means new,
And likewise the wealthy uncles — two,
And ditto the Push from Waterloo
That spotted the sunburnt bushman who
Came down from Goondiwindi, Q.

VII

This is the tale that has oft gone through
On Western plains where the skies are blue,
Till the native bear and the kangaroo
Have heard of the magistrate who knew
Not only the trooper dressed in blue,

But also the game by no means new,
And likewise the wealthy uncles — two,
And ditto the Push from Waterloo
That spotted the sunburnt bushman who
Came down from Goondiwindi, Q.

A Motor Courtship

Into her presence he gaily pranced,
A very fat spark, and a bit advanced.

With a Samson tread on the earth he trod,
He was stayed and gaitered, and fifty odd.

And she was a tulip just unfurled,
The sweetest thing in the motor world.

Her body was one of which poets dreamed;
Eighteen — twenty, or so she seemed.

Her air was haughty, her spirit proud,
But properly governed, as all allowed.

"Pity," he said, "my sad condition;
My heart's in a state of advanced ignition.

"Ask me to do some desperate deed,
And I'll do it at once at my topmost speed."

"Sir," said the maiden, "pray be seated;
I fear from your bearing you're somewhat heated.

"And I trust that a timely lubrication
Of throttle will cool your circulation."

As a well-made mixture she indicated,
With joy and gladness he radiated.

"Oh, come," said he, "in this soft spring weather,
Let us run over the world together!"

But she slipped his clutch with a gesture mocking,
"Your heart," she said; "I can hear it knocking.

"You haven't the gear at my pace to last;
Both men and motors — I like them fast.

"And I think that in me you have missed your mission;
You are only an old-style tube-ignition!"

With a sidelong motion he left the place;
For weal or woe he was off his base.

He drove his car to the cliffs of Dover,
Made one short circuit and ran her over.

And the stormy Petrol her rest is taking,
Where only the wild waves do the "brakeing".

"WE'RE ALL AUSTRALIANS NOW"

Australia takes her pen in hand,
  To write a line to you,
To let you fellows understand,
  How proud we are of you.

From shearing shed and cattle run,
  From Broome to Hobson's Bay,
Each native-born Australian son,
  Stands straighter up today.

The man who used to "hump his drum",
  On far-out Queensland runs,
Is fighting side by side with some
  Tasmanian farmer's sons.

The fisher-boys dropped sail and oar
  To grimly stand the test,
Along that storm-swept Turkish shore,
  With miners from the west.

The old state jealousies of yore
  Are dead as Pharaoh's sow,
We're not State children any more
  We're all Australians now!

Our six-starred flag that used to fly,
  Half-shyly to the breeze,
Unknown where older nations ply
  Their trade on foreign seas,

Flies out to meet the morning blue
  With Vict'ry at the prow;
For that's the flag the Sydney flew,
  The wide seas know it now!

The mettle that a race can show,
  Is proved with shot and steel,
And now we know what nations know
  And feel what nations feel.

The honoured graves beneath the crest
  Of Gaba Tepe hill,
May hold our bravest and our best,
  But we have brave men still.

With all our petty quarrels done,
  Dissensions overthrown,

We have, through what you boys have done,
  A history of our own.

Our old world diff'rences are dead,
  Like weeds beneath the plough,
For English, Scotch, and Irish-bred,
  They're all Australians now!

So now we'll toast the Third Brigade,
  That led Australia's van,
For never shall their glory fade
  In minds Australian.

Fight on, fight on, unflinchingly,
  Till right and justice reign.
Fight on, fight on, till Victory
  Shall send you home again.

And with Australia's flag shall fly
  A spray of wattle bough,
To symbolise our unity,
  We're all Australians now.

Australia Today 1916

They came from the lower levels
　　Deep down in the Brilliant mine;
From the wastes where the whirlwind revels,
　　Whirling the leaves of pine.

On the Western plains, where the Darling flows,
　　And the dust storms wheel and shift,
The teamster loosened his yokes and bows,
　　And turned his team adrift.

On the Western stations, far and wide,
　　There's many an empty pen,
For the "ringers" have cast the machines aside
　　And answered the call for men.

On the lucerne flats where the stream runs slow,
　　And the Hunter finds the sea,
The women are driving the mowers now,
　　With the children at their knee.

For the men have gone, as a man must go,
　　At the call of the rolling drums;
For the men have sworn that the Turks shall know
　　When the old battalion comes.

Column of companies by the right,
　　Steady in strong array,
With the sun on the bayonets gleaming bright,
　　The battalion marched away.

They battled, the old battalion,
　　Through the toil of the training camps,
Sweated and strove at lectures,
　　By the light of the stinking lamps.

Marching, shooting, and drilling;
　　Steady and slow and stern;
Awkward and strange, but willing
　　All of their job to learn.

Learning to use the rifle;
　　Learning to use the spade;
Deeming fatigue a trifle
　　During each long parade.

Till at last they welded
　　Into a concrete whole,

And there grew in the old battalion
  A kind of battalion's soul.

Brotherhood never was like it;
  Friendship is not the word;
But deep in that body of marching men
  The soul of a nation stirred.

And like one man with a single thought
  Cheery and confident;
Ready for all that the future brought,
  The old battalion went.

Column of companies by the right,
  Steady in strong array,
With the sun on the bayonets gleaming bright,
  The battalion marched away.

How shall we tell of their landing
  By the hills where the foe were spread,
And the track of the old battalion
  Was marked by the Turkish dead?

With the dash that discipline teaches,
  Though the hail of the shrapnel flew,
And the forts were raking the beaches,
  And the toll of the dead men grew.

They fixed their grip on the gaunt hillside
  With a pluck that has won them fame;
And the home-folks know that the dead men died
  For the pride of Australia's name.

Column of companies by the right,
  To the beat of the rolling drums;
With honours gained in a stirring fight
  The old Battalion comes!

THE ARMY MULES

Oh the airman's game is a showman's game for we all of us watch
    him go
With his roaring soaring aeroplane and his bombs for the blokes
    below,
Over the railways and over the dumps, over the Hun and the
    Turk,
You'll hear him mutter, "What ho, she bumps," when the Archies
    get to work.
But not of him is the song I sing, though he follow the eagle's
    flight,
And with shrapnel holes in his splintered wing comes home to his
    roost at night.
He may silver his wings on the shining stars, he may look from the
    throne on high,
He may follow the flight of the wheeling kite in the blue Egyptian
    sky,
But he's only a hero built to plan, turned out by the Army schools,
And I sing of the rankless, thankless man who hustles the Army
    mules.

Now where he comes from and where he lives is a mystery dark
    and dim,
And it's rarely indeed that the General gives a D.S.O. to him.
The stolid infantry digs its way like a mole in a ruined wall;
The cavalry lends a tone, they say, to what were else but a brawl;
The Brigadier of the Mounted Fut like a cavalry Colonel swanks
When he goeth abroad like a gilded nut to receive the General's
    thanks;
The Ordnance man is a son of a gun and his lists are a standing
    joke;
You order, "Choke arti Jerusalem one" for Jerusalem artichoke.
The Medicals shine with a number nine, and the men of the great
    R.E.,
Their Colonels are Methodist, married or mad, and some of them
    all the three;
In all these units the road to fame is taught in the Army schools,
But a man has got to be born to the game when he tackles the
    Army mules.

For if you go where the depots are as the dawn is breaking grey,
By the waning light of the morning star as the dust cloud clears
    away,
You'll see a vision among the dust like a man and a mule
    combined —

It's the kind of thing you must take on trust for its outlines aren't
defined,
A thing that whirls like a spinning top and props like a three-
legged stool,
And you find it's a long-legged Queensland boy convincing an
Army mule.
And the rider sticks to the hybrid's hide like paper sticks to a wall,
For a "magnoon" Waler is next to ride with every chance of a fall,
It's a rough-house game and a thankless game, and it isn't a game
for a fool,
For an army's fate and a nation's fame may turn on an army mule.

And if you go to the front-line camp where the sleepless outposts
lie,
At the dead of night you can hear the tramp of the mule train
toiling by.
The rattle and clink of a leading-chain, the creak of the lurching
load,
As the patient, plodding creatures strain at their task in the shell-
torn road,
Through the dark and the dust you may watch them go till the
dawn is grey in the sky,
And only the watchful pickets know when the "All-night Corps"
goes by.
And far away as the silence falls when the last of the train has
gone,
A weary voice through the darkness calls: "Get on there, men, get
on!"
It isn't a hero, built to plan, turned out by the modern schools,
It's only the Army Service man a-driving his Army mules.

Moving On

In this war we're always moving,
   Moving on;
When we make a friend another friend has gone;
Should a woman's kindly face
Make us welcome for a space,
Then it's boot and saddle, boys, we're
   Moving on.

In the hospitals they're moving,
   Moving on;
They're here today, tomorrow they are gone;
When the bravest and the best
Of the boys you know "go west",
Then you're choking down your tears and
   Moving on.

Hawker,
the Standard Bearer

The grey gull sat on a floating whale,
  On a floating whale sat he,
And he told his tale of the storm and the gale,
And the ships that he saw with steam and sail,
  As he flew by the Northern Sea.

"I have seen a sign that is strange and new,
  That I never before did see:
A flying ship that roared as it flew,
The storm and the tempest driving through,
It carried a flag and it carried a crew,
  Now what would that be?" said he.

"And the flag was a Jack with stars displayed,
  A flag that is new to me;
For it does not ply in the Northern trade,
But it drove through the storm-wrack unafraid,
  Now, what is that flag?" said he.

"I have seen that flag that is starred with white,"
  Said a southern gull, said he,
"And I saw it fly in a bloody fight,
When the raider *Emden* turned in flight,
  And crashed on the Cocos lee."

"And who are these folk whose flag is first
  Of all the flags that fly
To dare the storm and the fog accurst,
Of the great North Sea where the bergs are nursed,
  And the Northern Lights ride high?"

"The Australian folk," said a lone sea-mew,
  "The Australian flag," said he.
"It is strange that a folk that is far and few
Should fly their flag where there never flew
  Another flag!" said he.

"I have followed their flag in the fields of France,
  With its white stars flying free,
And no misfortune and no mischance
Could turn them back from their line of advance,
  Or the line that they held," said he.

"Wherever there's ever a rule to break,
  Wherever they oughtn't to be,

With a death to dare and a risk to take,
A track to find or a way to make,
  You will find them there," said he.

"They come from a land that is parched with thirst,
  An inland land," said he,
"On risk and danger their breed is nursed,
And thus it happens their flag is first
  To fly in the Northern Sea."

"Though Hawker perished, he overcame
  The risks of the storm and the sea,
And his name shall be written in stars of flame,
On the topmost walls of the Temple of Fame,
  For the rest of the world to see."

Boots

"The Australian boots were the best of any issued to the Allied forces."

We've travelled per Joe Gardiner, a humping of our swag
  In the country of the Gidgee and Belar.
We've swum the Di'mantina with our raiment in a bag,
  And we've travelled per superior motor car,
But when we went to Germany we hadn't any choice,
  No matter what our training or pursuits,
For they gave us no selection 'twixt a Ford or Rolls de Royce
  So we did it in our good Australian boots.

They called us "mad Australians"; they couldn't understand
  How officers and men could fraternise,
They said that we were "reckless", we were "wild, and out of
    hand",
  With nothing great or sacred to our eyes.
But on one thing you could gamble, in the thickest of the fray,
  Though they called us volunteers and raw recruits,
You could track us past the shell holes, and the tracks were all one
    way
  Of the good Australian ammunition boots.

The Highlanders were next of kin, the Irish were a treat,
  The Yankees knew it all and had to learn,
The Frenchmen kept it going, both in vict'ry and defeat,
  Fighting grimly till the tide was on the turn.
And our army kept beside 'em, did its bit and took its chance,
  And I hailed our newborn nation and its fruits,
As I listened to the clatter on the cobblestones of France
  Of the good Australian military boots.

THE OLD TIN HAT

In the good old days when the Army's ways were simple and
    unrefined,
With a stock to keep up their chins in front, and a pigtail down
    behind,
When the only light in the barracks at night was a candle of grease
    or fat,
When they put the extinguisher on the light, they called it the Old
    Tin Hat.

Now, a very great man is the C. in C., for he is the whole of the
    show —
The reins and the whip and the driver's hand that maketh the
    team to go —
But the road he goes is a lonely road, with ever a choice to make,
When he comes to a place where the roads divide, which one is the
    road to take.
For there's one road right, and there's one road wrong, uphill, or
    over the flat,
And one road leads to the Temple of Fame, and one to the Old
    Tin Hat.

And a very great man is the man who holds an Army Corps
    command,
For he hurries his regiments here and there as the C. in C. has
    planned.
By day he travels about in state and stirreth them up to rights,
He toileth early and toileth late, and sitteth up half the nights;
But the evening comes when the candle throws twin shadows upon
    the mat,
And one of the shadows is like a wreath, and one like an Old Tin
    Hat.

And a very proud man is the Brigadier at the sound of the stately
    tread
Of his big battalions marching on, as he rides with his staff ahead.
There's never a band to play them out, and the bugle's note is still,
But he hears two tunes in the gentle breeze that blows from over
    the hill.
And one is a tune in a stirring key, and the other is faint and flat,
For one is the tune of "My new C.B." and the other, "My Old Tin
    Hat".

And the Colonel heading his regiment is life and soul of the show,
It's "Column of route", "Form troops", "Extend", and into the fight
    they go;

He does not duck when the air is full of the "wail of the
    whimpering lead",
He does not scout for the deep dugout when the 'planes are
    overhead;
He fears not hog, nor devil, nor dog, and he'd scrap with a
    mountain cat,
But he goeth in fear of the Brigadier, and in fear of the Old Tin
    Hat.

THAT HALF-CROWN SWEEP

A Tale of the Territory

The run of Billabong-go-dry
  Is just beyond Lime Burner's Gap;
Its waterhole and tank supply
  Is excellent — upon the map.
But, lacking nature's liquid drench,
  The station staff are wont to try
With "Bob-in Sweeps" their thirst to quench,
  Or nearly quench, at Bong-go-dry.

The parson made five-yearly rounds
  That soil of arid souls to delve,
He wrote, "I'll come for seven pounds,
  Or I could stop away for twelve."
But lack of lucre brought about
  The pusillanimous reply:
"Our luxuries are all cut out,
  You'll have to come to Bong-go-dry."

Now rabbit skins were very high —
  There'd been a kind of rabbit rush —
And what with traps and sticks they'd shy,
  The station blacks were very flush,
And each was taught his churchman's job,
  "When that one parson's plate comes roun'
No good you put in sprat or bob,
  Too quick you put in harp-a-crown."

The parson's word was duly kept,
  He came and did his bit of speak;
The boss remarked he hadn't slept
  So sound and well for many a week.
But Gilgai Jack and Monkey Jaw
  Regarded preaching as a crime
Against good taste; they said, "What for
  That one chap yabber all the time?"

Proceedings ceased: the boss's hat
  Was raked from underneath his chair;
The coloured congregation sat
  And waited with expectant air.
At last from one far-distant seat
  Where Gilgai's Mary'd been asleep,
There came a kind of plaintive bleat,
  "Say, boss! Who won the harp-crown sweep?"

Australian Scenery

The Mountains
A land of sombre, silent hills, where mountain cattle go
By twisted tracks, on sidelings steep, where giant gum trees grow
And the wind replies, in the river oaks, to the song of the stream
  below.

A land where the hills keep watch and ward, silent and wide awake
As those who sit by a dead campfire, and wait for the dawn to
  break,
Or those who watched by the Holy Cross for the dead Redeemer's
  sake.

A land where silence lies so deep that sound itself is dead
And a gaunt grey bird, like a homeless soul, drifts, noiseless,
  overhead
And the world's great story is left untold, and the message is left
  unsaid.

The Plains
A land, as far as the eye can see, where the waving grasses grow
Or the plains are blackened and burnt and bare, where the false
  mirages go
Like shifting symbols of hope deferred — land where you never
  know.

Land of plenty or land of want, where the grey Companions dance,
Feast or famine, or hope or fear, and in all things land of chance,
Where Nature pampers or Nature slays, in her ruthless, red,
  romance.

And we catch a sound of a fairy's song, as the wind goes whipping
  by,
Or a scent like incense drifts along from the herbage ripe and dry
— Or the dust storms dance on their ballroom floor, where the
  bones of the cattle lie.

A Dog's Mistake

In Doggerel Verse

He had drifted in among us as a straw drifts with the tide,
He was just a wand'ring mongrel from the weary world outside;
He was not aristocratic, being mostly ribs and hair,
With a hint of spaniel parents and a touch of native bear.

He was very poor and humble and content with what he got,
So we fed him bones and biscuits, till he heartened up a lot;
Then he growled and grew aggressive, treating orders with disdain,
Till at last he bit the butcher, which would argue want of brain.

Now the butcher, noble fellow, was a sport beyond belief,
And instead of bringing actions he brought half a shin of beef,
Which he handed on to Fido, who received it as a right
And removed it to the garden, where he buried it at night.

'Twas the means of his undoing, for my wife, who'd stood his
    friend,
To adopt a slang expression, "went in off the deepest end",
For among the pinks and pansies, the gloxinias and the gorse
He had made an excavation like a graveyard for a horse.

Then we held a consultation which decided on his fate:
'Twas in anger more than sorrow that we led him to the gate,
And we handed him the beef-bone as provision for the day,
Then we opened wide the portal and we told him, "On your way."

Shearing with a Hoe

The track that led to Carmody's is choked and overgrown,
The suckers of the stringybark have made the place their own;
The mountain rains have cut the track that once we used to know
When first we rode to Carmody's, a score of years ago.

The shearing shed at Carmody's was slab and stringybark,
The press was just a lever beam, invented in the Ark;
But Mrs Carmody was cook — and shearers' hearts would glow
With praise of grub at Carmody's, a score of years ago.

At shearing time no penners-up would curse their fate and weep,
For Fragrant Fred — the billy-goat — was trained to lead the sheep;
And racing down the rattling chutes the bleating mob would go
Behind their horned man from Cook's, a score of years ago.

An owner of the olden time, his patriarchal shed
Was innocent of all machines or gadgets overhead:
And pieces, locks and super-fleece together used to go
To fill the bales at Carmody's, a score of years ago.

A ringer from the Western sheds, whose fame was wide and deep,
Was asked to take a vacant pen and shear a thousand sheep.
"Of course, we've only got the blades!" "Well, what I want to
    know:
Why don't you get a bloke to take it off 'em with a hoe?"

THE SILENT SHEARER

Weary and listless, sad and slow,
  Without any conversation,
Was a man that worked on The Overflow,
  The butt of the shed and station.

The shearers christened him Noisy Ned,
  With an alias "Silent Waters",
But never a needless word he said
  In the hut, or the shearers' quarters.

Which caused annoyance to Big Barcoo,
  The shed's unquestioned ringer,
Whose name was famous Australia through
  As a dancer, fighter and singer.

He was fit for the ring, if he'd had his rights
  As an agent of devastation;
And the number of men he had killed in fights
  Was his principal conversation.

"I have known blokes go to their doom," said he,
  "Through actin' with haste and rashness:
But the style that this Noisy Ned assumes,
  It's nothing but silent flashness.

"We may just be dirt, from his point of view,
  Unworthy a word in season;
But I'll make him talk like a cockatoo
  Or I'll get him to show the reason."

Was it chance or fate, that King Condamine,
  A king who had turned black tracker,
Had captured a baby porcupine,
  Which he swapped for a "fig tobacker"?

With the porcupine in the Silent's bed
  The shearers were quite elated,
And the things to be done, and the words to be said,
  Were anxiously awaited.

With a screech and a howl and an eldritch cry
  That nearly deafened his hearers
He sprang from his bunk, and his fishy eye
  Looked over the laughing shearers.

He looked them over and he looked them through
  As a cook might look through a larder;

"Now, Big Barcoo, I must pick on you,
    You're big, but you'll fall the harder."

Now, the silent man was but slight and thin
    And of middleweight conformation,
But he hung one punch on the Barcoo's chin
    And it ended the altercation.

"You've heard of the One-round Kid," said he,
    "That hunted 'em all to shelter?
The One-round Finisher — that was me,
    When I fought as the Champion Welter.

"And this Barcoo bloke on his back reclines
    For being a bit too clever,
For snakes and wombats and porcupines
    Are nothing to me whatever.

"But the golden rule that I've had to learn
    In the ring, and for years I've tried it,
Is only to talk when it comes your turn,
    And never to talk outside it."

THE BILLY-GOAT OVERLAND

Come all ye lads of the droving days, ye gentlemen unafraid,
I'll tell you all of the greatest trip that ever a drover made,
For we rolled our swags, and we packed our bags, and taking our
    lives in hand,
We started away with a thousand goats, on the billy-goat overland.

There wasn't a fence that'd hold the mob, or keep 'em from their
    desires;
They skipped along the top of the posts and cake-walked on the
    wires.
And where the lanes had been stripped of grass and the paddocks
    were nice and green,
The goats they travelled outside the lanes and we rode in between.

The squatters started to drive them back, but that was no good at
    all,
Their horses ran for the lick of their lives from the scent that was
    like a wall:
And never a dog had pluck or gall in front of the mob to stand
And face the charge of a thousand goats on the billy-goat overland.

We found we were hundreds over strength when we counted out
    the mob;
And they put us in jail for a crowd of thieves that travelled to steal
    and rob:
For every goat between here and Bourke, when he scented our
    spicy band,
Had left his home and his work to join in the billy-goat overland.

BLACK HARRY'S TEAM

No soft-skinned Durham steers are they,
  No Devons plump and red,
But brindled, black, and iron-grey
  That mark the mountain-bred;
For mountain-bred and mountain-broke,
  With sullen eyes agleam,
No stranger's hand could put a yoke
  On old Black Harry's team.

Pull out, pull out, at break of morn
  The creeks are running white,
And Tiger, Spot, and Snailey-horn
  Must bend their bows by night;
And axles, wheels and flooring boards
  Are swept with flying spray
As, shoulder-deep, through mountain fords
  The leaders feel their way.

He needs no sign of cross or kirn
  To guide him as he goes,
For every twist and every turn
  That old black leader knows.
Up mountains steep they heave and strain
  Where never wheel has rolled,
And what the toiling leaders gain
  The body bullocks hold.

Where eaglehawks their eyries make,
  On sidelings steep and blind,
He rigs the good old-fashioned brake —
  A tree tied on behind.
Up mountains, straining to the full,
  Each poler plays his part —
The sullen, stubborn, bullock pull
  That breaks a horse's heart.

Beyond the furthest bridle track
  His wheels have blazed the way;
The forest giants, burnt and black,
  Are earmarked by his dray.
Through belts of scrub where messmates grow
  His juggernaut has rolled,
For stumps and saplings have to go
  When Harry's team takes hold.

On easy grade and rubber tyre
    The tourist car goes through;
They halt a moment to admire
    The far-flung mountain view.
The tourist folk would be amazed
    If they could get to know
They take the track Black Harry blazed
    A hundred years ago.

THE WEATHER PROPHET

"'Ow can it rain," the old man said, "with things the way they are?
You've got to learn off ant and bee, and jackass and galah;
And no man never saw it rain, for fifty years at least,
Not when the blessed parakeets are flyin' to the East!"

The weeks went by, the squatter wrote to tell his bank the news.
"It's still as dry as dust," he said, "I'm feeding all the ewes;
The overdraft would sink a ship, but make your mind at rest,
It's all right now, the parakeets are flyin' to the West."

Buffalo Country

Out where the grey streams glide,
Sullen and deep and slow,
And the alligators slide
From the mud to the depths below
Or drift on the stream like a floating death,
Where the fever comes on the south wind's breath,
There is the buffalo.

Out on the big lagoons,
Where the Regia lilies float,
And the Nankin heron croons
With a deep ill-omened note,
In the ooze and the mud of the swamps below
Lazily wallows the buffalo,
Buried to nose and throat.

From the hunter's gun he hides
In the jungles dark and damp,
Where the slinking dingo glides
And the flying foxes camp;
Hanging like myriad fiends in line
Where the trailing creepers twist and twine
And the sun is a sluggish lamp.

On the edge of the rolling plains
Where the coarse cane grasses swell,
Lush with the tropic rains
In the noontide's drowsy spell,
Slowly the buffalo grazes through
Where the brolgas dance, and the jabiru
Stands like a sentinel.

All that the world can know
Of the wild and the weird is here,
Where the black men come and go
With their boomerang and spear,
And the wild duck darken the evening sky
As they fly to their nests in the reed beds high
When the tropic night is near.

CASTLEBAR

Bidding good morrow to all our cares,
  Riding along with a joyful heart,
Little we reck of the world's affairs,
  All that we ask is a decent start.
Though the jumps are big and the distance far
We will get to the finish on Castlebar.

Little Blue Peter goes sailing by;
  Little Blue Peter may stand or fall,
For his rider reckons no man can die
  Till his day comes round — so he chances all!
And away to the front where the good ones are
Go Little Blue Peter and Castlebar.

Bay and chestnut and brown and black,
  I hear in the timber their hoof beats drum,
As I clear the fence on the Prospect track
  I turn in the saddle and watch them come.
But the chestnut horse with the big white star,
Why isn't he following Castlebar?

Dear little woman with eyes of blue,
  With lissom figure and easy grace,
I turn in the saddle and long for you
  As the field sweeps on at a rattling pace.
But I know that away on the heights afar
Your heart is following Castlebar.

HERE'S LUCK

A Toast at a Hunt Club Dinner

It chanced one day I watched a steeplechase,
  And one horse singled out and led them all
Across the fences at a rattling pace
  Until he hit a fence and took a fall.
His rider laughed and muttered with a smile —
"Well, anyhow, I led 'em for a while."

And this the text is for my theme tonight —
  A moral that the wisest men have sung:
Our life is very short — and swift the flight
  Of time — so, comrades, go it while you're young.
And when old age comes on you'll find it good
To think you made the running while you could.

There's nothing now too solid or too high
  For some of you to take and chance a spill;
But we must funk the fences bye and bye,
  When limbs grow stiff and hands have lost their skill.
In wintry age we'll seek the hearthstone's blaze;
So let us make the most of youth's bright days.

So now, my friends, good luck and may you keep
  Stout hearts and true and honest kindly mirth,
When drawing nearer to the last great leap
  That lands us on the other side of earth,
Where many a gallant horseman and brave steed
Has gone before to give us all a lead.

QUEENSLAND MOUNTED INFANTRY

There's a very well-built fellow, with a swinging sort of stride,
  About as handy sort as I have seen.
A rough and tumble fellow that is born to fight and ride
  And he's over here a-fighting for the Queen.

He's Queensland Mounted Infantry — compounded 'orse and foot.
  He'll climb a cliff or gallop down a flat.
He's cavalry to travel but he's infantry to shoot.
  And you'll know him by the feathers in his hat!

CAPE MOUNTED RIFLES

Tune: "Botany Bay"

Now, when you've done talking of trifles,
   I'll sing you a song of the war —
A song of the Cape Mounted Rifles,
   The dandy South African Corps.
Though some of us haven't a penny,
   And others have acted the goat,
Yet, take us all round, there ain't many
   Will tread on the tail of our —

Chorus
Pom, pom, pom, pom, tooralido
Pom, pom, pom, pom, tooralay.
Yes, take us all round, there ain't many
Will tread on the tail of our coat.

They told us to stop on the border:
   We thought we were out of the hunt.
But quietly, they sent us an order —
   "The rifles are wanted in front."
And up in the front did they set us
   To fight all the Dutchmen afloat,
But ne'er a Commando that met us
   Could tread on the tail of our —

They sent us with Colonel Dalgety
   To fight with De Wet and old Steyn.
We've fought and we've beat them already —
   We'll fight and we'll beat them again.
Oom Paul has been picking up trifles —
   With millions of cash he's afloat —
If he meets with the Cape Mounted Rifles
   They'll jump for the tail of his coat!

Maxims of War

Firstly, when fighting the Dutchman, make it your cardinal rule —
Think he's a rogue if it please you: *never believe he's a fool.*

Never be needlessly reckless — he who does this is a dunce —
Stopping a bullet is easy — but you don't stop 'em well more than
    once.

Make better use of your cover — don't ride about in full view.
God made the kopjes for Dutchmen — likewise he made 'em for
    you.

Parties of twenty for scouting — easy to see and to smother:
Neither can fight nor keep hidden — neither one thing nor the
    other.

If reconnoitring a kopje, you feel the least shadow of doubt,
Send up one man to inspect it — send up a Rimington scout!
Don't send a *troop* as a target for Dutchmen to hustle about.

Never hold more than you've need of — kopjes all round you are
    strown.
If they can't help you, they'll hurt you — leave 'em severely alone.

If you should find a position, when it would suit you to fight,
Keep it! Don't shift! If you leave it, the Boers will come down in
    the night.
Then you'll go back and they'll shoot you — and serve you most
    damnably right!

Why should you load up with "Bully", bringing your transport to
    grief?
Look at the veldt all around you, stocked with the primest of beef!

Finally, never get jumpy — e'en though the fighting is hot!
Think of how often you're shot at — think of how seldom you're
    shot!

Our Own Flag

They mustered us up with a royal din,
  In wearisome weeks of drought.
Ere ever the half of the crops were in,
  Or the half of the sheds cut out.

'Twas down with saddle and spurs and whip;
  The swagman dropped his swag.
And we hurried us off to an outbound ship
  To fight for the English flag.

The English flag — it is ours in sooth
  We stand by it wrong or right.
But deep in our hearts is the honest truth
  We fought for the sake of a fight.

And the English flag may flutter and wave
  Where the World-wide Oceans toss,
But the flag the Australian dies to save
  Is the flag of the Southern Cross.

If ever they want us to stand the brunt
  Of a hard-fought, grim campaign,
We will carry our own flag up to the front
  When we go to the wars again.

CAMPIN' ROUND COONAMBLE

Written when reporting for the Sydney Morning Herald
on the shearing troubles at Coonamble

Campin' round Coonamble,
  Keepin' up the strike,
Through the black soil country
  Plugging on the "bike";
Half a thousand shearers,
  What had we to gain
Campin' round Coonamble,
  Campin' in the rain?

Twenty bob a hundred
  Shearing with machines!
Good enough in these times
  We know what it means —
Sinking tanks and fencing,
  Shearing's better pay
Twenty bob a hundred,
  Twenty bob a day!

Every little farmer
  Up Monaro side
Sends the boys a-shearing,
  Hoping to provide
Something for the homestead;
  All his hopes are vain,
While we're round Coonamble,
  Campin' in the rain.

Up at old man Tobin's,
  First pen on the right,
Don't I know his wethers,
  Know 'em all by sight!
Many a year I shore 'em
  Like to shear again,
Better game than campin',
  Campin' in the rain.

What's the use of talking
  Five-and-twenty bob,
While there's hundreds hungry
  Looking for a job?
Darling Harbour casuals,
  Hollow in the cheek,
Cadging from the Government
  Two days' work a week.

When with peal of trumpets,
  And with beat of drums,
Labour's great millennium
  Actually comes;
When each white Australian,
  Master of his craft,
Keeps a foreign servant
  Just to do the graft;

When the price of shearing
  Goes to fifty bob,
And there's no man hungry
  Looking for a job;
Then, if they oppress us,
  Then we'll go again
Campin' round Coonamble,
  Campin' in the rain.

A Grain
of Desert Sand

Beneath the blue Egyptian skies,
  With ramp and roller, guide and stay,
I saw the Pyramids arise
  And I shall see them pass away.

I watched when Alexander passed;
  I saw Napoleon's flag unfurled —
The greatest and perhaps the last
  Of men whose footsteps shook the world.

To each his hour of pride and place,
  Arab and Persian, Greek and Jew;
Mahomet trod upon my face,
  Darius spurned me with his shoe.

And yet I am not Priest or King,
  Sultan or Chief in high command.
I am that one unchanging thing,
  A grain of desert sand.

SONG OF MURRAY'S BRIGADE

Small birds singing in the tree tops tell
  Where runs the river of my home;
And the wistful wishing of the folk who love us well
  And follow us wherever we may roam.

And our hearts go back to the folk beside the river
  To the land where the sheep and cattle roam.
It's a long, long job, but we'll finish it together
  For every mile we travel leads us home.

No songs greet us for the birds are mute
  The aeroplane's the only thing to fly.
Upward to the pilot send a special brand salute
  For we may need him badly bye and bye.

Soldiers singing as their fancies come
  New songs, old songs, they sang another day.
Thus they sing and march to the beating of the drum
  Till orders come to put the drums away.

And our hearts go back to the folk beside the river
  To the land where the sheep and cattle roam.
It's a long, long job, but we'll finish it together
  For every mile we travel leads us home.

THE UPLIFT

When the drays are bogged and sinking, then it's no use sitting
  thinking,
  You must put the teams together and must double-bank the pull.
When the crop is light and weedy, or the fleece is burred and seedy,
  Then the next year's crop and fleeces may repay you to the full.

  So it's lift her, Johnny, lift her,
  Put your back in it and shift her,
While the jabber, jabber, jabber of the politicians flows.
  If your nag's too poor to travel
  Then get down and scratch the gravel
For you'll get there if you walk it — if you don't, you'll feed the
  crows.

Shall we waste our time debating with a grand young country
  waiting
  For the plough and for the harrow and the lucerne and the
  maize?
For it's work alone will save us in the land that fortune gave us.
  There's a no crop but what we'll grow it; there's no stock but
  what we'll raise.

  When the team is bogged and sinking
  Then it's no use sitting thinking.
There's a roadway up the mountain that the old black leader
knows:
  So it's lift her, Johnny, lift her,
  Put your back in it and shift her,
Take a lesson from the bullock — he goes slowly, but he goes!

INDEX TO
FIRST LINES